T0190228

Developing 2D Games with Unity

Independent Game Programming with C#

Jared Halpern

Apress®

Developing 2D Games with Unity: Independent Game Programming with C#

Jared Halpern
New York, NY, USA

ISBN-13 (pbk): 978-1-4842-3771-7
https://doi.org/10.1007/978-1-4842-3772-4

ISBN-13 (electronic): 978-1-4842-3772-4

Library of Congress Control Number: 2018963589

Managing Director, Apress Media LLC: Welmoed Spahr
Acquisitions Editor: Aaron Black
Development Editor: James Markham
Coordinating Editor: Jessica Vakili

Cover image designed by Freepik (www.freepik.com)

Distributed to the book trade worldwide by Springer Science+Business Media New York, 233 Spring Street, 6th Floor, New York, NY 10013. Phone 1-800-SPRINGER, fax (201) 348-4505, e-mail orders-ny@springer-sbm.com, or visit www.springeronline.com. Apress Media, LLC is a California LLC and the sole member (owner) is Springer Science + Business Media Finance Inc (SSBM Finance Inc). SSBM Finance Inc is a **Delaware** corporation.

For information on translations, please e-mail rights@apress.com, or visit http://www.apress.com/rights-permissions.

Apress titles may be purchased in bulk for academic, corporate, or promotional use. eBook versions and licenses are also available for most titles. For more information, reference our Print and eBook Bulk Sales web page at http://www.apress.com/bulk-sales.

Any source code or other supplementary material referenced by the author in this book is available to readers on GitHub via the book's product page, located at www.apress.com/978-1-4842-3771-7. For more detailed information, please visit http://www.apress.com/source-code.

Printed on acid-free paper

Table of Contents

About the Author xiii

About the Technical Reviewer xv

Acknowledgments..xvii

Preface xix

About This Book...xxi

Chapter 1: Games and Game Engines...1

  Game Engines—What Are They? 1

    The First Way to Build a House...4

    The Second Way to Build a House 4

    About the First Approach 5

    About the Second Approach 5

    In conclusion 6

  Game Engines Historically 6

  Game Engines Today 8

  The Unity Game Engine..10

  Summary..12

Chapter 2: Introduction to Unity 13

  Install Unity 13

  Configure Unity 14

    On Disk 15

    In the Cloud 15

The Script Editor: Visual Studio 17

Navigating the Unity Interface...18

Understanding the Different Window Views.............................18

Configure and Customize the Layout 22

The Transform Toolset..23

Handle Position Controls..25

Play, Pause, and Step Controls...26

Unity Project Structure...28

Unity Documentation..29

Summary..29

Chapter 3: Foundations **31**

Game Objects: Our Container Entities 31

Entity-Component Design 33

Components: Building Blocks 35

Sprites..35

Animations 45

    The Animator State Machine 49

Colliders 54

The Rigidbody Component 56

Tags and Layers 57

    Tags 57

    Layers...58

    Sorting Layers 59

Introducing: Prefabs..63

Scripts: Logic for Components 65

State and Animations 75

    More State Machines 75

    Animation Parameters 78

Summary 90

Chapter 4: World Building 91

Tilemaps and Tile Palettes 91

Creating Tile Palettes 93

Painting with Tile Palettes 96

    The Tile Palette 97

Working with Multiple Tilemaps 101

Graphics Settings 106

The Camera 107

Using Cinemachine 111

    Installing Cinemachine in Unity 2017 111

    Installing Cinemachine in Unity 2018 112

    After Installing Cinemachine 113

Virtual Cameras 114

    Cinemachine Confiner 120

Stabilization 125

Materials 129

Colliders and Tilemaps 130

    Tilemap Collider 2D 130

    Composite Colliders 133

    Editing Physics Shapes 137

Summary 141

Chapter 5: Assembling the Nuts and Bolts 143

Character Class...143

Player Class 145

Focus on Prefabs 147

    Create a Coin Prefab..147

    Set Up the Circle Collider 2D 148

    Set Up a Custom Tag..149

Layer-Based Collision Detection 151

Triggers and Scripting..154

Scriptable Objects..156

    Creating a Scriptable Object...157

    Build the Consumable Script 161

    Assembling Our Item 162

    Player Collisions 164

    Creating a Heart Power-Up 165

    Summary 173

Chapter 6: Health and Inventory 175

Creating a Health Bar...175

    Canvas Objects..175

    UI Elements 176

    Building the Health Bar..176

    Anchors 179

    Adjusting the Anchor Points 181

    UI Image Masks...184

    Importing Custom Fonts 188

    Adding Hit-Points Text 189

    Scripting the Health Bar 192

Scriptable Object: HitPoints...192

Update the Character Script..193

Update the Player Script...194

Create the HealthBar Script..198

Configure the Health Bar Component...202

Inventory...206

Import the Inventory Slot Image..209

Configure the Inventory Slot...210

Create the Inventory Script...218

Summary..231

Chapter 7: Characters, Coroutines, and Spawn Points **233**

Create a Game Manager...233

Singletons...234

Creating the Singleton...235

Build a GameManager Prefab...238

Spawn Points...238

Build a Spawn Point Prefab..241

Configure the Player Spawn Point...245

Spawn the Player...246

In Summary..248

A Spawn Point for Enemies...249

Camera Manager..251

Using the Camera Manager..253

Character Class Design..256

The Virtual Keyword..256

The Enemy Class 257

    Refactoring 257

    The Internal Access Modifier 258

Coroutines 259

    Invoking Coroutines 260

    Pausing or "Yielding" Execution 260

    A Complete Coroutine 260

    Coroutines with Time Intervals 261

    The Abstract Keyword 261

    Implementing the Enemy Class 263

    The DamageCharacter() method 263

    ResetCharacter() 266

    Calling ResetCharacter() in OnEnable() 266

    KillCharacter() 267

Updating the Player Class 267

    Refactoring Prefab Instantiation 269

    Review 270

    Using What We've Built 271

    OnCollisionEnter2D 272

    OnCollisionExit2D 273

    Configure the Enemy Script 274

Summary 275

Chapter 8: Artificial Intelligence and Slingshots **277**

The Wander Algorithm 277

    Getting Started 278

    Create the Wander Script 279

    Wander Variables 280

Build Out Start()...282

The Wander Coroutine 283

Choosing a New Endpoint..285

Angles to Radians to Vectors!..287

Enemy Walk Animation...287

The Move() Coroutine 291

Configure Wander Script..294

OnTriggerEnter2D()...295

OnTriggerExit2D()..297

Gizmos...299

Self-Defense 302

Classes Needed 303

Ammo Class 303

Import the Assets...304

Add Components, Set Layers..304

Update the Layer Collision Matrix..305

Build the Ammo Script...306

Before We Forget ... Make the AmmoObject Prefab 308

Object Pooling...308

Building the Weapon Class..310

Stubbing-Out Methods 313

The SpawnAmmo Method 315

The Arc Class and Linear Interpolation..317

Screen Points and World Points...320

The FireAmmo Method 321

Configure the Weapon Script...323

Arcing 324

Animating the Slingshot..326

    Animation and Blend Trees..326

Blend Trees 327

    Clean Up the Animator...328

    Build the Walking Blend Tree..329

    Layers, All the Way Down 332

    A Note About Blend Types..333

    Animation Parameters...333

    Use the Parameters..335

    Ok, but *Why*? 337

    Loop Time..339

    Create the Transitions...339

Updating the Movement Controller 340

    Import the Fight Sprites...342

    Create Animation Clips 342

    Build the Fighting Blend Tree...344

    Exit Time...346

    Update the Weapon Class..347

    Add the Variables...347

    Start()...349

    Update Update()...350

    Determining Direction 350

    The Slope Method...353

    Calculate the Slopes...354

    Comparing *y*-Intercepts...355

    HigherThanNegativeSlopeLine() 356

The GetQuadrant() method 357

The UpdateState() Method 359

Flicker When Damaged 362

Update the Player and Enemy Classes 363

Building for Platforms 364

Exiting the Game 367

Summary 367

What's Next 368

Communities 368

Learn More 369

Where to Find Help 369

Game Jams 370

News and Articles 371

Games and Assets 371

Beyond! 371

Index 373

About the Author

Jared Halpern is a software developer with a background in Computer Science and over 12 years of experience working in a wide range of technologies. Lately he has specialized in Apple and Unity. Jared has built many iPhone apps over the years, including games, augmented reality, photography, eCommerce, video, and GIF apps. His interests include Swift, Unity, AR, Game Development, and the creative application of these technologies. He has an immense passion for the potential of games as an interactive medium to tell stories and give experiences in ways that other mediums cannot. He currently enjoys working as a freelance software developer. Jared is on Twitter: @JaredEHalpern and his website: `https://JaredHalpern.com`.

About the Technical Reviewer

Jason Whitehorn is an experienced entrepreneur and software developer and has helped many oil and gas companies automate and enhance their oilfield solutions through field data capture, SCADA, and machine learning. Jason obtained his bachelor of science in computer science from Arkansas State University, but he traces his passion for development back many years before then, having first taught himself to program BASIC on his family's computer while still in middle school.

When he is not mentoring and helping his team at work, writing, or pursuing one of his many side projects, Jason enjoys spending time with his wife and four children and living in the Tulsa, Oklahoma region. More information about Jason can be found on his website: `https://jason.whitehorn.us`.

Acknowledgments

Above all, I want to thank my wife Drew for her boundless support, love, advice, patience, snacks, and encouragement over the past year while I worked evenings and weekends on this book. I could never have done this without you.

I would like to thank Apress Publishing for the opportunity to write this book. The experience of working with editors Aaron Black and Jessica Vakili was a true pleasure from start to finish. The impact of their professionalism, insight, and assistance at every step of the way cannot be overstated. This book benefited immensely from the guidance and attention to detail from my technical reviewer Jason Whitehorn and development editor James Markham. Thank you to Liz Arcury from the Apress social team for all your help.

My programming knowledge has benefited greatly from the community over at gamedev.stackexchange.com, especially moderator Douglas Gregory. I also thank the folks at Unity who lent their expertise during discussions in Unity Forums, in particular Gregory Labute.

I owe a tremendous debt to my parents, who have always supported my interests in technology and writing, my sister Sam whose work ethic inspires me, and my brother Zach who always has my back.

I also thank my friends and family, especially Derina and Justin Man, Brian Wesnofske, George Peralta, Nelson Pereira, Jolene and Maris Schwartz, Melissa Gordon, Constantinos Sevdinoglou, Ben Buckley, and Gene Goykhman for their never-ending support, positivity, and enthusiasm.

Preface

My video game "history" started in the public library when I discovered a series of beat-up, paperback books with titles resembling, "How to Write Your Own Computer Games in BASIC." By copying code from the book into an editor, I was able to create rudimentary adventure games. In college, I used C++ and Direct-X to create a *Bejeweled* clone with a *Star Trek* theme. As an iOS Developer, I eventually worked on a virtual-pet game using Apple's SceneKit and SpriteKit frameworks. When I discovered the Unity game engine, everything I had been attempting to do just came together. Instead of spending half a week writing the code to parse and slice sprites, Unity allowed me to drag and drop a spritesheet, click a button, then get on with development. I could finally focus on *making games*, instead of spending the majority of my time writing code.

It's possible to create video games—great video games, without Unity or any game engine. But it will take much, much longer than it needs to. You'll spend time and effort solving problems that aren't necessary to solve any more. It may take years to finish. Because life will also be happening during those years, it's possible, and in fact likely, that you'll never finish the game. Speaking from experience—I rarely finished any of the game projects that I started before I was introduced to Unity.

Teddy Roosevelt once was quoted in his autobiography, "Do what you can, with what you've got, where you are." I subscribe to that mindset, and I also believe that hard work alone won't always help you accomplish your goals. Success in life can often be about leverage: leveraging whatever resources you have, where ever you are, for maximum impact. The trick for making the most of your time is to find multipliers: things that allow you to produce a *multiple* of what you'd otherwise be capable of producing. Unity is one such multiplier. Unity allows you to take whatever time you have—nights, weekends, a 30-minute lunch break, and maximize the usage of that time toward making games. By using Unity to get the most out of your time, you're more likely to actually finish your game.

When I set out to write this book, I wanted to write the type of book I'd want to read if I were learning Unity for the first time. Hopefully I succeeded. In the following pages, you'll learn the fundamental skills required to create your own video games in Unity, and perhaps leave your own mark on the future of gaming. Let's get started.

About This Book

Who Is This Book For?

This book was written for programmers interested in making video games with Unity. It's not recommended that you learn to program for the first time while reading this book.

The programming language used in this text is C#. Although this text does not include a C# tutorial, the C# language is syntactically similar to many other popular programming languages. If you're already familiar with a language such as Java, then the syntax of C# will come naturally to you. Explanations of pertinent aspects of C# are included with the code examples used while building the game in this book.

What Are We Building?

This book is structured toward building a 2D RPG-style game in Unity over the course of eight chapters. The game is in the style of those top-down RPGs from the 1990s, but the concepts can be carried over to create other types of games as well.

You should feel free to tinker with the code, break things, change things around, and tweak values. If you break something and can't figure out how to fix it, refer to the source code from the Apress GitHub account to fix things. As you're working your way through this book, remember that it can be helpful to have something explained a different way. If you're not content with an explanation in this book, or if you would benefit from an alternate explanation, look to the Unity documentation online. Look at gamedev.stackexchange.com and the official Unity forums and ask questions. Make sure you understand what's going on. Don't settle for half of an understanding—you'll do yourself a disservice.

What You Will Need for This Book

The hardware requirements for this book are minimal: a PC or MacBook made in the past few years. The software requirements to run Unity 2018 are Windows 7 SP1+, 8, 10, 64-bit versions only; or macOS 10.11+. We'll be using the personal edition of the Unity software, which is free.

Art Sources

The Enemy sprites in this book were created using a wonderful procedural-generation sprite tool created by Robert Norenberg. The tool can be found here: `https://0x72.itch.io/pixeldudesmaker`

The typeface used in this book's sample game is called Silkscreen. Silkscreen was created by Jason Kottke and can be found here: `https://www.1001fonts.com/silkscreen-font.html`

The heart and coin sprites are sourced from the sprite set on OpenGameArt.org created by user: ArMM1998 and licensed CC0, public-domain.

The map tile artwork was created by the author, Jared Halpern, based heavily on pixel-style art from the heart and coin sprite set on OpenGameArt.org. The player sprites were all created from scratch by the author as well. Both the map tile artwork and the player sprites are licensed by CC0, public-domain.

CHAPTER 1

Games and Game Engines

In this introductory chapter, I'll talk a bit about game engines: what they are, and why they're used. I'll also discuss a few game engines of historical significance, as well as introduce the high-level capabilities of Unity. If you want to get straight to making games, feel free to skim or skip this chapter and come back to it later.

Game Engines—What Are They?

Game engines are software development tools designed to reduce the cost, complexity, and time-to-market required in the development of video games. These software tools create a layer of abstraction on top of the most common tasks in developing video games. The layers of abstraction are packaged together into tools designed to function as interoperable components that can be replaced outright or extended with additional third party components.

Game engines provide tremendous efficiency benefits by reducing the depth of knowledge required to make games. They can be minimal in their prebuilt functionality or full-featured, allowing game developers to focus entirely on writing gameplay code. Game engines offer an incredible advantage over starting from scratch for solo developers or teams who just want to focus on making the best game possible. When building the

© Jared Halpern 2019
J. Halpern, *Developing 2D Games with Unity*, https://doi.org/10.1007/978-1-4842-3772-4_1

sample game in this book, you won't need to build complex mathematical libraries from the ground up or figure out how to render individual pixels on-screen, because the developers who created Unity have already done that work for you.

Well-designed modern game engines do a good job of separating functionality internally. The game play code, which consists of code describing the player and inventory, is kept separate from the code that decompresses an .mp3 file and loads it into memory. Game play code will call on well-defined engine API interfaces to request things like "draw this sprite at this location" and so forth.

The component-based architecture of a well-designed game engine allows for extensibility that encourages adoption, because the development team is not locked into a predetermined set of engine capabilities. This extensibility is especially important if the game engine source code is not available as open-source or is prohibitively expensive to license. The Unity game engine is purpose built to allow for third party plug-ins. It even goes so far as to provide an Asset Store containing plug-ins, accessible through the Unity Editor.

Many game engines allow for cross-platform compilation as well, meaning that your game code is not constrained to a single platform. The engine does this by not making assumptions about the underlying computer architecture and letting the developer specify which platform they're using. If you wanted to release your game for console, desktop, and mobile, the game engine allows you to flip a few switches to set the build configuration to that platform.

There are caveats to the miracles of cross-platform compilation though. Although cross-platform compilation is an amazing feature and testament to how far game technology has come, keep in mind that if you're building a game for multiple platforms, you'll need to provide different image sizes and allow for the code reading in the controls to accept different kinds of peripherals such as a keyboard. You might need to adjust the layout of your game on-screen as well as numerous other tasks. It can actually be a lot of work just to port a game from one platform to another, but you probably won't have to touch the game engine itself.

Some game engines are so visually oriented that they allow for the creation of games without writing a single line of code. Unity has the ability to customize user-interfaces that can be configured for use by other nonprogrammer members of the development team such as level designers, animators, art directors, and game designers.

There are many different types of game engines, and there are no rules as to which functionality is absolutely *required* to be considered a game engine. The most popular game engines contain some or all of the following functionality:

- Graphics rendering engine, supporting 2D or 3D graphics

- Physics engine that supports collision detection

- Audio engine to load and play sounds and music files

- Scripting support to implement gameplay logic

- A world object model defining the contents and properties of the game world

- Animation handling to load animation frames and play them

- Networking code to allow for multiplayer, downloadable content, and leaderboards

- Multithreading to allow game logic to execute simultaneously

- Memory management because no computer has unlimited memory

- Artificial intelligence for pathfinding and computer opponents

If you're not fully sold yet on using a game engine, consider the following analogy.

Say you want to build a house. To start with, this house will have a concrete foundation, a nice wood floor, sturdy walls, and a weather-treated wooden roof. There are two ways of going about building this house:

The First Way to Build a House

Excavate the ground using a hand shovel until you've dug sufficiently deep to plant the foundation. Make concrete by heating limestone and clay at 2,640 °F in a kiln, grind it, and mix in a bit of gypsum. Take the powdered concrete you've created, mix it with water, crushed stone or fine sand, and lay your foundation.

At the same time you lay the foundation, you'll need steel rebars to strengthen the concrete. Gather the iron ore required to make steel rebar and smelt it in a blast furnace to make ingots. Melt and hot-roll those ingots into sturdy reinforcement bars for the concrete foundation.

After that, it's time to build the frame on which you'll hang your walls. Take your axe and start chopping down trees. Felling a few hundred or so timber will be enough to supply the raw materials, but next you'll need to take each timber and mill them into lumber. When you're done, don't forget to treat the lumber so it's weatherproof and doesn't rot or become infested with insects. Build out your joists and girders on which you'll lay the floor, and are you exhausted yet? We're just getting started!

The Second Way to Build a House

Purchase bags of premixed concrete, steel rebar, treated lumber from a mill, a dozen boxes of paper-tape galvanized nails, and a pneumatic nail gun. Mix and pour your concrete to create your foundation, lay down the premade steel rebar, let the concrete set, then build out your floor with the treated lumber.

About the First Approach

The first way of building a house requires tremendous amount of knowledge simply to create the materials needed to begin building a house. This approach requires that you know the precise ratio of raw materials needed and techniques to make concrete and steel. You'll need to know how to fell trees without ending up pinned underneath one, and you'll have to know the proper chemicals required to treat the lumber, which you've taken great pains to cut into hundreds of uniform beams. Even if you possessed all the knowledge required to build a house this way, it would still take you thousands of hours.

This first approach is analogous to sitting down to write a video game without using a game engine. You must do everything from scratch: write the math libraries, graphics rendering code, collision detection algorithms, network code, asset loading libraries, audio player code, and much more. Even if you knew how to do all these things from the get-go, it would still take you a long time to write the game engine code and debug it. If you aren't familiar with linear algebra, rendering techniques, and how to optimize culling algorithms, you should expect that it could take you years before you have enough of a game engine that you can actually start writing the game to go along with it.

About the Second Approach

The second way of building a house assumes that you aren't starting entirely from scratch. It doesn't require that you know how to work a blast furnace, fell hundreds of timbers, or mill them to make lumber. The second way allows you to focus entirely on building the house instead of making the materials that you'll need to build the house. Your house will be constructed faster, cost less as a result, and probably be higher quality, provided you carefully selected the materials and know how to use them.

The second approach is analogous to sitting down to write a video game and using a prebuilt game engine. The game developers are able to focus on the game's content and don't need to know how to do complex calculations to figure out if two objects collided as they're flying through the air because the game engine will do that for them. There's no need to construct an asset-loading system, write low-level code to read user-input, decompress sound files, or parse animation file formats. It's unnecessary to build this functionality common to all video games because the game engine developers have already put thousands of hours into writing, testing, debugging, and optimizing code to do these things already.

In conclusion ...

It is impossible to overstate the advantage that game engines give to the independent developer or the big-studio team working on the next hit game. Some developers want to write their own game engines as a programming exercise to learn how everything works under the hood, and they will learn a tremendous amount. But if your intention is to ship a game, then you're doing yourself a disservice by not using a premade game engine.

Game Engines Historically

Historically game engines have sometimes been closely tied to the games themselves. In 1987, Ron Gilbert, along with some help from Chip Morningstar, created the SCUMM, or Script Creation Utility for *Maniac Mansion* game engine, while working at Lucasfilm Games. SCUMM is a great example of a game engine that was custom-made for a specific *type* of game. The "MM" in SCUMM stands for *Maniac Mansion*, which was a critically acclaimed adventure game and the first to use the point-and-click style interface, which Gilbert also invented.

The SCUMM game engine was responsible for converting scripts consisting of human-readable tokenized words such as "walk character to door" into byte-sized programs to be read by the game engine interpreter. The interpreter was responsible for controlling the games' actors on screen and presenting the sound and graphics. The ability to script gameplay instead of coding it, facilitated rapid prototyping and allowed the team to begin building and focusing on the gameplay from an early stage. Although the SCUMM engine was developed specifically for *Maniac Mansion* (Figure 1-1), it also was used for other hit games such as *Full Throttle, The Secret of Monkey Island, Indiana Jones and the Last Crusade: The Graphic Adventure*, and more.

Figure 1-1. *Maniac Mansion, from Lucasfilm Games, uses the SCUMM Engine*

When compared with modern day game engines like Unity, the SCUMM Engine lacks a great deal of flexibility, as it was custom-made for point-and-click style games. However, like Unity, the SCUMM engine allowed game developers to focus on gameplay instead of continuously rewriting graphics and sound code for each game, saving untold amounts of time and effort.

Sometimes game engines can have an enormous impact on the industry as a whole. In mid-1991, a seismic shift in the industry occurred at a company named id Software, when 21-year-old John Carmack built a 3D game engine for a game called *Wolfenstein 3D*. Up until then, 3D graphics were generally limited to slow-moving flight simulation games or games with simple polygons, because the available computer hardware was too slow to calculate and display the number of surfaces necessary for a fast-paced 3D action game. Carmack was able to work around the current hardware limitations by using a graphics technique called *raycasting*. This allowed for fast display of 3D environments by calculating and displaying only the surfaces visible to the player, instead of the entire area around the player.

This unique approach allowed Carmack, along with John Romero, designer Tom Hall, and artist Adrian Carmack to create a violent, fast-paced game about mowing down Nazis that spawned the first-person shooter (FPS) genre of video games. The Wolfenstein 3D engine was licensed by id Software to several other titles. They have produced seven game engines to date, which have been used in influential titles such as *Quake III Arena*, a *Doom* reboot, and *Wolfenstein II: The New Colossus*.

These days, building a rough 3D FPS-game prototype is something an experienced game developer can do in a few days using a powerful game engine like Unity.

Game Engines Today

Modern-day AAA game development studios such as Bethesda Game Studios and Blizzard Entertainment often have their own in-house, proprietary game engines. Bethesda's in-house game engine is called: Creation Engine and was used to create *The Elder Scrolls V: Skyrim* as well as *Fallout 4*. Blizzard has their own proprietary game engine used to make games such as *World of Warcraft* and *Overwatch*.

A proprietary in-house game engine may start out as built for a specific game project. After that project is released, the game engine often finds a new life when it's reused for the next game coming out of that game studio. The engine might require upgrades to stay current and take advantage of the latest technology, but it doesn't need to be rebuilt from the ground-up.

If a game development company doesn't have an in-house engine, they typically use an open-source engine, or license a third-party engine such as Unity. To create a significant 3D game these days without the use of a game engine would be an incredibly demanding task—financially as well as technologically. In fact, game studios with in-house game engines require separate programming teams dedicated entirely to building out engine features and optimizing them.

Having said all of this, why would an AAA-studio choose not to use a game engine like Unity, but instead elect to build their own in-house engine? Companies such as Bethesda and Blizzard have an enormous body of pre-existing code to draw from, financial resources, and a wealth of deeply talented programmers. For certain types of projects, they want complete control over every facet of their game and game engine.

Even having all of these advantages over the typical small game studios, Bethesda still used Unity to develop the mobile game: *Fallout Shelter*; and Blizzard used Unity to develop a little cross-platform collectible card game: Hearthstone. When time equals money, a game engine like Unity can be used to quickly prototype, build out, and iterate on functionality. The time = money equation is especially relevant if your plan is to release a game to multiple platforms. Porting an in-house engine to specific platforms such as iOS and Android can be time consuming. If a project doesn't require the same level of control over the game engine that you would need when developing a game like *Overwatch*, using a cross-compatible game engine like Unity is a no-brainer.

The Unity Game Engine

Unity is an extremely popular game engine that affords a huge number of advantages over other game engines available in the market today. Unity offers a visual workflow with drag-and-drop capabilities and supports scripting with C#, a very popular programming language. Unity has long supported 3D and 2D graphics, and the toolsets for both grow more sophisticated and user-friendly with each release.

Unity has several tiers of licenses and is free for projects with revenues up to $100k. It offers cross-platform support for 27 different platforms and takes advantage of graphics APIs specific to the system architecture, including Direct3D, OpenGL, Vulkan, Metal, and several others. Unity Teams offers cloud-based project collaboration and continuous integration.

Since its debut in 2005, Unity has been used to develop thousands of desktop, mobile, and console games and applications. A small sampling of some well-known titles developed over the years with Unity would include: *Thomas Was Alone* (2010), *Temple Run* (2011), *The Room* (2012), *RimWorld* (2013), *Hearthstone* (2014), *Kerbal Space Program* (2015), *Pokémon GO* (2016), and *Cuphead* (2017), which is seen in Figure 1-2.

Figure 1-2. *Cuphead, developed by StudioMDHR, uses the Unity Game Engine*

For game developers who want to customize their workflow, Unity affords the ability to extend the default visual editor. This extremely powerful mechanism allows for the creation of custom tools, editors, and inspectors. Imagine creating a visual tool for your game designers to easily tweak values for in-game objects like hit-points for a character class, skill-trees, attack range, or item drops, without having to go into the code and modify values or use an external database. This is all made possible and straightforward by the Editor Extension functionality that Unity provides.

Another Unity advantage is the Unity Asset Store. The Asset Store is an online storefront where artists, developers, and content creators can upload content to be bought and sold. The Asset Store contains thousands of free and paid Editor Extensions, models, scripts, textures, shaders, and more, which teams can use to accelerate their development timelines and enhance a final product.

Summary

In this chapter we learned about the many advantages to using a premade game engine as opposed to writing your own. We touched on a couple of interesting game engines of yesteryear and the impact they had on game development as a whole. We also outlined the specific advantages that Unity offers and mentioned some of the better-known games developed using the Unity engine. Perhaps one day soon, someone will mention your game as one of the better known games made with Unity!

CHAPTER 2

Introduction to Unity

This chapter covers the Unity Editor—installing, configuring, navigating its windows, using its toolset, and getting familiar with the project structure. Not all of this material will be immediately relevant to your everyday work in Unity, and you'll probably have to refer back to this chapter a few times in the future anyway, so don't try to commit it all to memory on the first go.

Install Unity

First thing's first: head over to `https://store.unity.com` and download Unity. Because we're just learning to use Unity, get the Personal version, which is free.

For our purposes in this book, the main difference between the free version and the Plus tier is that the free version flashes the "Made with Unity" on the splash screen, while the Plus version allows you to create a custom splash screen. The Plus, Pro, and Enterprise versions get gradually more expensive, but offer interesting benefits such as better analytics and control over your data, multiplayer features, test builds using the Unity Cloud service, and even access to the source code at the Enterprise level.

You should remember that these tiers your qualification for each tier is determined by revenue. If you or your game company generate less than $100k/year USD, you qualify to use Unity Personal Edition free of charge. If your company generates less than $200k/year USD, you're required to use the Unity Plus tier. Finally, if your company generates more than $200k/year USD you must use Unity Pro. Not a bad deal at all.

© Jared Halpern 2019
J. Halpern, *Developing 2D Games with Unity*, https://doi.org/10.1007/978-1-4842-3772-4_2

While installing Unity, the Unity Download Assistant will prompt you to select which components of the Unity Editor you want to install. Ensure that the following components are checked off: Unity 2018 (or the most recent version), Documentation, Standard Assets, and Example Project. We'll be building our sample game to run stand-alone on your desktop (PC, Mac, or Linux) in this book. If you'd like, you can also check off boxes to install the components for WebGL, iOS, or Android Build Support to build for those platforms as well.

Configure Unity

After installing Unity and running for the first time, you'll be prompted to sign in to your account (Figure 2-1). Creating and signing into an account isn't really necessary unless you want to take advantage of some more advanced features such as Cloud Builds and Ads, but there's no harm in creating an account and signing in anyway. You'll need an account if you want to use anything from the Unity Asset Store.

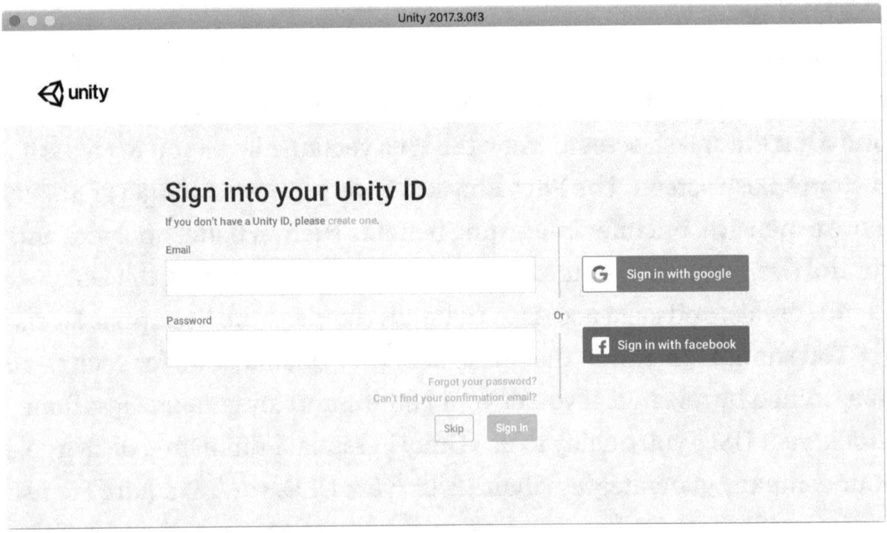

Figure 2-1. Unity sign in screen

Let's go through Unity's Projects and Learning screen, as seen in Figure 2-2, and point out a few things. On the upper left, you'll notice two tabs—Projects and Learn.

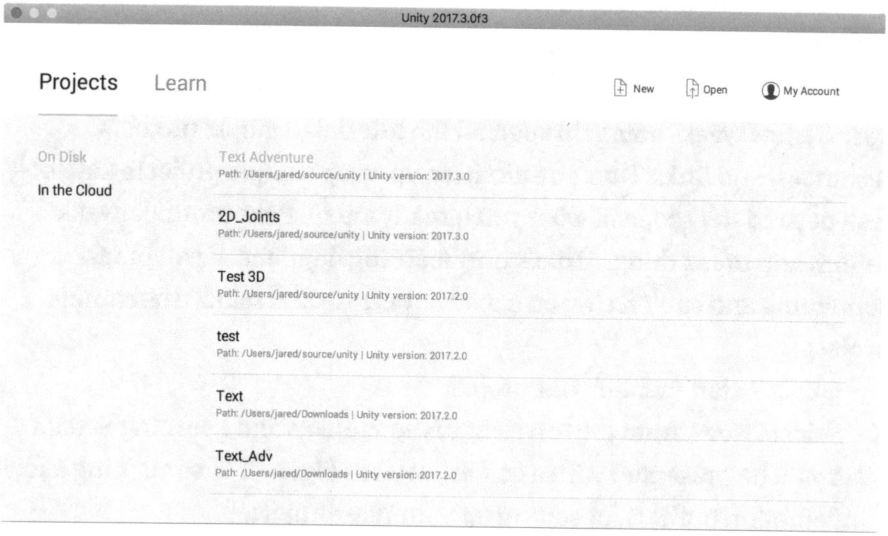

Figure 2-2. *Unity Projects and Learning screen*

Select Projects and let's go through the options:

On Disk

A history of the last six projects you've worked on will appear, and can be opened by selecting them.

In the Cloud

This refers to using cloud-based collaborative projects, which we won't be covering. Unity Teams has a feature called Unity Collaborate that allows team members to update files in a project and publish those changes to the cloud. Other team members can then view those changes and decide whether to sync their local project with the changes or ignore them. If you've ever worked with Git, Unity Collaborate is very similar, but whereas Git has a bit of a learning curve, Unity Collaborate is intentionally designed to be very visual and easy to use.

Now select the Learn tab.

The Learn section has a wealth of information and you could easily spend a few weeks going through all the tutorials, sample projects, resources, and links. Don't be afraid to open up sample projects that look well beyond the scope of what you already know. Poke around, tweak things, and break things. That's how learning happens. If you break something and can't fix it, you can always close and reload the sample project.

Ok, let's start creating our project.

Select "New" from the top right of the Projects and Learning Screen.

You'll be presented with a screen, seen in Figure 2-3, containing a few configuration options for setting up your new project.

The default name of a new Unity project is, "New Unity Project." Change the Project Name to be "RPG" or "Greatest RPG Ever", as seen in Figure 2-3. Select the radio button next to 2D to configure the project to show a side view in 2D at all times. Don't worry if you forget to set this—it's easy to switch once our project is created.

Note the file path in the Location text box. That's where Unity will save your project. I like to organize source code on my computer inside a parent directory called "source" with Unity code inside a "Unity" subdirectory, but you can organize your directory structure however you wish. If you're logged in, you'll see a toggle switch to turn on Unity Analytics. You can leave this setting turned off, as we won't be using it.

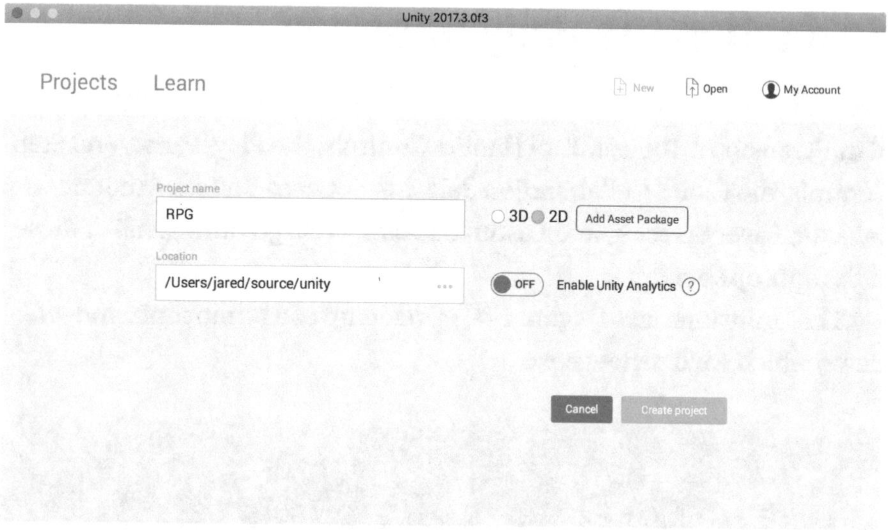

Figure 2-3. *Project creation*

Hit the "Create Project" button to create a new project with these settings and open it in the Unity Editor.

The Script Editor: Visual Studio

As of Unity 2018.1, Visual Studio is now the default Script Editor for developing C# scripts. Historically, the built-in Script Editor shipped with Unity was MonoDevelop, but starting with Unity 2018.1, Unity ships with Visual Studio for Mac instead of MonoDevelop on macOS. On Windows, Unity ships with Visual Studio 2017 Community and no longer ships with MonoDevelop.

Next up, we'll get to know the Unity Editor.

Navigating the Unity Interface

Stretching across the top of the Unity Editor is the Tool Bar, which consists of the Transform Toolset, Tool Handle Controls, the Play, Pause, and Step Controls, the Cloud Collaboration Selector, Services Button, Account Selector, Layer Selector, and Layout Selector. We'll go through all of these at the appropriate time.

The Unity interface (Figure 2-4) is made up of a number of window views, which we'll review next.

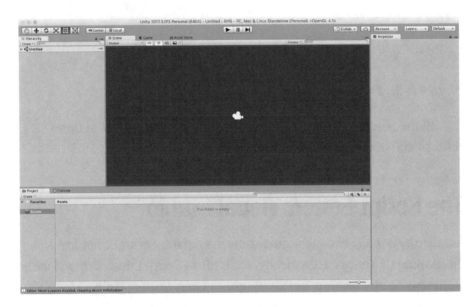

Figure 2-4. *The Unity Editor*

Understanding the Different Window Views

Let's go through the various views displayed in the Default Editor Layout. There are many views available other than those we discuss below, and we'll cover some of them later in this book.

- Scene View

Scenes can be thought of as the foundation of Unity Projects, so you'll have the Scene View open most of the time while you're working in the Unity Editor. Everything that happens in your game takes place in a Scene. The Scene View is where we'll construct our game and do most of our work with sprites and colliders. Scenes contain GameObjects and they hold all the functionality relevant to that Scene. We'll cover GameObjects in more detail in Chapter 3, but for now just know that every object in a Unity Scene is a GameObject.

- Game View

The Game View renders your game from the currently active camera's point of view. The Game View is also where you'll view and play your actual game while you're working on it in Unity Editor. There are ways of building and running your game outside of Unity Editor as well, such as a stand-alone application, in a Web browser, or on a mobile phone, and we'll cover some of these platforms later in this book.

- Asset Store

A compelling factor when choosing Unity to build games is the Unity Asset Store. As discussed in Chapter 1, the Unity Asset Store is an online storefront where artists, developers, and content creators can upload content to be bought and sold. The Unity Editor has a built-in tab that connects to the Asset Store for convenience, but you can also access the Asset Store via the Web at `https://assetstore.unity.com`. Although there's no harm in having this pane available in your Layout, there's also no harm in hiding it and only opening it when you need something from the Asset Store.

- Hierarchy Window

The Hierarchy Window displays a list of all objects in the current Scene in a hierarchical format. The Hierarchy Window also allows for the creation of new GameObjects via the "Create" drop-down menu in the top-left corner. The search field allows a developer to search for specific GameObjects by name.

In Unity, GameObjects can contain other GameObjects in what's called a "parent–child" relationship. The Hierarchy Window will display these relationships in a helpful nested format. Figure 2-5 portrays the Hierarchy Window view in an example Scene.

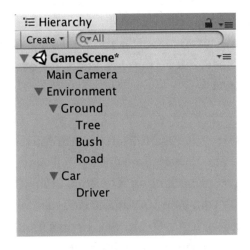

Figure 2-5. *The Hierarchy Window*

Here's a brief explanation about what we mean by "parent–child" relationships in the Hierarchy Window. The example Scene in Figure 2-5 is called GameScene, and it contains a GameObject called Environment. Environment is a parent object to several GameObjects, including one called Ground. Ground is a child object with respect to Environment. However, Ground contains several child objects of its own, including Tree, Bush, and Roads. Ground is the parent object with respect to these child objects.

- Project Window

The Project Window gives an overview of all the content in the Assets folder. It's helpful to create folders in the Project Window to organize items such as audio files, materials, models, textures, scenes, and scripts. Throughout the lifetime of your project, you'll spend a lot of time dragging and rearranging assets in folders and selecting those assets to view them in the Inspector Window. In this book, we'll demonstrate a suggested project folder structure, but you should feel free to rearrange things in a way that makes logical sense to you and the way you like to work.

- Console View

The Console View will display errors, warnings, and other output from your Unity application. There are C# scripting functions that can be used to output information to the Console View at runtime to aid in debugging. We'll cover those later on when we discuss debugging. You can toggle the various forms of output on and off via the three buttons in the top-right of the Console View.

Tip   Sometimes you'll get an error message that occurs with every Unity frame update, and those messages will clog up your Console View in a hurry. In situations like this, it's helpful to hit the Collapse toggle button to collapse all identical error messages into a single message.

- Inspector Window

The Inspector Window is one of the most useful and important windows in the Unity Editor; be sure to familiarize yourself with it. Scenes in Unity are made up of GameObjects, which consist of Components such as Scripts, Meshes, Colliders, and other elements. You can select a GameObject and use the Inspector to view and edit the attached Components and their respective properties. There are even techniques to create your own properties on GameObjects that can then be modified. We'll cover this more in later chapters. You can also use the Inspector to view and change properties on Prefabs, Cameras, Materials, and Assets as well. If an Asset is selected, such as an audio file, the Inspector will show details such as how the file was loaded, its imported size, and the compression ratio. Assets such as Material Maps will allow you to inspect the Rendering Mode and Shader.

Tip   Notice that you can access many of the more commonly used panes via the shortcut: Control (PC) or Cmd / ⌘ (Mac) + number. For example, ⌘ + 1, and ⌘ + 2 to switch between the Scene View and Game View, respectively on a Mac. This is a good way to save some time and avoid having to use the mouse for more common pane switching.

Configure and Customize the Layout

Each pane can be rearranged by grabbing the tab on the top-left of the pane and dragging it. Unity allows a user to create a custom Editor layout by dragging around panes, locking them into place, resizing them to your liking, and then saving that layout.

To save the layout, you have two options:

- Go to the menu option: Window ➤ Layouts ➤ Save Layout. When prompted, give your custom layout a name, and hit the Save button.

- Click the layout selector in the top-right-most corner of the Unity Editor (Figure 2-6). It will say Default at first. Then select Save Layout and give your custom layout a name and hit the Save button.

You can load any layout in the future from the same menu: Window ➤ Layouts, or use the Layout selector. If you want to reset your layout, simply select Default from the Layout selector.

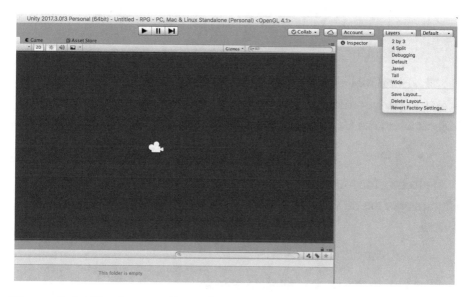

Figure 2-6. *The Layout drop-down menu*

The Transform Toolset

Next, we'll go through the different buttons and toggles that make up
the Tool Bar. The three things to note with the Tool Bar for now are: the
Transform Toolset; the Tool Handle Controls; and the Play, Pause, and
Step Controls. There are other controls on the Tool Bar but we'll get to
those when we start to use them.

The Transform tools (Figure 2-7) allow a user to navigate around the
Scene View and interact with GameObjects.

Figure 2-7. *The Transform Toolset*

The six Transform tools, from left to right, are:

- Hand

The Hand tool allows you to left-click and drag the mouse around the screen to pan around the view. Note that you won't be able to select any objects when the Hand Tool is selected.

- Move

Selecting the Move tool and selecting a GameObject in either the Hierarchy or Scene View will allow you to move that object around the screen.

- Rotate

The Rotate tool rotates selected objects.

- Scale

The Scale tool scales selected objects.

- Rect

The Rect tool allows for the moving and resizing of selected objects using 2D Handles, which will appear on the selected object.

- Move, Rotate, or Scale Selected Objects

This tool is a combination of the Move, Rotate, and Scale tools, consolidated into one set of Handles.

At any time, you can temporarily switch to the Hand tool (only in 2D projects) by pressing Option (Mac) or Alt (PC) and move around the Scene.

Tip   The six controls in the Transform toolset are individually mapped to the following six keys: Q, W, E, R, T, Y. Use these hot-keys to quickly switch between the tools.

A useful trick when using the Move tool (hot-key: W) is to have the GameObject snap to specific increments by holding down Control (PC) or Cmd / ⌘ (Mac). Adjust the snap increment settings in Edit ➤ Snap Settings menu.

Handle Position Controls

To the right of the Transform Toolset you'll find the handle position controls, as seen in Figure 2-8.

Figure 2-8. *The handle position controls*

Handles are the GUI controls on objects used to manipulate them in a Scene. The Handle position controls allow you to adjust the position of the Handles for selected objects and how they are oriented.

The first toggle button (see Figure 2-8) allows you to set the position of the Handles.

The two options for position are:

- Pivot: this places the Handles at the selected object's pivot point.

- Center: this places the Handles at the center of the selected object.

The second toggle button allows you to set the orientation of the Handles. Note that the orientation button will be grayed out if the Scale tool is selected, as orientation doesn't pertain to scale. The two orientation options are:

- Local: when selected, a Transform tools functionality will be relative to the GameObject.

- Global: when selected, a Transform tools functionality will be relative to the world space orientation.

Tip It's possible to change the pivot point of a Sprite by selecting the Sprite in the Project window, switching the Sprite Mode to Multiple in the Inspector, and clicking the Sprite Editor button. Tap the Slice button in the Sprite Editor and select a Pivot point from the drop-down menu.

Play, Pause, and Step Controls

The Unity Editor has two modes: Play Mode and Edit Mode. When the Play button is pressed, provided there are no bugs preventing the game from building, the Unity Editor enters Play Mode and switches to the Game View (see Figure 2-9). The shortcut to enter play mode is Control (PC) or Cmd / ⌘ (Mac) + P.

Figure 2-9. *Play, Pause, and Step controls*

While still in Play Mode, you can switch back to Scene View by selecting the tab at the top of the Scene Pane if you want to inspect GameObjects in the running Scene. This is helpful if you need to debug a Scene. While in Play Mode, you also can press the Pause button at any time to pause the running Scene. The shortcut to pause the scene is Control + Shift + P on PC, and Cmd / ⌘ (Mac) + Shift + P on Mac.

The Step button allows Unity to advance a single frame, and then pause again. This is helpful for debugging as well. The shortcut to Step ahead by a single frame is Control + Alt + P on PC, and Cmd / ⌘ (Mac) + Option + P on Mac.

Pressing the Play button again while in Play Mode will stop playing the Scene, switch the Unity Editor back to Edit Mode, and switch back to Scene View.

An important thing to always remember when working in Play Mode is that any changes you make to objects will not be saved or reflected in the Scene once the Editor switches back to Edit mode. It's very easy to forget about this while a Scene is running, make some changes and tweak things until they're perfect, only to have those changes lost when you stop playing.

Tip   To make it super obvious that you're in Play Mode, it's useful to configure Unity preferences to switch the background tint color of the Editor automatically when entering Play Mode. To do so, go to the menu option as seen in Figure 2-10: Unity ➤ Preferences. Select Colors from the options on the left, and look for the section header, "General." Select your preferred background tint color and exit out. Now hit the Play button to see the results. The background of the Unity Editor should be tinted to your selected color.

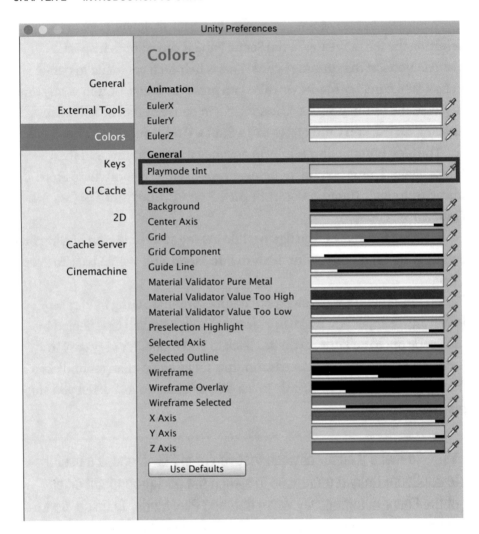

Figure 2-10. *Unity Preferences menu*

Unity Project Structure

The main two Unity project folders to know are the Assets/ folder and the ProjectSettings/ folder. If you're using any form of source version control, these are the two folders you should check in.

The Assets/ folder is where all game resources are located including scripts, images, sound files, and so forth.

The ProjectSettings/ folder, as the name suggests, contains all types of project settings pertaining to physics, audio, networking, tags, time, meshes, and so on. Everything set from the menu Edit ➤ Project Settings is stored in this folder.

There are other folders and files in the Unity project structure but they're all generated based off of the contents of Assets/ or ProjectSettings/. The Library/ folder is a local cache for imported assets, and Temp/ is used for temporary files generated during the build process. Files ending with a .csproj extension are C# project files, and files ending with .sln are solution files used for the Visual Studio IDE.

Unity Documentation

Unity is very well documented, and the documentation available on Unity's website (https://docs.unity3d.com/) covers the scripting API as well as working with the Unity Editor. Unity also has dozens of video tutorials with content appropriate for all levels of developer experience in the Learn portal (https://unity3d.com/learn). The Unity Forums (https://forum.unity.com/) are the place for discussions about Unity topics, and Unity Answers (https://answers.unity.com) is a great resource to post questions and get help from fellow Unity developers in the community.

Summary

We've covered a lot of material in this chapter that will be relevant to your future as a Unity Game Developer. We introduced the most commonly used windows and views in the Unity Editor such as Scene View, where you construct your game, and Game view, where you can view your game running. We discussed how the Hierarchy Window gives an overview of all GameObjects in the current scene, how to edit the properties of these GameObjects in the Inspector, and how to manipulate them via the Transform Toolset, and Handle Position controls. Along the way, we discussed how to change the layout of these windows and views and save that layout for future use. We learned how the console view will display error messages and can be used for debugging when issues arise with our game. We concluded the chapter by pointing out the extensive Unity documentation, video tutorials, discussion forums, and Q&A resources.

CHAPTER 3

Foundations

Now that we're familiar with the Unity Editor, it's time to starting making our game. This chapter will walk you through how to construct the objects and write the code that will comprise our game. We'll talk about software design patterns used in Unity, along with some higher-level principles in Computer Science and how they're relevant to making games. You'll also learn how to control the player on-screen and play the player animations.

Game Objects: Our Container Entities

Games in Unity consist of Scenes, and everything in a Scene is called a GameObject. You'll encounter Scripts, Colliders, and other types of elements in your Unity adventures, and all of these are GameObjects. It's helpful to think of GameObjects as a sort of container, composed of many pieces of individually implemented functionalities. As we discussed in Chapter 2, GameObjects can even contain other GameObjects in parent–child relationships.

We're going to create our first GameObject, then talk about why Unity uses GameObjects as a fundamental aspect of building games.

In the Hierarchy view, select the Create button in the top-left (Figure 3-1), and select Create Empty. This creates a new GameObject in the Hierarchy view.

© Jared Halpern 2019
J. Halpern, *Developing 2D Games with Unity*, https://doi.org/10.1007/978-1-4842-3772-4_3

Figure 3-1. *One way of creating a new GameObject in the Hierarchy view*

There are a few different ways to create GameObjects. You also could have right-clicked on the Hierarchy view pane itself, or gone to the GameObject ➤ Create Empty in the top menu.

Right-click the new GameObject and select Rename. Call it "PlayerObject." This PlayerObject will contain all the logic related to the courageous player in our RPG!

Make a second GameObject and call it "EnemyObject." This EnemyObject will contain all the logic related to an enemy that our player must defeat.

As we learn how to build a game in Unity, we're also going to learn Computer Science concepts that will make you a better programmer overall, and how those concepts will make your life easier as a game developer.

Entity-Component Design

There is a concept in Computer Science known as "separation of concerns." Separation of concerns is a design principle that describes how software is divided into modules based on the functionality they perform. Each module is responsible for a single functional "concern" that should be completely encapsulated by that module. When it comes down to implementation, a concern can be a somewhat loose and interpretive term—these concerns can be as broad as the responsibility for rendering graphics on-screen, or as specific as calculating when one triangle in space overlaps with another triangle.

One of the primary motivations for separating concerns in software design is to reduce wastefulness seen when a developer writes duplicated or overlapping functionality. For example, if you have code that renders an image on-screen, you should only have to write that code once. A video game will have dozens or hundreds of situations where rendering graphics to screen is needed, but the developer only had to write that code once and can reuse it everywhere.

Unity builds on the philosophy of separation of concerns with a very popular design pattern in game programming called Entity-Component design. Entity-Component design favors "composition over inheritance," which is the notion that objects or "entities" should encourage code reuse by containing instances of classes that encapsulate specific functionality. Entities gain access to functionality via instances of these component classes. When used appropriately, composition can result in less code and be easier to understand and maintain.

This is different from the common design approach in which an object inherits functionality from a parent class. A disadvantage to using inheritance is that it can lead to deep and wide inheritance trees, where changing one small thing in a parent class can have ripple-down effects with unintended consequences.

In Unity's Entity-Component design, something called a GameObject is the Entity and the Components are actually called "Components." Everything in a Unity Scene is considered a GameObject, but GameObjects by themselves don't do anything. We implement all of our functionality in Components, then add these Components to our GameObjects to give them the behaviors that we want. Adding functionality and behaviors to an entity becomes as straightforward as adding a component to that entity. The Components themselves can be thought of as distinct modules, only focused on one thing, and decoupled from other concerns and code.

Take a look at the following diagram to get a better idea of how we might use Entity-Component design in a hypothetical game setting. The Components that provide behaviors are in the top x-axis, and the Entities in our game are in the y-column on the left.

	Graphics Renderer	Collision Detection	Physics Integration	Audio Player
Player	X	X	X	X
Enemy	X	X	X	X
Spear (weapon)	X	X	X	
Tree	X	X		
Villager	X	X		X

As you can see, the player and the enemy will need all four component functionalities. The spear weapon will need most of the functionality, especially physics for when it's thrown, but not audio. The tree doesn't require physics or audio—just graphics rendering and collision detection to ensure that anything bumping into it cannot pass through it. The villager in the preceding example requires graphics and collision detection, but will just be walking around the scene, so they don't need physics. They might need audio though, if we want our game to play an audio track of the villager interacting with the player.

The Unity Entity-Component design is not without its limitations, especially for large projects, and after many years has begun to show its age. It is due to be replaced in the future by a more data-oriented design. Now let's put this newfound knowledge to use.

Components: Building Blocks

Select our PlayerObject in the Hierarchy view, and notice how the values in the Inspector have changed. You should see something that looks like Figure 3-2.

Figure 3-2. *The Transform component*

The one element universal to all GameObjects in Unity is the Transform component, which is used to determine the position, rotation, and scale of that GameObject in the scene. We will be using the Transform component in our game when we want to move our Player character.

Sprites

If you're new to game development, you might be asking, "What's a sprite?" A *sprite* in the context of video game development is just a 2D image. If you've ever seen *Super Mario Brothers* on Nintendo (Figure 3-3), or played a game like *Stardew Valley* (Figure 3-4), *Celeste, Thimbleweed Park,* or *Terraria,* you've played games that used sprites.

Figure 3-3. *An individual sprite of Mario, the heroic plumber from Super Mario Brothers, (Nintendo)*

Figure 3-4. *The chickens, ducks, scarecrow, vegetables, trees, and all the other images in this image of Stardew Valley are individual sprites*

Animation effects in 2D games can be achieved using a technique similar to how animated films, anime, or cartoons are made. Just like individual cells (frames) of a cartoon, sprites are illustrated and saved to a disk ahead of time. Displaying individual sprites in a rapid sequence can convey the impression of motion, such as a character walking, fighting, jumping, or inevitably dying.

To see the player character on screen, we need to display the images using a Sprite Renderer Component. We will add this Sprite Renderer Component to the Player GameObject. There are a few different ways of adding a Component to a GameObject but we're going to use the Add Component button the first time.

Select the Add Component button from the Inspector, then type in "sprite" and select Sprite Renderer (Figure 3-5). This adds the Component to our Player GameObject. Instead we could have created a GameObject with the Sprite Renderer already attached by going to the GameObject menu, then selecting 2D Object ➤ Sprite.

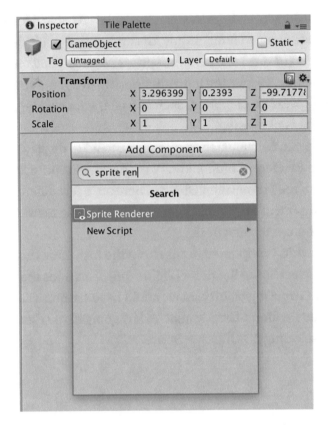

Figure 3-5. *Add a Sprite Renderer Component to the Player GameObject*

Add a Sprite Renderer Component to the EnemyObject using the same technique.

Saving the scene is a good habit to get into, so let's save the Scene right now. Type Control (PC) / CMD (Mac) + s, then create a new folder and name it "Scenes". Save the Scene as "LevelOne". We've created a new folder to hold this Scene and other Scenes that we'll create for our game.

Next, create a folder called, "Sprites" in the Project view. As you might have guessed, this will hold all the sprite assets for our project. Create another folder underneath this Sprites folder called, "Player" and another called "Enemies". Select the Sprites folder in the Project view and then go to the folder in your Downloads directory, Desktop, or where ever you've placed the unzipped folder with the downloaded game assets for this book.

In the downloaded assets for Chapter 3, select the file named Player. png, EnemyWalk_1.png, and EnemyIdle_1.png, and drag them into the Sprites folder in the Project view. Once they're in the main Sprites folder, drag them into their respective Player and Enemies folders. Your Project view should resemble Figure 3-6.

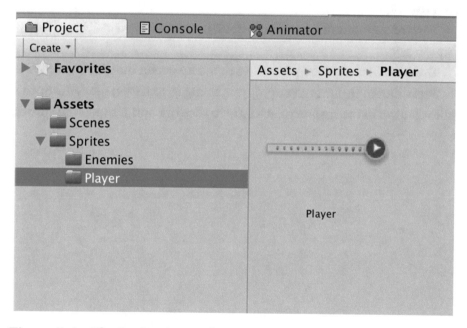

Figure 3-6. *The Project view after adding the Player sprite sheet. The Enemy sprite sheets are in the Enemies folder*

Now select the Player sprite sheet in the Project view. Notice how its properties have appeared in the Inspector on the right. We're going to configure the Asset Import Settings in the Inspector and then use the Sprite Editor to slice up this sprite sheet into individual sprites.

Set the Texture Type to "Sprite (2D and UI)" and select the Sprite Mode dropdown picker and select "Multiple." This indicates that there are multiple sprites in that sprite sheet asset.

Change the pixels per unit to 32. We'll explain the pixels per unit, or PPU, settings when we talk about cameras.

Change Filter Mode to "Point (no filter)." This will make the sprite texture appear blocky up close, which is perfect for the pixelated look of our artwork.

Toward the bottom, press the Default button, and select "None" for Compression.

Double-check that the properties in the Inspector match Figure 3-7.

Press the Apply button to apply our changes, and then press the Sprite Editor button in the Inspector. It's time to slice our sprite sheet into sprites.

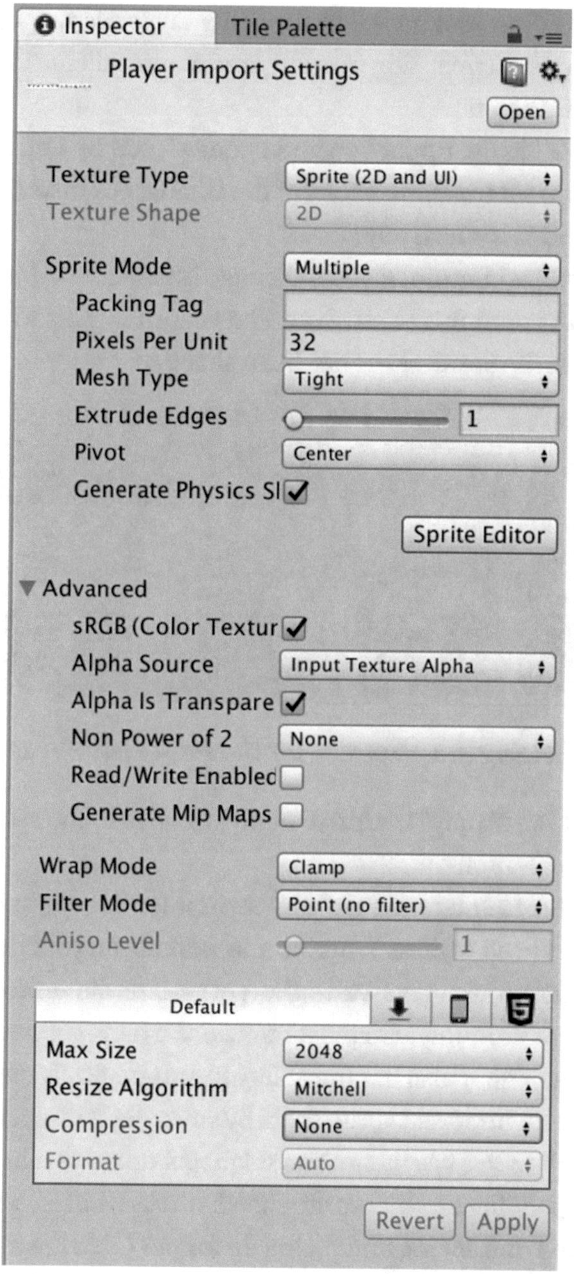

Figure 3-7. *Properties for the Player sprite sheet, as shown in the Inspector*

The Sprite Editor tool built into the Unity Engine is very convenient for taking sprite sheets, consisting of many sprites, and slicing them up into individual sprite assets.

Select "Slice" in the upper left, and choose "Grid By Cell Size" for Type. This allows us to set the dimensions of the slicing. For Pixel Size, enter 32 and 32 for X and Y, respectively.

Press the "Slice" button. If you look closely at Figure 3-8 you'll see a faint white line outlining each of our Player sprites. This white line indicates where the sprite sheet has been sliced.

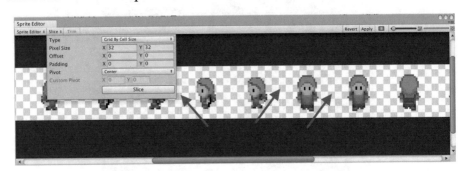

Figure 3-8. *Setting the pixel size for the imported Player sprite sheet*

Now press the "Apply" button to apply the slice to the sprite sheet. Close the Sprite Editor.

We were able to enter the exact dimensions for this sprite sheet because we knew them ahead of time. When you're working on your own games, you'll encounter sprite sheets with sprites of various dimensions and you might have to play around with the dimensions a bit to get them just right. The Unity Sprite Editor also has the ability to automatically detect sprite dimensions on an imported sprite sheet by selecting "Automatic" from Type in the Sprite Editor ➤ Slice menu. You might get mixed results from this technique, depending on what sprite sheets you use, but it's a starting point.

What did all that slicing and dicing do for us? Click the little triangle next to the Player sprite sheet and take a look at all the individual sprites extracted from the sprite sheet (Figure 3-9). We're going to create some animations using our freshly cut player sprites.

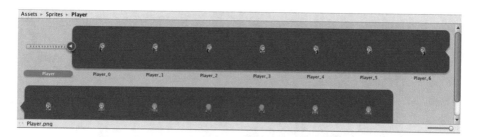

Figure 3-9. *The resulting sliced sprites from the Player sprite sheet*

Let's put these sprites to work. Select the PlayerObject. In the Inspector view, all the way to the right of the Sprite property you'll see a little circle (Figure 3-10). Click that circle to bring up the Sprite Selector screen as seen in Figure 3-11.

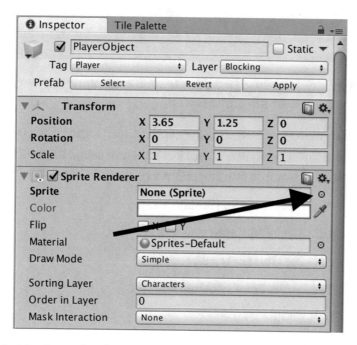

Figure 3-10. *Press this button to bring up the Select Sprite screen*

In the Sprite Selector screen, double-click to select one of the Player sprites to use as a stand-in for our PlayerObject in the Scene when we're editing our game (Figure 3-11).

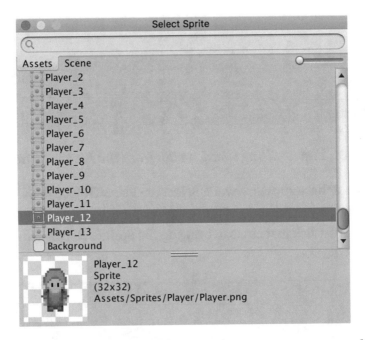

Figure 3-11. *Select one of the Player sprites to represent our player in the Scene view when the game isn't playing*

Now that we have all of our player sprites, let's import the enemy sprite sheets. Select the "EnemyIdle_1" sprite sheet and set its Import Settings in the Inspector the same as our PlayerObject:

> Texture Type: Sprite (2D and UI)
>
> Sprite Mode: Multiple
>
> Pixels Per Unit (PPU): 32
>
> Filter Mode: Point (no filter)
>
> Compression: None

Press the Apply button.

Use the Sprite Editor to slice the sprite sheet into individual 32 × 32 pixel sprites. Ensure the white slice lines appear in the right place, then press the Apply button and close the Sprite Editor. Follow the same steps for the "EnemyWalk_1" sprite sheet to slice it into individual sprites.

Animations

Let's create a new folder to hold the animations we're about to create. You remember how to do that, right? Select Assets from the Project view, right click, and then select Create ➤ Folder. Or you can click the Create button in the top-left of the Project view. Call this folder, "Animations". Select the Animations folder and create another two subfolders within it, titled "Animations" and "Controllers".

Expand the Player sprites by clicking the little arrow next to it in the Project view. Select the first Player sprite—this should be a sprite of the player walking east. Hold down the shift-key to select the three sprites next to it. Drag these four sprites together onto the PlayerObject as seen in Figure 3-12.

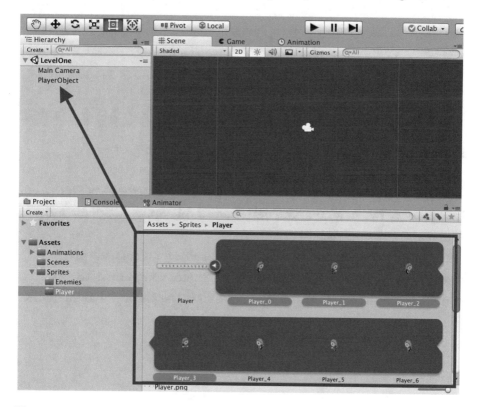

Figure 3-12. *Dragging sprites onto the PlayerObject to create a new Animation*

A screen prompting you to Create New Animation will appear (Figure 3-13). Navigate to the Animations ➤ Animations subdirectory that we created previously, and save this Animation as "player-walk-east".

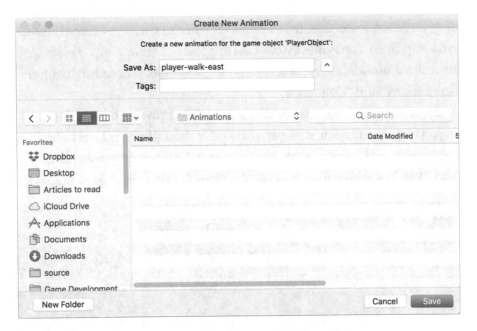

Figure 3-13. *Create and save a new Animation object*

Now select the PlayerObject and look at the Inspector view. Notice how we have two new components (Figure 3-14): Sprite Renderer and Animator.

A Sprite Renderer component is responsible for displaying or rendering a sprite. Unity also added an Animator component, which contains an Animator Controller, which allows the playing of animations.

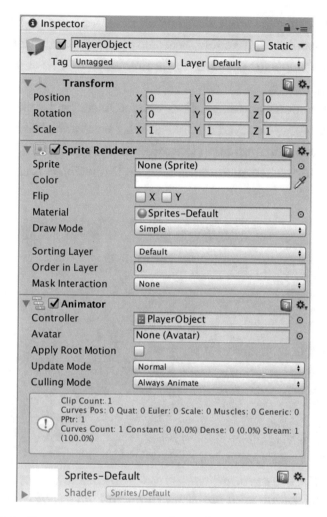

Figure 3-14. *Two new components have been automatically added: Sprite Renderer and Animator*

Dragging the sprites to the PlayerObject and creating a new Animation resulted in these two components being added to the PlayerObject.

When we added an Animation to our PlayerObject, the Unity Editor was smart enough to know that we would need some way of playing and controlling that animation. So it automatically created an Animator component to play the animation, and attached an Animation Controller object, "PlayerObject". We could have also pressed the Add Component button in the Inspector, searched for "Animator," and then added an Animator manually.

The Animation Controller called, "PlayerObject", will appear by default in the folder where we saved the "player-walk-east" animation. The default name for the Animation Controller is "PlayerObject" (Figure 3-15), which is confusing because our main Player GameObject is also called "PlayerObject."

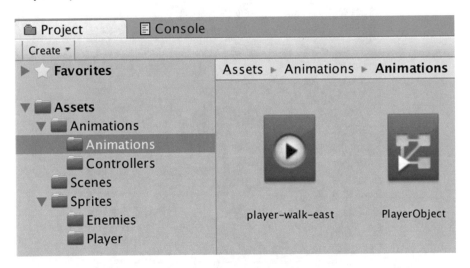

Figure 3-15. *The automatically created Animation Controller: PlayerObject, along with our first animation object: player-walk-east*

Let's rename the Animation Controller to something slightly more descriptive. Select the PlayerObject, and press the Enter-key, or right-click, and rename the object to "PlayerController".

Select, drag, and move that PlayerController object into the Controllers folder we created.

Double-click on the PlayerController object to open the Animator window.

The Animator State Machine

The Animation Controller maintains a set of rules, called a State Machine, used to determine which Animation Clip to play for an associated object based on which state the Player is in. Some examples of states used by a Player object might be: walk, attack, idle, eat, and die. We further divide up these states into directions because our player might be facing north, south, east, or west when they are in these states. A visual flow-like representation of these states is displayed in the Animator window, as seen in Figure 3-16.

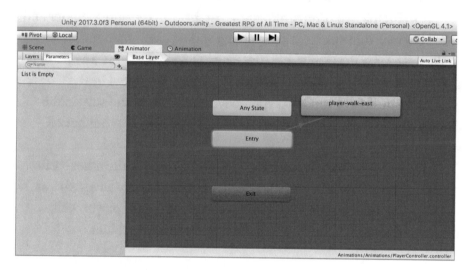

Figure 3-16. *The Animator window*

It's helpful to think of the Animation Controller as the "brain" controlling the animation. Each state in the Animation State Machine is represented by an Animation object attached to it. This Animation object contains the actual Animation Clip to play for that state. The Animation Controller also maintains the details of how to transition between the animation states.

As you can see in the Animator window, our Animation Controller has the following states: Entry state, Any, Exit, and the state we just added: player-walk-east. The "Any state" is used when you want to transition to a state, such as "jump" from any other state.

If you don't see the Exit state, you might need to scroll around the window a bit to find it. You can also zoom in and zoom out with the scroll button on your mouse or trackpad to get a better view of things, and hold the Option / Alt-key while dragging the background, to move around the Animator window. At any time, feel free to move around these Animation objects and arrange them in a way that makes sense to you.

Let's add the rest of our animations. Go back to the Sprites folder and select the next four sprites. These are the sprites used when the player walks west. Drag these four onto the PlayerObject, the same way we did to create the previous walking animation. When prompted by the Create New Animation save window, type "player-walk-west" and save to the Animations ➤ Animations folder. You should see this new animation appear in the Animator window.

Follow the same steps to create new animations for the other sprites. Note that the walk south and walk north animations only have two frames, not four. Call their animations "player-walk-south" and "player-walk-north", and save them to the Animations ➤ Animations folder.

At this point, your Animator window should resemble Figure 3-17 with all four Animation objects shown. These four Animation objects represent four different states of walking, and hold references to the Animation Clips as well.

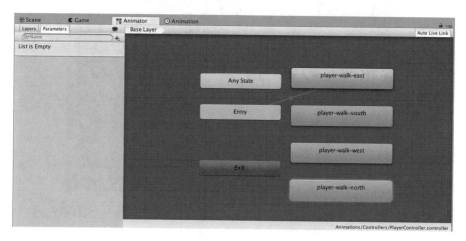

Figure 3-17. *The Animator window showing all four player walk animations, after adding them to the PlayerObject*

We've done all this work, but we still don't have anything animating on screen yet. There's one last step—in the Hierarchy view, select the Main Camera GameObject and set the size property to 1. This is temporary so you can clearly see the player animating. We'll explain more about Cameras later on in the book.

Press the Play button in the toolbar. If all goes well, you should see our intrepid Player frantically running in place as in Figure 3-18.

Figure 3-18. *We have sampled the sweet taste of pixelated victory*

Let's slow down our frantic Player. Open the Animator window by double-clicking the PlayerObject Animator, or by selecting the Animator window tab. Select the "player-walk-east" Animation and change the value for Speed to 0.6 as in Figure 3-19.

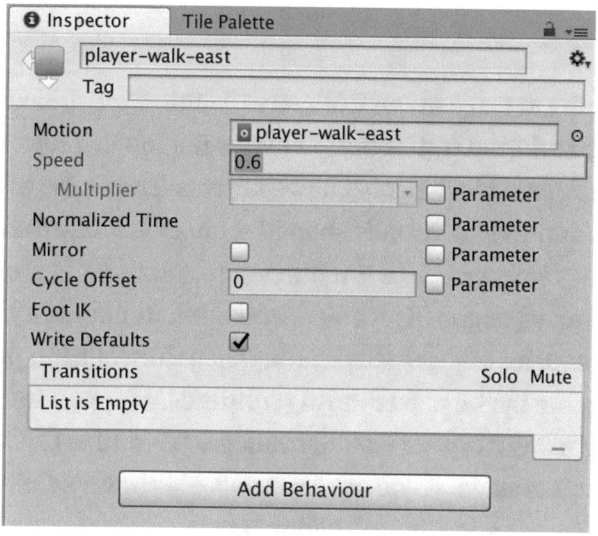

Figure 3-19. *Changing the Animation Speed*

Then press play again to see her walking at a more sustainable pace. You can adjust this speed to whatever you feel looks natural.

Stop the Playing Scene by pressing the Play button again.

Now create and save the animations for our EnemyWalk_1 and EnemyIdle_1 animations. Each of these animations contains five sprites each. Name the animations: enemy-walk-1, and enemy-idle-1. Rename the EnemyObject Animation Controller to EnemyController, and move it to the Animations ➤ Controllers subfolder. Move the enemy animations to the Animations ➤ Animations subfolder.

Colliders

Next we're going to learn about Colliders. Colliders are added to GameObjects and used by the Unity Physics Engine to determine when a collision has taken place between two objects. The shape of a Collider is adjustable, and they're usually shaped more or less like the outline of the object they represent. It's sometimes computationally prohibitive to outline the exact shape of an object and often unnecessary, as an approximation of an object's shape is sufficient for collision purposes and indistinguishable by the player during runtime. An approximation of the objects shape using a type of Collider called a "Primitive Collider" is also less processor intensive. There are two types of Primitive Colliders in Unity 2D: Box Collider 2D and Circle Collider 2D.

Select the PlayerObject and then select the Add Component button in the Inspector. Search for and select "Box Collider 2D" to add a Box Collider 2D to the PlayerObject as seen in Figure 3-20.

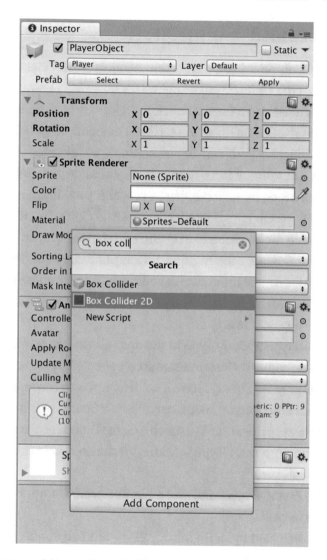

Figure 3-20. *Adding a Box Collider 2D to the PlayerObject*

We'll need to know when the player collides with an enemy, so add a Box Collider 2D to the EnemyObject as well.

The Rigidbody Component

A Rigidbody Component added to a GameObject allows that GameObject to interact with the Unity Physics Engine. It's how Unity knows to apply forces such as gravity to a GameObject. A Rigidbody also allows you to apply forces to the GameObject via scripts. For example, your game may have a GameObject called "car," which contains a Rigidbody. You could apply a certain amount of force to the car object to move it in the current direction, depending on which button a player is pressing: gas or turbo.

With the PlayerObject selected, click the Add Component button in the Inspector, search for "Rigidbody 2D," and add it to the PlayerObject. In the Body Type dropdown for the Rigidbody Component, select "**Dynamic.**" Dynamic Rigidbody will interact and collide with other objects. Set the following properties of the Rigidbody 2D to 0: Linear Drag, Angular Drag, and Gravity Scale. Set Mass to 1.

The second type of Body Type in the drop-down menu is **Kinematic**. Kinematic Rigidbody 2D Components aren't affected by external physics forces such as gravity. They do have a velocity but only move when we move their Transform component, usually via a Script. This is a different approach from applying forces to move a GameObject, as we described previously. The third Body Type is **Static**, for the objects in the game that won't move at all.

Select the EnemyObject and add a Rigidbody 2D Component of type Dynamic to it as well.

Now that we've added a Rigidbody 2D to our player and enemy, they will be affected by gravity. Because our game uses a top-down perspective, let's turn off gravity so our player doesn't go flying off the screen. Go to Edit ➤ Project Settings ➤ Physics 2D and change the value for Gravity Y from –9.81 to 0.

Tags and Layers

Tags

Tags allow us to label GameObjects for easy reference and comparison while our game is running.

Select the PlayerObject. Under the Tag drop-down menu on the very top left of the Inspector, select the Player tag to add a tag to our PlayerObject, as seen in Figure 3-21.

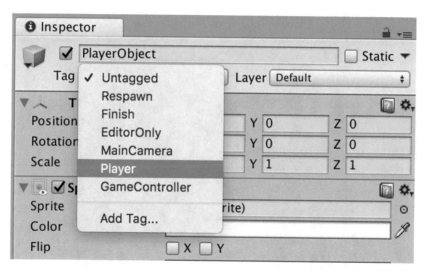

Figure 3-21. *Select the Player Tag in the Inspector to assign it to our PlayerObject*

The Player tag is a default tag that comes with every Scene in Unity but you also can add tags as you need.

Create a new Tag called "Enemy" and use it to set the EnemyObject Tag. We'll add Tags for other items later as our game develops.

Layers

Layers are used to define collections of GameObjects. These collections are used in collision detection to determine which layers are aware of each other and thus can interact. We can then create logic in a Script to determine what to do when two GameObjects collide. As we can see in Figure 3-22, we want to create a new "User Layer" called "Blocking". Type "Blocking" into the User Layer 8 field.

Select the Layers drop-down menu and select, "Add Layer." You should see the Layers window appear as in Figure 3-22.

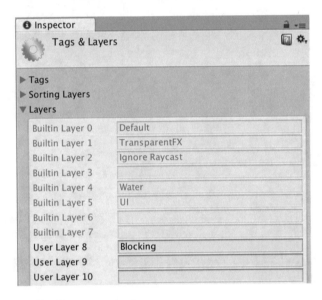

Figure 3-22. *The Layers window*

Now select the PlayerObject again to view its properties in the Inspector. Select the Blocking Layer we just created from the drop-down menu (see Figure 3-23) to add our PlayerObject to that Layer. Select the EnemyObject and set the Layer to "Blocking" in the Inspector as well.

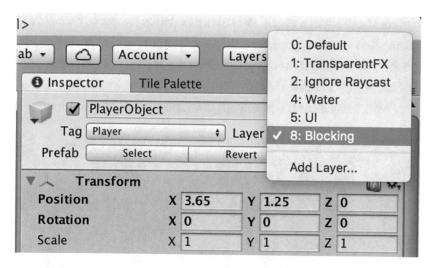

Figure 3-23. *Select Blocking Layer from the drop-down menu*

Later on, we'll configure our game to enforce the condition that certain GameObjects will not be able to pass through any object in the Blocking Layer. For example the Player will be in the Blocking Layer, as will any walls, trees, or enemies. Enemies should not be able to pass through the player, and the player should not be able to pass through any walls, trees, or enemies.

Sorting Layers

Let's look at a different type of Layer now: Sorting Layers. Sorting Layers are different than regular Layers in that they allow us to tell the Unity Engine what order our various 2D Sprites on the screen should be "rendered" or drawn. Because the Sorting Layer relates to rendering, you'll always see the Sorting Layer drop-down menu inside the Renderer component.

To get a better idea of what we mean by the "order" in which sprites are rendered, take a look at the screenshot in Figure 3-24 of the point-and-click adventure *Thimbleweed Park*. The screenshot shows two player characters standing in a room. We can see various pieces of furniture in the room such as a filing cabinet and a table. In the *Thimbleweed Park* screenshot, the female detective, Agent Ray, appears to be standing in front of the filing cabinet. This effect is accomplished by rendering the sprite of Agent Ray after the game engine renders the filing cabinet.

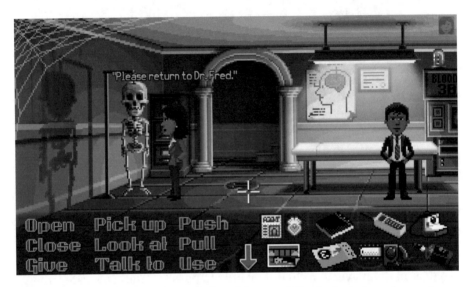

Figure 3-24. A screenshot of Thimbleweed Park showing characters standing in front of objects

Thimbleweed Park uses its own proprietary game engine instead of Unity, but all engines must have some sort of logic describing the order in which to render pixels.

In our RPG, we're going to be looking from the top-down, in what's called an "orthographic" perspective. We'll talk more about what that means when we talk about cameras, but for now know that we want Unity to draw pixels for the ground first, then any characters such as the player or enemies on top of the ground, so the characters appear to be walking on it.

We're going to add a Sorting Layer called "Characters" that we'll use for our player and all enemies.

In the Sprite Renderer Component in the Inspector, select the Sorting
Layer dropdown and select "Add Sorting Layer" as seen in Figure 3-25. The
Sorting Layer that we create will be available throughout our game, even
though we're creating it from the menu on the PlayerObject.

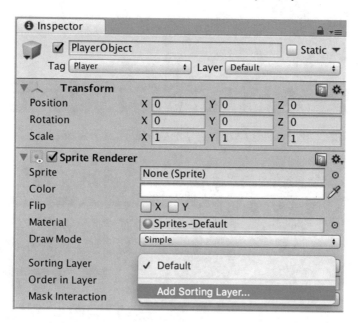

Figure 3-25. *Adding a Sorting Layer*

Add a Sorting Layer named, "Characters" (Figure 3-26), and then
click on the PlayerObject again to view its Inspector and select our new
Characters Sorting Layer from the Sorting Layer drop-down menu, as seen
in Figure 3-27.

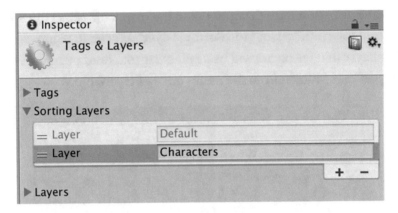

Figure 3-26. *Add a new Sorting Layer called Characters*

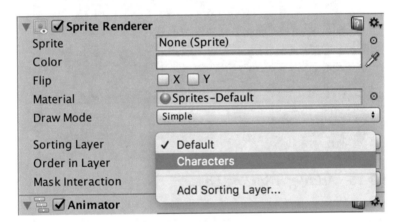

Figure 3-27. *Use the new Characters Sorting Layer in our PlayerObject*

Select our EnemyObject and set its Sorting Layer to Characters, because we want enemies to also be rendered on top of things like ground tiles.

Introducing: Prefabs

Unity allows you to construct GameObjects with embedded Components and then create something called a "Prefab" out of that GameObject. Prefabs can be thought of as pre-fabricated templates from which you can create, or "instantiate," new copies of already-made GameObjects. This asset has a very useful feature that allows you to edit all of the Prefabs at once by changing the Prefab template. On the other hand, you could choose to change a single Prefab and leave the rest of them identical to the original.

For example, imagine if you had a Scene where the player is inside a tavern. There are numerous props inside this tavern such as chairs, tables, and mugs of ale. If you created individual GameObjects for all of these props, each one of them would be independently editable. If you should ever want to change a single property on every table, for example, to make them dark wood instead of light wood, you'd have to select and edit each one of the tables and change that property. If the table objects were Prefab instances, you'd only have to change the property on a single object—the Prefab, then click the button to apply that change to all the instances derived from that Prefab.

We're going to use this straightforward technique of Prefabs constantly throughout the process of building our game.

It's really easy to create a Prefab out of a GameObject. First, create a Prefabs folder under our Assets folder in the Project view. Then select our PlayerObject from the Hierarchy view and simply drag it into our Prefabs folder.

The screenshot in Figure 3-28 shows a Prefab after we've dropped our PlayerObject into the Prefabs folder.

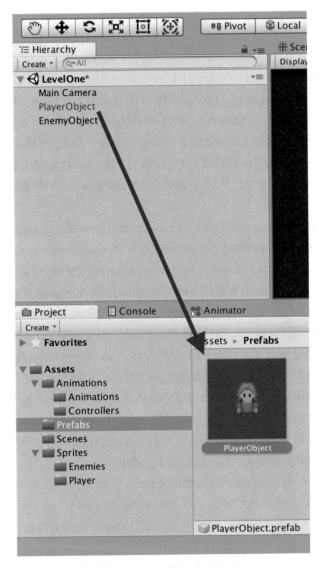

Figure 3-28. *Create a Prefab by dragging any GameObject into the Prefabs folder*

Take a look at the Hierarchy view in Figure 3-28. You'll notice that the PlayerObject text is light blue. This indicates that PlayerObject is based on a Prefab. This also means that going forward, if you make any changes to the PlayerObject Prefab and you want to apply the changes to all instances of the Prefab, you need to press the Apply button in the Inspector while that GameObject is selected in the Project view (see Figure 3-29).

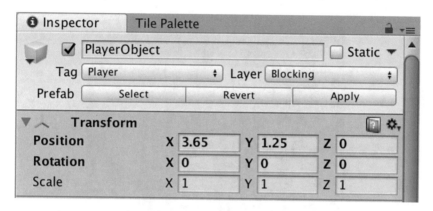

Figure 3-29. *Press the Apply button to apply any changes you make to the PlayerObject, to all instances of the Prefab*

You can now safely delete the PlayerObject from the Hierarchy view, as we now have a Prefab PlayerObject which we can always use to recreate the PlayerObject. If you want to edit all instances of the Prefab, simply drag the Prefab object back into the Hierarchy view and make your changes, then press Apply.

Do the same for the EnemyObject: drag it into the Prefabs folder and delete the original EnemyObject from the Hierarchy view.

Now's a good time to save our Scene again, so make sure to do that.

Scripts: Logic for Components

So we have our PlayerObject and we have our EnemyObject. Let's make them move! Select our PlayerObject Prefab and drag it into the Hierarchy view. You'll notice that the Inspector has once again been populated with the properties for the PlayerObject.

Scroll to the bottom of the Inspector and press the Add Component button. Type in the word, *script* and select "New Script". Name the new script, "MovementController" as seen in Figure 3-30.

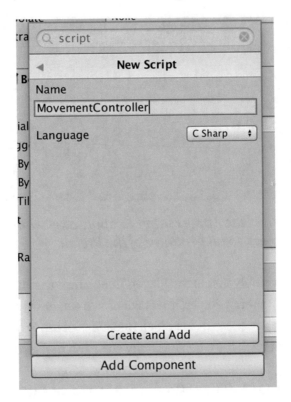

Figure 3-30. *Name the new Script: "MovementController"*

Create a new folder called "Scripts" in the Project view. The new script will have been created in the top-level Assets folder in the Project view. Drag the MovementController script into the Scripts folder, and then double-click it to open it in Visual Studio.

It's time to program our first script. Scripts in Unity are written in a language called C#. Once you've opened up our MovementController script in Visual Studio, it should resemble Figure 3-31.

Figure 3-31. *The MovementController script in Visual Studio*

Note   Up until relatively recently, Unity allowed developers to write scripts in two different languages: C# as well as a language resembling JavaScript called "UnityScript." Starting with the Unity 2017.2 beta, Unity began the process of deprecating UnityScript, but it's possible you might find some UnityScript samples out there in the wild. Going forward, you should only use C# to write scripts for Unity. You can read more about the reasons for deprecation in Unity's blog: `https://blogs.unity3d.com`.

Let's go through the structure of a typical Unity Script. All of the following lines should be typed exactly as you see them, and every line in C# should end with a semicolon. Programming languages are very literal and don't take kindly to omitted semicolons, returns, or extra letters or numbers. The lines prefaced with // are comments, written only for clarification, and you don't have to type those. Comments in C# can be written using two forward slashes: // or with a: /* followed by your comment, and closed with: */

```
// 1
using System.Collections;
using System.Collections.Generic;
using UnityEngine;

// 2
public class MovementController : MonoBehaviour
{

// 3
    // Use this for initialization
    void Start()
    {

    }

// 4
    // Update is called once per frame
    void Update()
    {

    }
}
```

Here's a breakdown of each preceding section:

```
// 1
```

```
using System.Collections;
using System.Collections.Generic;
using UnityEngine;
```

Namespaces are used to organize and control the scope of classes in a C# project to avoid conflicts as well as make the developers lives easier. The keyword **Using** is used to describe a specific Namespace in the .NET Framework, and saves the developer the trouble of having to type the fully qualified name every time a method from that Namespace is used.

For example, if we include the System namespace, as in the following example:

```
using System;
```

instead of having to type the cumbersome:

```
System.Console.WriteLine("Greatest RPG Ever!");
```

We can simply type the shorter version:

```
Console.WriteLine("Greatest RPG Ever!");
```

This is possible because the: using System; declaration clarifies that code in this class file will be using the System namespace.

Namespaces in C# are also nestable. This means you can refer to namespaces within namespaces like Collections, within System. This is written as follows:

```
using System.Collections;
```

The UnityEngine Namespace contains many Unity-specific classes, some of which we've already used in our Scene, such as MonoBehaviour, GameObject, Rigidbody2D, and BoxCollider2D. By declaring the UnityEngine Namespace, we can reference and work with these classes in our C# script.

```
// 2
public class MovementController : MonoBehaviour
```

For a class to be attached to a GameObject within a Scene as a Component, it needs to inherit from the **UnityEngine** class **MonoBehaviour**. By inheriting from **MonoBehaviour**, a class gets access to methods such as Awake(), Start(), Update(), LateUpdate(), and OnCollisionEnter() along with guarantees that those methods will be invoked at a certain point in Unity's event function execution cycle.

```
// 3
void Start()
```

One of the methods provided by the parent **MonoBehaviour** class is Start(). We'll describe the event function execution cycle later but as you can imagine from its name, the Start() function is one of the first methods to be called as a script executes. The Start() method is called before the first frame update provided a few conditions are met:

1. The script must inherit from MonoBehaviour. Our MovementController does inherit from MonoBehaviour.

2. The script must be enabled at initialization time. By default, scripts will be enabled, but it is possible for a script not to be enabled initialization time, which could be a possible error source.

```
// 4
void Update()
```

The Update() method is called once per frame and is used to update game behaviors. Because Update() is called once per frame, a game with a 24 frames-per-second rate will call Update() 24 times in a second, however the time between update calls may vary. If you require a consistent time between method calls, then use the FixedUpdate() method.

Now that we're familiar with the default MonoBehaviour script, replace the MovementController class with the following:

```
using System.Collections;
using System.Collections.Generic;
using UnityEngine;
```

```
public class MovementController : MonoBehaviour
{
    //1
    public float movementSpeed = 3.0f;

    // 2
    Vector2 movement = new Vector2();

    // 3
    Rigidbody2D rb2D;

    private void Start()
    {
        // 4
        rb2D = GetComponent<Rigidbody2D>();
    }

    private void Update()
    {
        // Keep this empty for now
    }

    // 5
    void FixedUpdate()
    {
        // 6
        movement.x = Input.GetAxisRaw("Horizontal");
        movement.y = Input.GetAxisRaw("Vertical");

        // 7
        movement.Normalize();

        // 8
        rb2D.velocity = movement * movementSpeed;
```

```
    }
}
```

```
// 1
public float movementSpeed = 3.0f;
```

Declare a public float that we'll use to adjust and set the characters movement speed. By declaring it public, we allow this variable movementSpeed to appear in the Inspector when the GameObject to which it is attached is selected.

Take a look at Figure 3-32 to see how the public variable appears in the Inspector, in the Movement Controller (Script) section. Unity will automatically capitalize the first letter of a public variable, and add a space right before the first uppercase letter. That means "movementSpeed" will appear as "Movement Speed" in the Inspector.

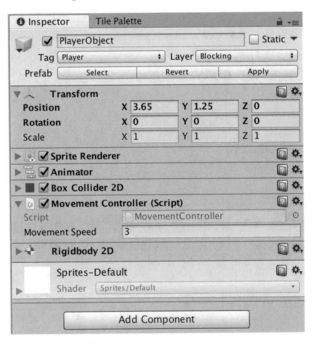

Figure 3-32. *The public variable movementSpeed appears capitalized and with a space*

```
// 2
Vector2 movement = new Vector2();
```

A Vector2 is a built-in data structure that holds 2D vectors or points. We're going to use it to represent a Player or Enemy character's location in 2D space or where the character is moving to.

```
// 3
Rigidbody2D rb2D;
```

Declare a variable to hold a reference to the Rigidbody2D.

```
// 4
rb2D = GetComponent<Rigidbody2D>();
```

The method GetComponent takes a parameter of Type, and will return the component attached to the current object of that type, if one is attached. We call GetComponent<Rigidbody2D> to grab a reference to the Rigidbody2D component that we attached to the PlayerObject in the Unity Editor. We're going to use this component to move the player around.

```
// 5
FixedUpdate()
```

As we discussed a few pages earlier, FixedUpdate() is called at fixed intervals by the Unity Engine. This contrasts with the Update() method that is called once per frame. On slower hardware devices, a games framerate could slow down, in which case Update() may be called less frequently.

```
// 6
movement.x = Input.GetAxisRaw("Horizontal");
movement.y = Input.GetAxisRaw("Vertical");
```

The Input class gives us several ways to capture user input. We capture user input using the method GetAxisRaw() and assign the values to the x and y values of our Vector2 structure. The GetAxisRaw() method takes a parameter specifying which 2D axis we are interested in, horizontal or vertical, and retrieves a -1, 0, or 1 from the Unity Input Manager and returns it.

A "1" indicates that the right key, or "d" (using the common w, a, s, d input configuration) was pressed, while a "-1" indicates that the left key or "a" was pressed. A "0" indicates that no key was pressed. This input key mapping is configurable via the Unity Input Manager, which we'll explain later.

```
// 7
movement.Normalize();
```

This will "normalize" our vector and keep the player moving at the same rate of speed whether they're moving diagonally, vertically, or horizontally.

```
// 8
rb2D.velocity = movement * movementSpeed;
```

Multiplying the movementSpeed by the movement Vector will set the velocity of the Rigidbody2D attached to the PlayerObject and move it.

Go back to the Unity Editor and ensure that you see our PlayerObject in the Hierarchy view. If not, drag the PlayerObject from the Prefabs folder into the Hierarchy view.

There's one last very important step: we need to add the script to the PlayerObject.

To add the script to our PlayerObject, drag the MovementController script from the Scripts folder, onto the PlayerObject in the Hierarchy view, or drag it into the Inspector when the PlayerObject is selected. This is how we can attach a script to an object in the Unity Editor. The MovementController script gets access to the other components in the PlayerObject when it is attached to a specific object.

Now press the play button. You should see our player character walking in place. Press either the arrow keys or W, A, S, D on your keyboard and watch her move around.

Congratulations! You've just breathed life into what was once just electronic impulses. You know what they say about *what comes with great power...*

State and Animations

More State Machines

Now that we know how to move our character around the screen, we're going to talk about how to switch between animations based on the current player state.

Go to the Animations ➤ Controllers folder and double-click the PlayerController object. You should be looking at the Animator window, displaying the State Machine we set up earlier. As we discussed earlier, Unity's Animation State machine allows us to view all the various player states and their associated animation clips.

Click and drag your Animation State objects around until it resembles the screen in Figure 3-33, with the player-idle off to the side, and the player-walk animations grouped together. There's no need to get too precise when lining them up, as the only thing that really matters is the directional arrows between the Animation State objects.

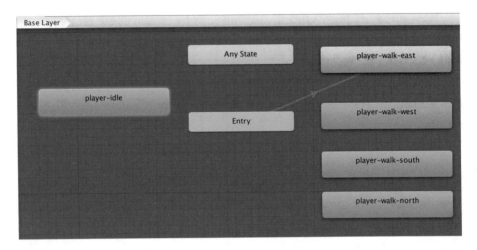

Figure 3-33. *Organization of the Animations in the Animator window*

In Figure 3-33, you can see how the player-walk-east Animation State is orange. The orange color indicates that it's the default state for this Animator. Select then right-click on the "player-idle" Animation State and select "Set as Layer Default State" as seen in Figure 3-34. The color should change to orange.

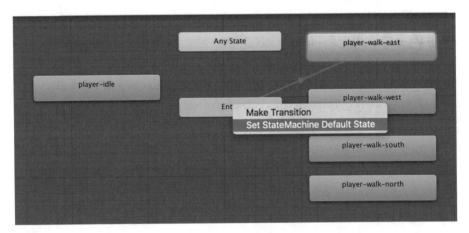

Figure 3-34. *Right-click and select Set as Layer Default State to set the player-idle animation as the default*

We want player-idle to be the default state because when we're not touching a directional key, we want the player facing south toward the user in an idle state. This will look as if the player character is awaiting the user.

Now select and right-click on the "Any State" and select "Make Transition." A line with an arrow will appear, attached to and following around your mouse. Click on "player-walk-east" to create a transition between the Any State object and player-walk-east.

If you've done this correctly, it should look like Figure 3-35.

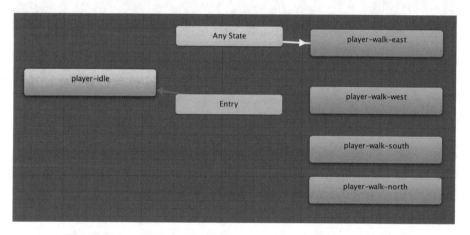

Figure 3-35. *Create a transition from Any State to player-walk-east*

Now do the same for the rest of the Animation States: right-click Any State, Create Transition, and select each one of the Animation States to create a transition. As we mentioned earlier, the "Any State" is used when you want to transition to a state, such as "jump" from any other state.

You should create a total of five white transition arrows pointing from Any State to all four player-walk Animation States and the player-idle Animation State. There also should be a orange-colored default-state arrow from the Entry Animation State, leading to the player-idle Animation State, as seen in Figure 3-36.

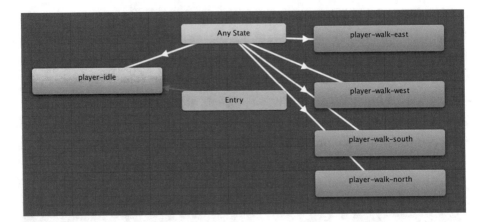

Figure 3-36. *Create transitions from Any State to all the Animation States*

Animation Parameters

To use these transitions and states, we want to create something called an Animation Parameter. Animation Parameters are variables defined in the Animation Controller and are used by scripts to control the Animation State Machine.

We're going to use this Animation Parameter that we create in our Transitions and in our MovementController script to control the PlayerObject and make her walk around the screen.

Select the Parameters tab (Figure 3-37) on the left side of the Animator window. Press the plus symbol and select "Int" from the drop-down (Figure 3-38). Rename the created Animation Parameter to "AnimationState" (Figure 3-39).

Figure 3-37. *The Parameters tab in the Animator window*

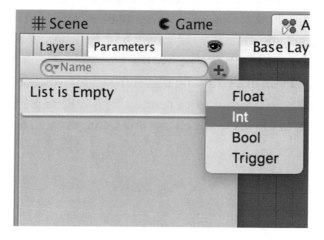

Figure 3-38. *Select Int from the drop-down menu*

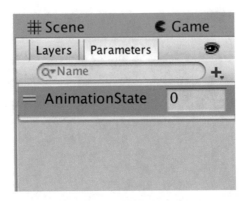

Figure 3-39. *Name the Animation Parameter: AnimationState*

We're going to set the Animation Parameter in each Transition to a specific condition. If during gameplay this condition is ever true, then the Animator will transition to that Animation State and the corresponding Animation Clip will play. Because this Animator component is attached to the PlayerObject, the Animation Clips will be displayed at the Transform component's location in the Scene. We use a script to set this Animation Parameter condition to be true and trigger the state transition.

Select the white Transition line connecting Any State to the player-walk-east state. In the Inspector, change the settings so that they match Figure 3-40.

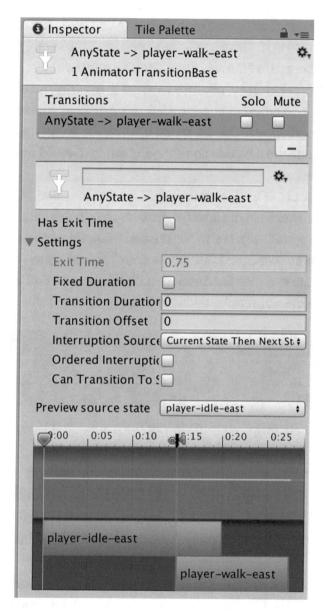

Figure 3-40. *Configuring the Transition in the Inspector*

We want to uncheck boxes such as Exit Time, Fixed Duration, and Can Transition to Self. Make sure to set Transition Duration (%) to 0, and Interruption Source to "Current State Then Next State."

Uncheck Has Exit Time because we want to interrupt an animation if our user presses a different key. If we left Has Exit Time checked, then the animation would have to finish playing up until the % entered in the Exit Time box, before the next one could begin, and that would result in poor player experience.

On the bottom of the inspector, you'll see an area titled, "Conditions." Click the plus symbol in the lower-right and select AnimationState, Equals, and enter 1 (Figure 3-41). We've just created a condition that says: if the Animation Parameter called "AnimationState" equals 1, then enter this Animation State and play the Animation. This is how we will trigger state changes from the script we're about to write.

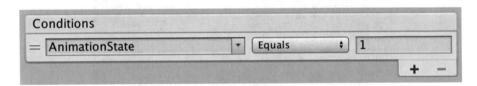

Figure 3-41. *Setting the condition of the Animation Parameter: AnimationState*

Note   It's really easy to accidentally leave the AnimationState drop-down box as "Greater" instead of "Equals" so watch out for that. Our transitions won't work properly if we don't set the condition to Equals.

The next item we're going to do is actually set that AnimationState parameter equal to 1 in our script. Go back to Visual Studio and our MovementController.cs script.

Replace the MovementController class with:

```
using System.Collections;
using System.Collections.Generic;
using UnityEngine;

public class MovementController : MonoBehaviour
{
    public float movementSpeed = 3.0f;
    Vector2 movement = new Vector2();

// 1
    Animator animator;

// 2
    string animationState = "AnimationState";
    Rigidbody2D rb2D;

// 3
    enum CharStates
    {
        walkEast = 1,
        walkSouth = 2,
        walkWest = 3,
        walkNorth = 4,

        idleSouth = 5
    }

    private void Start()
    {
// 4
        animator = GetComponent<Animator>();
        rb2D = GetComponent<Rigidbody2D>();
    }
```

```
    private void Update()
    {
```
// 5
```
        UpdateState();
    }

    void FixedUpdate()
    {
```
// 6
```
        MoveCharacter();
    }

    private void MoveCharacter()
    {
        movement.x = Input.GetAxisRaw("Horizontal");
        movement.y = Input.GetAxisRaw("Vertical");

        movement.Normalize();
        rb2D.velocity = movement * movementSpeed;
    }

    private void UpdateState()
    {
```
// 7
```
        if (movement.x > 0)
        {
            animator.SetInteger(animationState, (int)
            CharStates.walkEast);
        }
```

```
    else if (movement.x < 0)
    {
        animator.SetInteger(animationState, (int)
        CharStates.walkWest);
    }
    else if (movement.y > 0)
    {
        animator.SetInteger(animationState, (int)
        CharStates.walkNorth);
    }
    else if (movement.y < 0)
    {
        animator.SetInteger(animationState, (int)
        CharStates.walkSouth);
    }
    else
    {
        animator.SetInteger(animationState, (int)
        CharStates.idleSouth);
    }
}
}
// 1
Animator animator;
```

We create a variable called "animator" that we'll use later on to store a reference to the Animator component in the GameObject to which this script is attached.

```
// 2
string animationState = "AnimationState";
```

Typing a string directly into the code where it will be used is called "hard-coding" the value. It's also a common source of bugs when the inevitable typos happen, so let's avoid the possibility altogether by only typing it once, then using the variable when we need to refer to the string.

```
// 3
enum CharStates
```

The data type "enum" is used to declare a set of enumerated constants. Each enumerated constant corresponds to an underlying typed value, such as int (integer), and you can reference the enum to get the corresponding value.

Here we declare an enum called CharStates and use it to map the various states of a character (walk east, walk south, etc.) along with a corresponding int. We'll use this int value to set our Animation State soon.

```
// 4
animator = GetComponent<Animator>();
```

Grab a reference to the Animator component in the GameObject to which this script is attached. We want to save this component reference so we can quickly access it later on via this variable, and don't have to retrieve it every time we need it. Using GetComponent is most common way of accessing other components from within a script. You can even use it to access other scripts.

```
// 5
UpdateState();
```

Call a method that we've written to update the animation state machine. We've moved this logic into a separate method to keep the codebase clean and easily readable. The more code you have in a single method, the harder it is to read. Harder to read code is harder to debug, test, and maintain.

```
// 6
MoveCharacter();
```

We've moved the code to move the player into another method to keep the code clean and readable.

```
// 7
```

This series of if-else-if statements will determine if our call to Input.GetAxisRaw() returns a -1, 0, or 1, and move the character accordingly.

For example:

```
if (movement.x > 0)
{
        animator.SetInteger(animationState, (int)
CharStates.walkEast);
      }
```

If movement along the *x* axis is greater than 0, then the player is pressing the key to go right.

We want to tell the Animator object that it should change the state to walk-east, so we call the SetInteger() method to set the value of the Animation Parameter we created earlier and trigger the transition of states.

SetInteger() takes two parameters: a string, and an int value. The first value is the Animation Parameter (Figure 3-42) we created earlier in the Unity Editor called, "AnimationState."

Figure 3-42. *We set this Animation Parameter from our script*

We've conveniently stored the name of this Animation Parameter in a string called "animationState" in our script and we'll pass that as the first parameter to SetInteger().

The second parameter to SetInteger() is the actual value to set for AnimationState. Because each value in our CharStates enum corresponds with an int value, when we type:

```
CharStates.walkEast
```

We are actually using whatever value walkEast corresponds with in the enum. In this case, walkEast corresponds with 1. We still need to explicitly cast (or convert) this to an int by writing (int) to the left of the variable. The reason why we need to cast the enum is beyond the scope of this book but has to do with the way the C# language is implemented under the hood.

Save your script and switch back to the Unity Editor so we can put all of this to use. Select the white transition arrows leading to player-walk-south, and in the Conditions area, click that plus symbol. Select AnimationState, Equals, and enter the value 2. This value 2 corresponds with the value 2 in the enum in the script we just wrote.

Now select each white transition arrow one-by-one for player-walk-west, player-walk-north, and all of the player-idle state transition arrows. Add a Condition to each of them via the Inspector window and enter the corresponding value from the CharStates enum:

```
enum CharStates
    {
        walkEast = 1,
        walkSouth = 2,
        walkWest = 3,
        walkNorth = 4,

        idleSouth = 5
    }
```

As you're going through each transition arrow, remember to uncheck boxes such as Exit Time, Fixed Duration, Can Transition to Self, and set Transition Duration (%) to 0.

One last thing, I promise! Select each player-walk Animation State object and adjust the speed to 0.6, and adjust each idle animation to 0.25. This will make our player animations look just right.

You've now set up a large portion of the player animations required for our game. Press the Play button and move our character around the screen with the arrow keys or W, A, S, D.

Go on and stretch your pixelated legs.

Tip   If you forget the exact parameters for a method in C#, Visual Studio will show a helpful pop-up with this information (Figure 3-43). You can press return to auto-complete the method call.

```
// 6
if (movement.x > 0)
{
    animator.SetInteger()
} else if (movement.x <
{
    animator.SetInteger(
}
else if (movement.y > 0)
{
    animator.SetInteger(
} else if (movement.y <
```

```
public void SetInteger(        ▲ 1 of 2 ▼
    string name,
    int value
)
Summary
See IAnimatorControllerPlayable.SetInteger.
```

Figure 3-43. *Visual Studio displays a pop-up with the methods parameter names and types*

Summary

In this chapter we've covered a lot of the core knowledge required to make games in Unity. We covered some of the design philosophy and computer science principles behind how Unity works. We covered how games in Unity are made of Scenes, and everything in a Scene is a GameObject. We learned about how Colliders and Rigidbody components work together to determine when two GameObjects collide and how Unity's physics engine should handle the interaction. We learned how Tags are just labels used to refer to GameObjects, such as the PlayerObject, from Scripts while our game is running. Another useful tool we added to our toolkit is Layers, which are used to group together GameObjects. We can then impose logic onto these Layers via Scripts.

One of the most useful concepts we learned in this chapter was Prefabs, which we think of as premade asset templates which we use to create new copies of these assets. For example, our game might have hundreds of enemy objects appear over the course of the game, or even at once (if you *really* want to kill the player). Instead of creating hundreds of individual enemy GameObjects, we create one enemy prefab and instantiate new copies of the enemy GameObject from that prefab. We've started the process of learning how to write Unity scripts, and we'll continue building on that knowledge throughout this book. We even wrote our first script to walk the player around the screen by moving the PlayerObject Transform component. Our script also set the Animation Parameters used by the Animator state machine to control the transitions between player states and animation clips. We covered a lot in this chapter, but we're really just getting started!

CHAPTER 4

World Building

Now that we've learned how to create basic character animations and change the state between them, it's time to create a world for these characters to inhabit. Two-dimensional (2D) worlds are often created by placing a series of tiles together to paint a background, then placing other tiles on top of that background to create the illusion of depth. These tiles are really just sprites that have been segmented or "sliced" into convenient dimensions and usually placed using a Tile Palette. The designer or developer can build up multiple layers of these Tilemaps to create effects such as trees, birds flying overhead, or even mountains in the distance. We're going to learn how to do many of these things in this chapter. You'll even get to create your own custom Tilemaps for our RPG game. You'll also learn how the Unity Camera works, and how to create behavior to follow the player as she walks around the level.

Tilemaps and Tile Palettes

With the introduction of the Tilemap feature, Unity took a significant step forward with their 2D workflow toolchain. Unity Tilemaps make it easy to create levels natively within the Unity Editor, instead of relying on outside tools. Unity also has a number of tools that augment the Tilemap feature, some of which we'll get into in this chapter.

© Jared Halpern 2019
J. Halpern, *Developing 2D Games with Unity*, https://doi.org/10.1007/978-1-4842-3772-4_4

Tilemaps are data structures that store sprites in a particular arrangement. Unity abstracts away the details of the underlying data structure and makes it easy for the developer to focus on working with the Tilemap.

To get started, we'll need to import the Tilemap assets, just as we imported the sprite assets used for our player and enemy in Chapter 3.

Before we start importing, let's get organized: create new folders in the Sprites directory called: "Objects" and "Outdoors." We'll use these folders to hold the spritesheets and sliced sprites used for our outdoor Tilemap and various objects we'll place in our world.

From the downloaded book assets, in the Chapter 4 folder, find the spritesheet titled "OutdoorsGround.png". Drag the spritesheet into the Sprites ➤ Outdoors folder. The Outdoors Import Settings in the Inspector should be set to the following:

> Texture Type: Sprite (2D and UI)
>
> Sprite Mode: Multiple
>
> Pixels Per Unit: 32
>
> Filter Mode: Point (no filter)
>
> Ensure the Default button is selected at the bottom and set Compression to: None

Press the Apply button.

Now we want to slice the spritesheet that we've just imported. Go into the Sprite Editor by clicking its respective button in the Inspector. Press the Slice button in the upper-left and then the Grid by Cell Size from the Type menu. Use 32 × 32 for the X and Y pixel size. Press the Slice button.

Check that the resulting slice lines look good, and then press the Apply button in the top-right corner of the Sprite Editor. We now have our outdoor tile set.

Next we want to create our Tilemap. In the Hierarchy view, right-click and Select 2D Object ➤ Tilemap to create a Tilemap GameObject. You should see a GameObject appear called "Grid" with a child GameObject called, "Tilemap." This Grid object is used to configure the layout of its child Tilemaps. The child Tilemaps are made up of a Transform component just like all GameObjects, a Tilemap component, and a Tilemap Renderer component.

This Tilemap component is where we actually "paint" our tiles.

Creating Tile Palettes

Before we can paint, we need to create a tile palette, which is made of individual tiles. Go to the menu Window ➤ Tile Palette to show the Tile Palette pane. Dock the Tile Palette pane in the same area as the Inspector.

We want our project to stay organized, so create a folder in our Project view under the main Assets folder called "TilePalettes," then create another folder called "Tiles" under the Sprites folder. In the Tiles folder, create two folders called, "Outdoors" and "Objects." Your Project view should resemble Figure 4-1.

Figure 4-1. *Project View after creating folders*

Select the "Create New Palette" button in the Tile Palette window. Name the Palette, "Outdoor Tiles" and leave the Grid and Cell Size settings as shown in Figure 4-2.

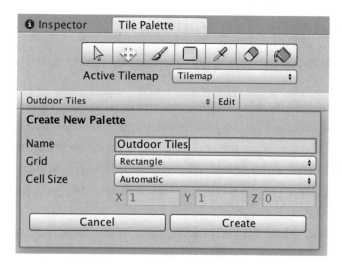

Figure 4-2. *Create a new Tile Palette*

Press "Create" and save the Tile Palette to the newly created
TilePalettes folder. This will create a TilePalette GameObject.

Select the Sprites ➤ Outdoors folder in the Project view, then select the
Tile Palette view from wherever you've docked it. We're going to create a
Tile Palette using the Outdoors spritesheet we imported and sliced earlier.

Select the Outdoors spritesheet and drag it into the Tile Palette area to
where it says, "Drag Tile, Sprite or Sprite Texture assets here."

When prompted to "Generate Tiles into folder", navigate to the Sprites
➤ Tiles ➤ Outdoor Tiles folder we created earlier, and press the Choose
button. Unity will now generate the TilePalette tiles from the individually
sliced sprites. In a few moments, you should see the tiles from our
Outdoors spritesheet appear in the Tile Palette.

Painting with Tile Palettes

Now comes the fun part: we're going to use our Tile Palette to paint a Tilemap.

Select the paintbrush tool from the Tile Palette, and then select a tile from the Tile Palette. Use the paintbrush to paint on the Tilemap in the Scene view. If you make a mistake, you can hold down the *Shift* key to use the tile paintbrush as an eraser. When the paintbrush is selected, you can hold down Option (Mac)/Alt (PC) + the left mouse button to pan around the Tilemap.

Use Option (Mac)/Alt (PC) + left mouse button to pan around the Tile Palette, left-click to select a tile, and left-click and drag to select a group of tiles. If your mouse has a scroll wheel, you can use that to zoom in and out on the Tile Palette, or you can hold down Option / Alt + swipe up/down on a touchpad to zoom in and out. These same keys and gestures will work for the Tile Map as well.

Paint your Tilemap and have fun! You can make your Tilemap look however you'd like, but here's a suggestion for how to get started (Figure 4-3).

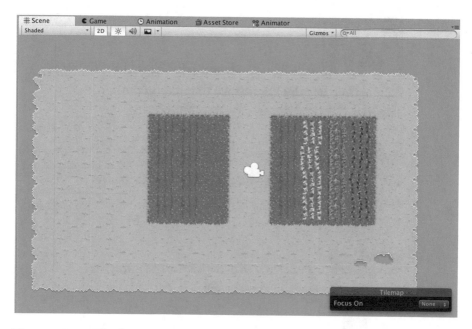

Figure 4-3. *The beginnings of a Tilemap*

Now that we've done a little bit of painting, let's take a closer look at the tools in the Tile Palette.

The Tile Palette

 Select—Select areas of the grid or specific tiles

 Move Selection—Move around selected areas

Paintbrush—Select a tile from the Tile Palette then use the Paintbrush to paint on the Tilemap

Box Fill—Paint a filled area using the actively selected tile

Pick New Brush—Use an existing tile from the Tilemap as a new brush

Erase—Remove a painted tile from the Tilemap (Shortcut: hold down Shift)

Flood Fill—Fill an area with the actively selected tile

Let's get back to building our level.

From the assets you downloaded for this book, drag the file titled, "OutdoorsObjects.png" into the Sprites ➤ Objects folder. The Import Settings in the Inspector should be set to the following:

Texture Type: Sprite (2D and UI)

Sprite Mode: Multiple

Pixels Per Unit: 32

Filter Mode: Point (no filter)

Ensure the Default button is selected at the bottom
and set Compression to: None

Press the Apply button.

Now go into the Sprite Editor by clicking its respective button in the
Inspector. Press the Slice button in the upper-left and then Grid by Cell
Size from the Type menu. Use 32 × 32 for the X and Y pixel size. We are
reusing the Sprite slicing techniques we learned in Chapter 3.

Press the Slice button and check that the resulting white slice lines look
like they're dividing the sprite sheet in the right positions. Press the Apply
button in the top-right corner of the Sprite Editor. We now have a set of
outdoor-themed object sprites to place in our scene.

Now we're going to create a Tile Palette to paint with these object
sprites. Go back to our Tile Palette and select Create New Palette from the
drop-down. Name the new palette, "Outdoor Objects" and press the Create
button. When prompted, save this Palette to the TilePalettes folder where
we saved our Outdoor Tiles Palette earlier.

Now we'll do the same as we did for the Outdoor Tiles: select the
Outdoor Objects spritesheet and drag it into the Tile Palette area where it
says, "Drag Tile, Sprite or Sprite Texture assets here."

When prompted to "Generate Tiles into folder", navigate to the Sprites
➤ Tiles ➤ Objects folder we created and press the Choose button. Unity
will now generate the Tile Palette tiles from the individually sliced sprites.
In a few moments, you should see the tiles from our Objects spritesheet
appear in the Tile Palette.

Tip   Sometimes sprites are made of multiple tiles. To select multiple tiles at once, make sure the Paintbrush tool is chosen then click and drag a rectangle around the tiles you want to use. Then you can just paint normally with the paintbrush. The large rock in the Objects spritesheet is made of four separate sprite tiles.

Select one of the rocks from the Outdoor Objects Tile Palette by clicking and dragging a rectangle around all four tiles. Use the paintbrush to place a single rock on your Tilemap. You'll immediately notice that something looks wrong: you can actually see the background of the Unity Scene view around the outline of the rock sprite (Figure 4-4).

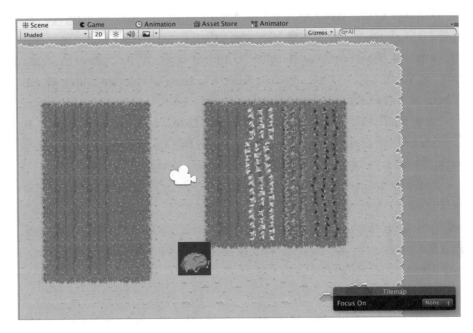

Figure 4-4. *Transparent border around the placed rock object sprite*

When we painted the rock tiles on the same Tilemap as the ground tiles, we didn't actually paint on top of the existing tiles. Instead, we replaced the existing tiles with new tiles. Because the rock sprites we painted with contain some transparent pixels, we can see the background of the Scene view. To avoid this, we'll use multiple Tilemaps and Sorting Layers.

Working with Multiple Tilemaps

Let's get our Tilemaps organized. Click on the Tilemap object in the Hierarchy view and rename it: "Layer_Ground."

We're going to create multiple Tilemaps and stack them on top of each other in layers. Right-click on the Grid object in the Hierarchy view and go to: 2D Object ➤ Tilemap to create a new Tilemap. Select this new Tilemap and rename it: "Layer_Trees_and_Rocks." As you may have guessed from the name, we're going to paint trees, bushes, shrubs, and rocks on this Tilemap.

At this point, if you started to paint, you'd notice that have run into the same transparency issue again. There are two things we have to do to fix this issue.

To paint on a specific Tilemap, it must be selected as the **Active Tilemap** in the Tile Palette view. In the Tile Palette window, you'll notice the drop-down menu for Active Tilemap (Figure 4-5). Use it to select our new layer, Layer_Trees_and_Rocks.

Figure 4-5. *Select Layer_Trees_and Rocks to make it the Active Tilemap*

If you recall our earlier discussion, the Sprite Renderer uses Sorting Layers to determine the order in which to render sprites. Before we can paint on our Layer_Trees_and_Rocks Tilemap, we need to set up the Sorting Layers for our Tilemaps. This will ensure that when we paint our trees and rocks, they will appear on top of the ground tiles.

Select Layer_Ground and find the Tilemap Renderer Component in the Inspector.

Press the Add Sorting Layer button in the Tilemap Renderer and create two layers: call the first layer "Ground" and the second layer "Objects". Rearrange these Sorting Layers by clicking and dragging them so that Ground is above Objects in the listing as seen in Figure 4-6.

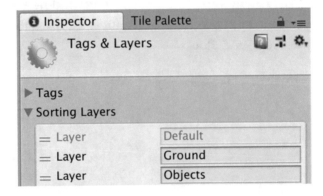

Figure 4-6. *Be sure the Ground Layer is above the Objects Layer*

Select the Layer_Ground Tilemap in the Hierarchy view again, to see its properties in the Inspector. In the Tilemap Renderer component, change the Sorting Layer to "Ground." Select the Layer_Trees_and_Rocks Tilemap and change its Sorting Layer to "Objects."

Delete the rock tiles we painted earlier by setting the Active Layer to Layer_Ground, and then select the Erase tool from the Tile Palette toolset. You also can delete items using the paintbrush by holding down shift and painting. Fill in the erased spot with some grass or whatever ground tile you like from the Outdoor Objects palette.

Now we're ready to paint. When you want to paint ground tiles, be sure that the Active Tilemap is set to Layer_Ground, and when you want to paint trees, rocks, and shrubs, be sure the Active Tilemap is Layer_Trees_and_Rocks.

Tip   Use the square-bracket keys, "[" and "]" to rotate a selected tile before using it to paint. You can also rotate tiles directly on the palette this way.

Then set the Active Tilemap to Layer_Trees_and_Rocks and paint some rocks and bushes using the Outdoor Objects Tile Palette (Figure 4-7).

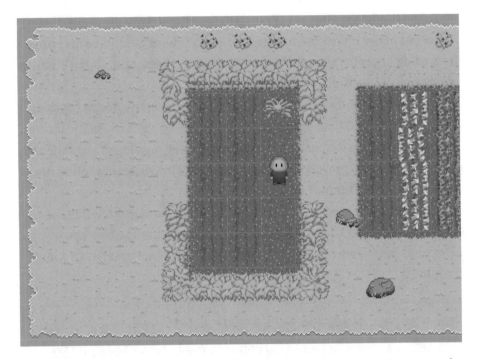

Figure 4-7. *Paint some rocks and bushes onto the Layer_Trees_and_
Rocks Tilemap*

Now our map is starting to look like a map. There are a few things we
have to do before our player can go exploring though.

We want to make sure the player is rendered in front of the ground
and rocks. We'll accomplish this by setting the player's sorting layer.
Select the PlayerObject, then look for the Sorting Layer property in the
Sprite Renderer Component and press the Add Sorting Layer button. Add
a Sorting Layer called "Characters" and move it to the bottom, after the
Ground and Objects layers. Now we've told the Sprite Renderer to render
objects in order from the first Sorting Layer, "Ground" to the last Sorting
Layer, "Characters."

Your Sorting Layers should look like Figure 4-8.

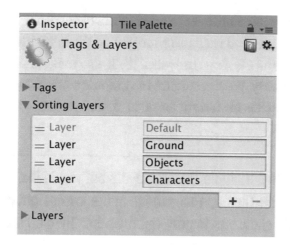

Figure 4-8. *Add the Characters Sorting Layer*

Select the PlayerObject and set its Sorting Layer to the Characters layer that we just created. This will render the player on top of the ground and any objects on the ground and give the appearance of the characters walking on top of the ground.

We'll explain how the camera works later in this chapter but for now, select the camera object and change the Size property to 3.75.

Press the Play button and take our Player for a walk around the little island.

You'll notice a few things immediately:

- The camera doesn't follow the Player. In fact, you can walk right off the screen and keep walking forever if you wanted to.

- The player can walk right through objects on the map.

- You might see a few strange-looking lines or "tears" on the Tilemap. If they appear, they will be located between where two tiles meet.

We're going to address all of these points in this chapter.

We'll learn to use **Colliders** to prevent the Player from walking through everything, and we'll use a tool called **Cinemachine** to make the Camera follows the Player as he walks. We'll also make sure the Camera is configured properly. We'll configure the graphic settings to ensure we get a crisp edge, which is important for pixel art and we'll use a Material to get rid of the tears.

Tip   If you have multiple Tilemap layers but would like to focus on just one, use the Tilemap focus mode in the lower-right of the Scene view. This will allow you to gray-out the other Tilemap layers and focus working on a specific layer.

Graphics Settings

Let's tweak the Unity Engine graphics settings so that our pixel art looks as good as possible. Unity uses an algorithm called anti-aliasing when the graphics output of the current device isn't powerful enough to render the edges of objects into perfectly smooth lines. Instead of rendering smooth lines, the edges of objects appear jagged or aliased. The anti-aliasing algorithm runs over the edges of an object and gives it a smooth appearance to compensate for the jagged graphics output.

Anti-aliasing is turned on by default in the Unity Editor regardless of the power of the device you're using. To turn off anti-aliasing, go to the Edit Menu ➤ Project Settings ➤ Quality, and set Anti-Aliasing to Disabled. As we've learned, the Unity Engine can be used for both 3D and 2D games, but we don't need anti-aliasing for our pixel-art style 2D game.

From within that same menu, Edit ➤ Project Settings ➤ Quality, also disable Anisotropic Textures. Anisotropic filtering is a way of enhancing image quality when using a specific type of camera perspective. It isn't relevant to what we're doing here with our project, so we should turn it off.

The Camera

All 2D projects in Unity use something called an Orthographic camera. Orthographic cameras render objects that are both near and far, the same size. By rendering all objects the same size, it appears to the onlooker as though everything is the same distance from the camera. This is different from how 3D projects render objects. In 3D projects, objects are rendered with different sizes to give the illusion of distance and perspective. We configured our Unity project to use an Orthographic camera in the very beginning, when we set up a 2D project.

To get the best results when rendering 2D graphics, it's important to understand how the camera works in a 2D game. Orthographic cameras have a property called **Size** that determines how many vertical "**world units**" can fit into **half** of the screen's height. World units are determined by setting the **PPU** or **pixels per unit** setting in Unity. As you may suspect from the name, the pixels per unit setting describes how many pixels the Unity Engine should render in a single world unit, that is, pixels *per* unit. PPU can be set during the import assets process. PPU is important because when you're creating art for your game, you'll want to make sure it all looks good at the same PPU.

The equation for camera size is:

(Vertical resolution / PPU) * 0.5 = Camera Size

Let's use a few simple examples to clarify this concept.

Given a screen resolution of 960 × 640, the vertical screen height is 640 pixels. Let's use a PPU of 64, to make our calculations simple: 640 divided by 64 equals 10. That means 10 world units stacked on top of each other would take up the entire vertical screen height and 5 world units would take up half of the vertical screen height. Thus, the camera size is 5, as seen in Figure 4-9.

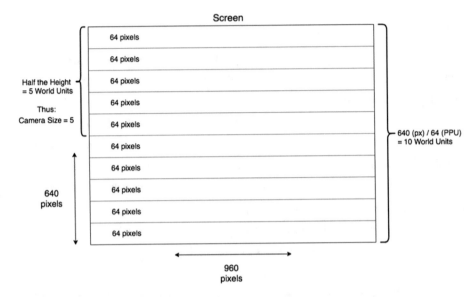

Figure 4-9. *Resolution of 960 × 640 and PPU of 64, results in a Camera Size of 5*

Let's do another example. If your game uses a screen resolution of 1280 × 1024, then the vertical screen height is 1024. Using a PPU of 32, we divide 1024 by 32 to get 32. That means 32 world units stacked on top of each other would take up the entire vertical screen height and 16 world units would take up half of the vertical screen height. Thus, the orthographic camera size is 16.

Here's one last example to reinforce the equation. Using a screen resolution of 1280 × 720, the vertical screen height would be 720. Using a PPU of 32, we divide 720 by 32 to get 22.5. That means 22.5 world units stacked on top of each other would fit into the vertical screen height: 22.5 divided by 2 equals 11.25, which is half of the screen height and our orthographic camera size.

Starting to get the hang of this? Orthographic size can seem bizarre at first but really, it's a pretty simple equation.

Here's that equation again:

(Vertical resolution / PPU) * 0.5 = Camera Size

The trick to getting a good-looking pixel art game is to pay attention to the orthographic camera size with respect to the resolution, and make sure the artwork looks good at a certain PPU.

In our game, we're going to use a resolution of 1280 × 720 but we'll use a trick to scale up the art a bit. We're going to multiply the PPU by a scaling factor of 3.

Our modified equation will look like this:

(Vertical resolution / (PPU * Scaling factor)) * 0.5 = Camera Size

Using a resolution of 1280 × 720 and a PPU of 32:

(720 / (32 PPU * 3)) * 0.5 = 3.75 Camera Size

This is why we set our camera size to be 3.75 earlier.

Now that we have a better understanding of how the camera works in Orthographic games, let's set our screen resolution. Unity comes with several screen resolution choices out of the box, but sometimes it's beneficial to set your own. We're going to set a resolution of 1280 × 720, which is considered "Standard HD" and should be sufficient for the style of game we are making.

Click on the Game window and look for the Screen Resolution drop-down menu. By default, it will probably be set to Free Aspect as seen in Figure 4-10.

Figure 4-10.   *The drop-down menu*

At the bottom of the drop-down menu, press the plus sign to open a window where you can enter new resolution. Create a custom resolution of 1280 × 720, as seen in Figure 4-11.

Figure 4-11. *Create a new custom resolution*

Press the play button and walk the character around the map to see our new resolution and camera in action.

Exciting stuff! Our game is starting to look like ... well, a game!

We've created a map for the player to walk around, but as you may have noticed, the camera stays in one place. This is fine for certain types of games such as puzzle games, but for an RPG, we'll need the camera to follow the player around. It's possible to write a C# script to direct the camera to follow the player, but we're going to use a Unity tool called Cinemachine instead.

Note Cinemachine was originally created by Adam Myhill and sold in the Unity Asset Store. Unity eventually acquired Cinemachine and made it part of their free offerings. As mentioned in Chapter 2, you can create your own tools, artwork, and content, and sell them in the Unity Asset Store.

Using Cinemachine

Cinemachine is a powerful suite of Unity tools for procedural in-game cameras, cinematics, and cutscenes. Cinemachine can automate all types of camera movements, blend and cut from camera to camera automatically, and automate all types of complex behaviors, many of them well beyond the scope of this book. We're going to use Cinemachine to automatically track the player as she walks around the map.

Cinemachine was made available through the Asset Store for Unity 2017.1, but starting with Unity 2018.1, Cinemachine was made available through the new Unity Package Manager. Earlier versions of Unity can still use Cinemachine from the Asset Store, but that version is no longer being updated and will contain no new features.

We'll talk about how to install Cinemachine in both Unity 2017 and Unity 2018 later. Refer to the instructions for the version of Unity that you're running.

Installing Cinemachine in Unity 2017

Go to the Window menu and select Asset Store to open the Asset Store tab. At the top of screen in the search field, type in, "Cinemachine" and press enter. You should get a result that looks like Figure 4-12.

Figure 4-12. *The Cinemachine Unity Package in the Asset Store*

Press on the Cinemachine icon to go to the asset page. On the asset
page, press the Import button to import the Cinemachine Unity Package
into your current project. Unity will present you with a pop-up screen as
seen in Figure 4-13 showing all the assets inside the package. Press the
Import button.

Figure 4-13. *Import the Cinemachine Unity Package*

Importing the Cinemachine package should have created a new folder
called, "Cinemachine".

Installing Cinemachine in Unity 2018

From the menus, select Window ➤ Package Manager. You should see
the Unity Package Manager window appear. Select the All tab, as seen in
Figure 4-14, then select Cinemachine.

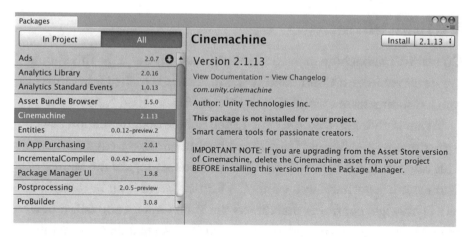

Figure 4-14. *Select the All Tab*

Click the Install button in the upper-right to install Cinemachine. After Cinemachine is finished installing, close out the Package Manager window. You should see a new Packages folder in the Project view.

After Installing Cinemachine

Regardless of which version of Unity you're running, when Cinemachine is done installing, you should see a Cinemachine menu at the top of the screen, between Component and Window.

Note   Unity Packages are collections of files that can be dropped into a project and will simply work out of the box. Packages come as modular, version, and automatically resolve dependencies. In May 2018, Unity announced that packages are the future and they intend to distribute many of their new features via packages.

Virtual Cameras

Go to the Cinemachine menu and select Create 2D Camera. This should create two objects: a **Cinemachine Brain**, attached to the main Camera, and a **Cinemachine Virtual Camera** GameObject called "CM vcam1".

What is a **Virtual Camera**? The Cinemachine documentation uses a great analogy—a Virtual Camera can be thought of as a cameraman. This cameraman controls the position and lens settings of the Main Camera but is not actually a camera. A Virtual Camera can be thought of as a lightweight controller that directs the Main Camera and tells it how to move. We can set a target for the Virtual Camera to follow, move the virtual camera along a path, blend from one path into another, and adjust all types of parameters around these behaviors. Virtual cameras are a very powerful tool to have in your Unity game development toolbox.

The **Cinemachine Brain** is the actual link between the Main Camera and the Virtual Cameras in a Scene. The Cinemachine Brain monitors for the currently active Virtual Camera, and then applies its state to the Main Camera. Switching on and off Virtual Cameras during runtime allows the Cinemachine Brain to blend together cameras for some pretty amazing results.

Select the virtual camera and drag the PlayerObject into the property called, "Follow" as seen in Figure 4-15.

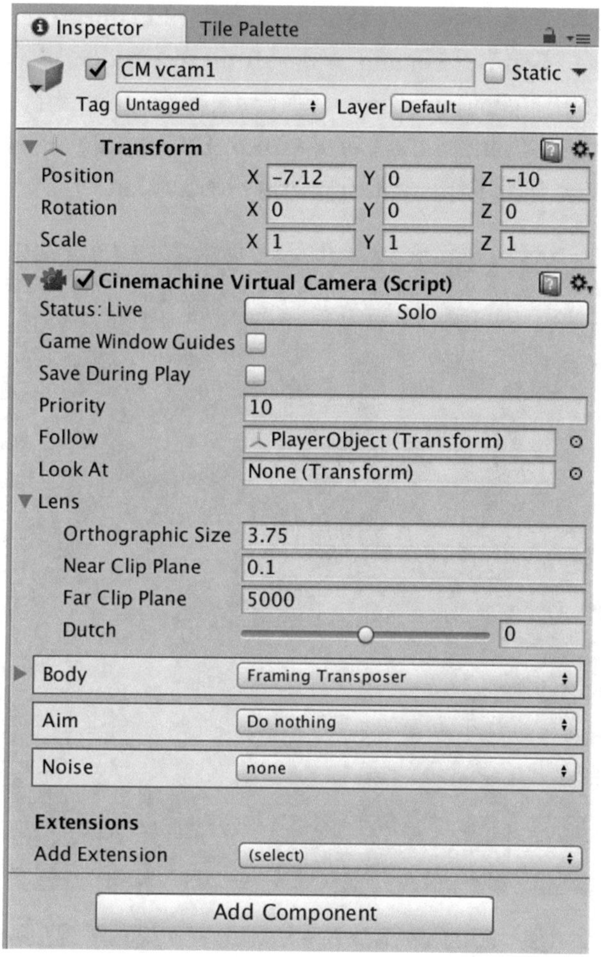

Figure 4-15. *Set the Virtual Camera Follow target to the PlayerObject*

This tells the Cinemachine Virtual Camera to follow and track the Transform component of the Player GameObject as she moves across the map.

Press play and watch the camera follow the player around. Pretty neat! With Cinemachine, we get some pretty sophisticated camera behaviors out of the box with just a few mouse clicks. To get a better idea of the hidden

115

parameters governing camera movement, let's hide the ground layer. Select the Layer_Ground Tilemap object from the Project view. Uncheck the box next to the Tilemap's Tilemap Renderer component to deactivate it. Now Unity won't render the Layer_Ground Tilemap. Your Scene should resemble Figure 4-16, with all the ground tiles hidden.

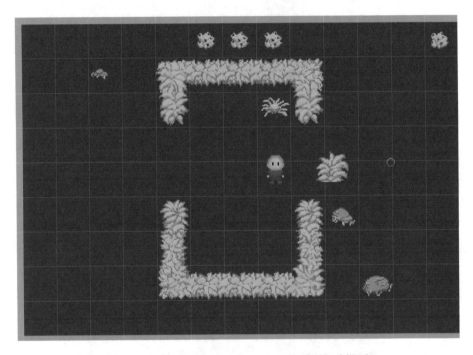

Figure 4-16. *After unchecking the box to the left of "Tilemap Renderer" to deactivate it*

Now click on the Main Camera object in the Hierarchy view and press the colored box that says Background. Change the background color to white (Figure 4-17). This will make it easier to see the Cinemachine follow frame in the next step.

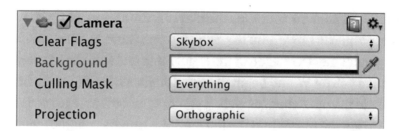

Figure 4-17. *Change the Camera background color to white*

Last, select the virtual camera and ensure that the "Game Window Guides" checkbox is checked. You'll see what Game Window Guides are in the next step.

Press the play button again. Notice how there's a white box in the middle encircling the player, surrounded by a light blue colored area, and a red area encompassing all of it (Figure 4-18). This white box is called the "Dead Zone." There's a yellow point inside the Dead Zone called the Tracking Point that will move directly with the player.

Figure 4-18. *The Dead Zone around the player contains a yellow tracking point*

The Dead Zone surrounding the player is the area in which the tracking point can move, and the camera won't move to follow. When the tracking point moves outside of the Dead Zone and into the blue area, the camera will move and begin to track. Cinemachine will add a bit of damping to the movement as well. If you're somehow able to move fast enough to get the player into the red area, the camera will track the player 1:1 and follow every movement with no delay.

Make sure the Game view is visible and click on the edge of the white box. Drag the white box out a bit, to resize the tracking area and make it a bit bigger. Now the player can walk a little further without the camera moving. You can play around with the size of these guides to get camera behavior that feels natural in your game.

With the Cinemachine object still selected in the Hierarchy view, look at the Cinemachine Virtual Camera component. You'll see an arrow to expand the "Body" section. Inside the Body section, (Figure 4-19) there are options to adjust the X and Y Damping for the virtual camera body. Damping is how quickly the Virtual Camera Dead Zone will move to catch up with the tracking point.

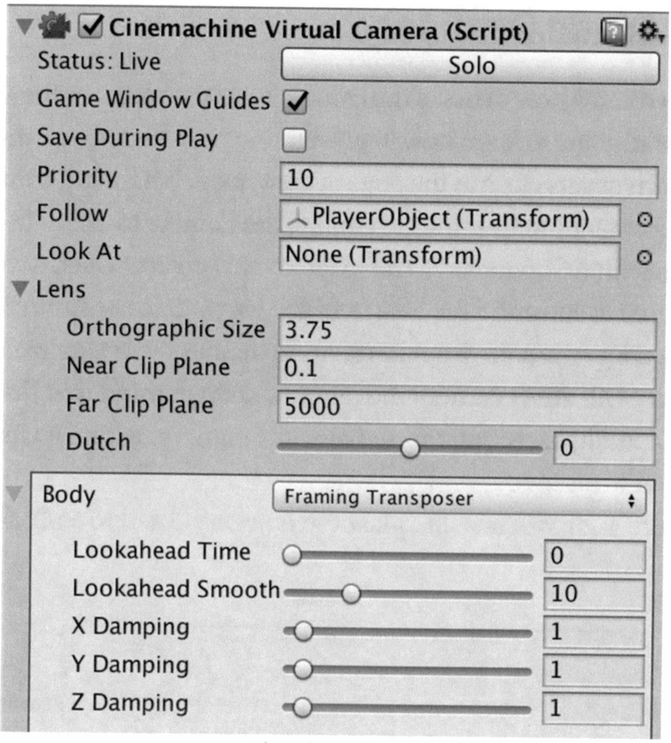

Figure 4-19. *The Damping properties from the Virtual Camera Body properties section*

The best way to understand Damping is to adjust the X and Y Damping as you walk the player around the map. Press Play and experiment with the Damping values.

If you walk the player to the edge of the map, you'll see the camera moves with the target and things don't look too bad. But we can do better.

Stop play and select the Layer_Ground object in the Hierarchy view. Check the box to the left of "Tilemap Renderer" to make the layer visible again.

Cinemachine Confiner

Now that we know how to make the camera track the player as they walk around, we're going to learn how to prevent the camera from moving when the player gets close to the edge of the screen. We'll use a component called a **Cinemachine Confiner** to confine the Camera to a certain area. The Cinemachine Confiner will use a Collider 2D object, which we've preconfigured to surround the area in which we want to constrain the camera.

Before we get into the implementation details, let's visualize how the Confiner will affect camera movement. Keep in mind that the virtual camera is actually directing the active scene camera, telling it where to move and at what speed.

In Figure 4-20, we have the player in a Scene, about to walk east.

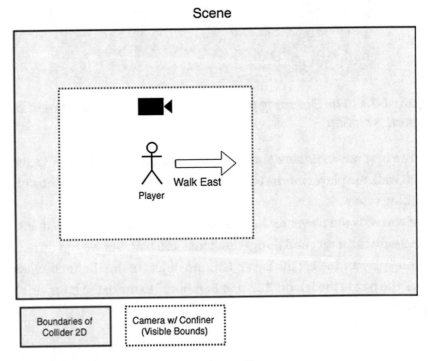

Figure 4-20. *The player is about to walk east*

The area in white is the visible viewport of the currently active camera. The area in gray is the rest of the map, outside of the camera's viewport and not currently visible. The perimeter of the area in gray is surrounded by a Collider 2D.

As the player walks east, the virtual camera directs the camera to move east and track the player as she walks through the scene, as seen in Figure 4-21.

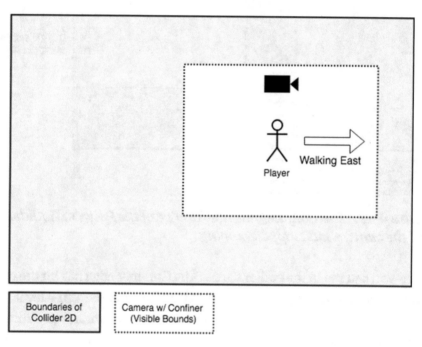

Figure 4-21. *The player is walking east*

The virtual camera movement will take into account player movement speed, the size of the Dead Zone, and the amount of Damping applied to the camera body.

The key thing to keep in mind is that we've encircled the perimeter of the area in gray with a Polygon Collider 2D and set the bounding shape of the Confiner to point to this Collider. When the Confiner edge hits the edge of that bounding shape, it will interact and tell the virtual camera to direct the active camera to stop moving, as seen in Figure 4-22.

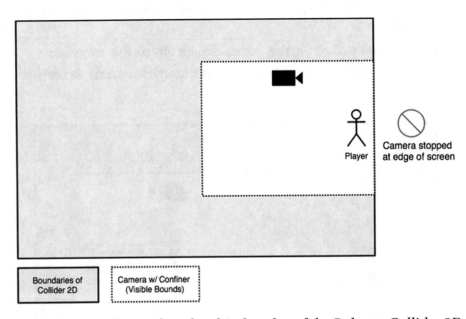

Figure 4-22. *The Confiner has hit the edge of the Polygon Collider 2D and the camera has stopped moving*

As you can see in the earlier figures, the Confiner edge has hit the edge of the bounding shape which is the Collider 2D, surrounding the level. The Virtual Camera has stopped moving, and the player continues to walk to the edge of the map.

Let's build a Cinemachine Confiner.

Select our Virtual Camera from the Hierarchy view. In the Inspector, next to Add Extension, select CinemachineConfiner from the drop-down menu. This will add a Cinemachine Confiner component to our Cinemachine 2D Camera.

The CinemachineConfiner requires either a Composite Collider 2D, or a Polygon Collider 2D to determine where the edges of the confinement begin. Select the Layer_Ground object and add a Polygon Collider 2D via the Add Components button. Click the Edit Collider button on the collider component and edit the collider so that it surrounds the edges of our Layer_Ground level as seen in Figure 4-23.

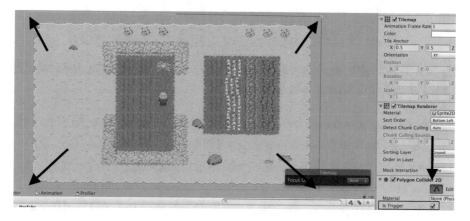

Figure 4-23. *Drag the corners of the Polygon Collider 2D to match the outline of Layer_Ground*

The arrows in Figure 4-23 are there to remind you to leave a little bit of a space between the collider and the edge of the map. This is so the camera will show a bit of water and won't be confined strictly to the edge of the land mass. Don't forget to press the Edit Collider button again when you're finished editing the collider. Check the "Is Trigger" property on the collider component and then select our Cinemachine Camera again. We want to use this Collider as a trigger because if we didn't, the player would be forcefully pushed out of the collider when the player's Collider and Tilemap Collider interacted. This is because two objects with Colliders can't occupy the same place unless one of them is being used as a Trigger.

Select and drag the Layer_Ground object into the Bounding Shape 2D field of the Cinemachine Confiner as seen in Figure 4-24.

Cinemachine Confiner (Script)

Confine Mode	Confine 2D ⬍
Bounding Shape 2D	⬦ Layer_Ground (Pol) ⊘
Confine Screen Edges	☐
Damping	⊙━━━━━━ 0

Figure 4-24. *The Polygon Collider 2D from the Layer_Ground will be used for the Bounding Shape 2D*

The Confiner will take the Collider 2D from the Layer_Ground object and use it as the Confiner's bounding shape. Make sure to check the "Confine Screen Edges" box to tell the Confiner to stop at the Polygon 2D edges.

Press the play button and walk toward the edge of the screen. If everything is set up properly, you'll see the Virtual Camera's Dead Zone stop moving as soon as the camera reaches the edge where we placed the Polygon Collider 2D earlier. The arrow in Figure 4-25 points to the edge of the Polygon Collider 2D. As you can see, the player has walked far out of the Dead Zone, and while the Tracking Point has continued moving with the Player, the Camera has stopped.

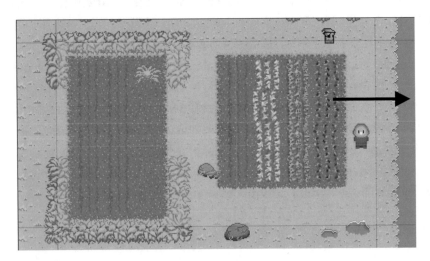

Figure 4-25. *The Dead Zone has stopped moving along with the player*

To review, the three steps to setting up a Cinemachine Confiner:

1. Add a CinemachineConfiner Extension to the Virtual Camera.

2. Create a Polygon Collider 2D on a Tilemap, edit its shape to determine the confinement edges, and set the "Is Trigger" property.

3. Use this Polygon Collider 2D as the Bounding Shape 2D field of the Cinemachine Confiner.

Forcing the camera to stop moving at the edge of the screen, while allowing the player to continue walking, is a common effect that you've probably seen in dozens of 2D games.

Note that using a Confiner won't prevent the player from walking off the map—just the camera from tracking them. We'll set up some logic soon to keep the player from walking off the map.

Stabilization

As you walk the player around the map, you may notice a slight jittering effect. The jittering is especially pronounced when you stop walking and the virtual camera damping slowly brings the tracking to a halt. This jittering effect is due to overly precise camera coordinates. The camera is tracking the player but it's moving to subpixel positions, whereas the player is only moving around from pixel to pixel. We made sure of that when we did the calculations for the Orthographic Camera size earlier.

To fix this jittering, we want to force the final Cinemachine Virtual Camera position to stay within pixel boundaries. We're going to script a simple "extension" component that we'll add to the Cinemachine Virtual Camera. Our extension component will grab the last coordinates of the Cinemachine Virtual Camera and round them to a value that lines up with our PPU.

Create a new C# Script called RoundCameraPos and open it up in Visual Studio. Type in the following script and refer to the following comments to better understand it. This is certainly one of the more advanced scripts you'll be writing, but if having your game look good is important to you, it pays to understand it.

```
using UnityEngine;

// 1
using Cinemachine;

// 2
public class RoundCameraPos : CinemachineExtension
{
    // 3
    public float PixelsPerUnit = 32;

    // 4
    protected override void PostPipelineStageCallback(
        CinemachineVirtualCameraBase vcam,
        CinemachineCore.Stage stage, ref CameraState state,
        float deltaTime)
    {
        // 5
        if (stage == CinemachineCore.Stage.Body)
        {
            // 6
            Vector3 pos = state.FinalPosition;

            // 7
            Vector3 pos2 = new Vector3(Round(pos.x),
            Round(pos.y), pos.z);
```

```
        // 8
        state.PositionCorrection += pos2 - pos;
    }
  }
  // 9
  float Round(float x)
  {
      return Mathf.Round(x * PixelsPerUnit) / PixelsPerUnit;
  }
}
```

And the explanation for the earlier code:

// 1

```
using Cinemachine;
```

Import the Cinemachine framework to write an extension component that we'll attach to the Cinemachine Virtual Camera.

// 2

```
public class RoundCameraPos : CinemachineExtension
```

Components that hook into Cinemachine's processing pipeline must inherit from CinemachineExtension

// 3

```
public float PixelsPerUnit = 32;
```

The Pixels Per Unit, or PPU. As we discussed earlier when we talked about the Camera, we're displaying 32 pixels in one world unit.

// 4

```
protected override void PostPipelineStageCallback(Cinemachine
VirtualCameraBase vcam, CinemachineCore.Stage stage, ref
CameraState state, float deltaTime)
```

This method is required by all classes that inherit from CinemachineExtension. It's called by Cinemachine after the Confiner is done processing.

```
// 5
if (stage == CinemachineCore.Stage.Body)
```

The Cinemachine Virtual Camera has a post-processing pipeline consisting of several stages. We perform this check to see what stage of the camera's post-processing we're in. If we're in the "Body" stage then we're permitted to set the Virtual Camera's position in space.

```
// 6
Vector3 finalPos = state.FinalPosition;
```

Retrieve the Virtual Camera's final position

```
// 7
Vector3 newPos = new Vector3(Round(finalPos.x),
Round(finalPos.y), finalPos.z);
```

Call the Rounding method we wrote (following) to round the position, and then create a new Vector with the results. This will be our new, pixel-bounded position.

```
// 8
state.PositionCorrection += newPos - finalPos;
```

Set the VC's new position to the difference between the old position and the new rounded position that we just calculated.

```
// 9
```

A method that rounds the input value. We use this method to make sure the camera always stays on a pixel position.

Materials

As you walk the player around the map, you may notice some lines or "tears" between the tiles. That's because they aren't snapping precisely to a pixel-perfect location. To fix this, we'll use something called a Material to tell Unity how we want our sprites rendered.

Create a new folder called, "Materials" then right-click and Create ➤ Material. Call this material, "Sprite2D."

Set the properties on the material as follows:

Shader: Sprites/Default

Ensure Pixel Snap is checked.

The new Material properties should look like Figure 4-26.

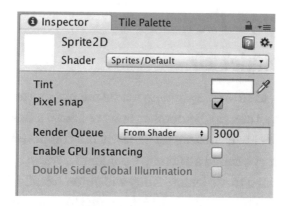

Figure 4-26. *Configure the new material*

We want the Renderer component in our GameObjects to use this Material instead of the default Material.

Select our Layer_Ground Tilemap and change the material in the Tilemap Renderer by clicking the dot next to the Material property. When you've selected the Sprite2D material, the Renderer component should look like Figure 4-27.

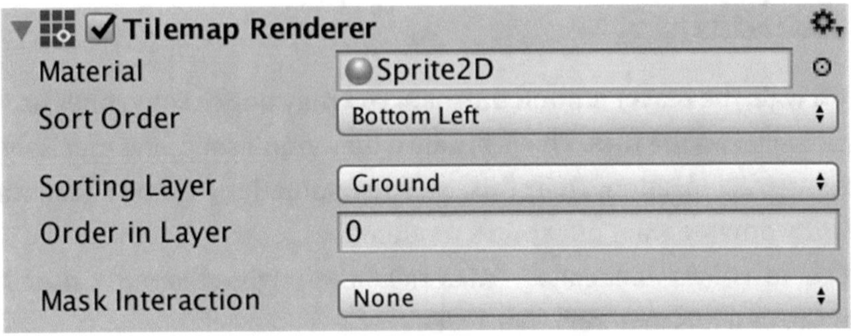

▼ ⊞ ☑ Tilemap Renderer		⚙
Material	⊙ Sprite2D	⊙
Sort Order	Bottom Left	↕
Sorting Layer	Ground	↕
Order in Layer	0	
Mask Interaction	None	↕

Figure 4-27. *Use the Sprite2D Material in our Tilemap Renderer component*

Do this for all of our Tilemap layers, and then press the Play button and the tears should have disappeared.

Colliders and Tilemaps

Tilemap Collider 2D

Now we're going to solve the problem where the player can walk through everything on the Tilemap. Remember how we added a Box Collider 2D to our PlayerObject back in Chapter 3? There is a component specially tailored for Tilemaps called a Tilemap Collider 2D. When a Tilemap Collider 2D is added to a Tilemap, Unity will automatically detect and add a Collider 2D to each sprite tile it detects on that Tilemap. We are going to use these Tilemap colliders to determine when the PlayerObject collider comes in contact with a tile collider and prevent the player from walking through it.

Select Layer_Trees_and_Rocks from the Hierarchy view then press the Add Component button in the Inspector. Search for and add a component called "Tilemap Collider 2D".

You'll notice that all the sprites on your Layers_Objects Tilemap now have a thin green line surrounding them, indicating a Collider component, similar to Figure 4-28.

Figure 4-28. *The Tilemap Collider 2D added Colliders to the rocks, as shown by the arrow*

Note   If you see a box surrounding every tile on the Tilemap, then you had the wrong Tilemap (Layer_Ground) selected. This is a common mistake. Remove the Tilemap Collider 2D Component by clicking the gear icon in the top right of the Component in the Inspector, then select Remove Component from the menu as seen in Figure 4-29.

▼ ⦂⦂⦂ ☑ **Tilemap Collider 2D** ⚙▾

Material	None (P	Reset
Is Trigger	☐	
Used By Effector	☐	Remove Component
Used By Composite	☐	Move Up
		Move Down
Offset	X 0	Copy Component
▶ Info		Paste Component As New
		Paste Component Values

Sprites−Default

Figure 4-29. *Removing the misplaced Tilemap Collider 2D Component*

Now select the desired Tilemap: Layer_Trees_and_Rocks in the
Hierarchy view and add a Tilemap Collider 2D Component to it.

We've just added a Collider 2D to every tile sprite on Layer_Objects.
Take a look at Figure 4-30 and notice how the bushes around the garden
have seven separate colliders. The problem with this is that it's pretty
inefficient for Unity to be keeping track of all these colliders.

Figure 4-30. *Every sprite in the Layer_Trees_and_Rocks now has its
own Collider*

Composite Colliders

Fortunately, Unity comes with a tool called a Composite Collider that will combine all of these separate colliders into one large collider, which is more efficient. Keeping the Layer_Trees_and_Rocks Tilemap Layer selected in the Hierarchy view, select Add Component and add a Composite Collider 2D component to Layer_Trees_and_Rocks. You can leave all the default settings as they are. Now check the box in the Tilemap Collider 2D that says, "Used By Composite" and watch how all the separate Colliders for the bushes are merged together like magic.

When we added a Composite Collider 2D to the Tilemap layer, Unity automatically added a Rigidbody 2D component. Set this Rigidbody 2D component Body Type to Static because it won't be moving.

Before we press Play, let's make sure that when the player collides with something, she doesn't rotate around, as seen in Figure 4-31. Because the PlayerObject has a Dynamic Rigidbody 2D component, it is subject to forces imposed by the physics engine when it interacts with other colliders.

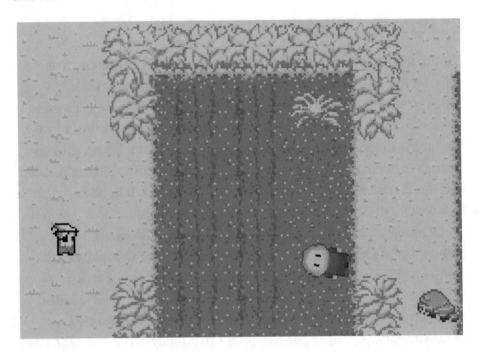

Figure 4-31. *This ridiculous-looking rotation is due to Rigidbody 2D collisions*

Select the PlayerObject and in the attached Rigidbody 2D component, check the "Freeze Rotation Z" checkbox as seen in Figure 4-32.

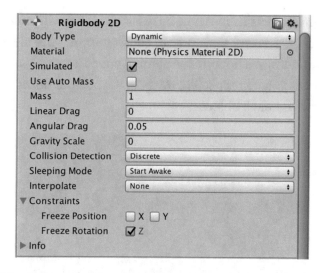

Figure 4-32. *Freeze the Z axis rotation to prevent the Player from spinning*

Press the Play button and walk the Player around the map. You'll notice that she can no longer walk through shrubbery, rocks, or anything you placed on the Layer_Trees_and_Rocks level. This is because the collider that we added to the PlayerObject in Chapter 3 is colliding with the Tilemap collider we added just a few moments ago.

You'll also notice that for some objects there is a noticeable gap between where the Player has stopped and the object on the Tilemap. To better view the bounds of each Collider, keep the game running and switch to Scene view by selecting the Scene tab.

Zoom in to the Player using the scroll-wheel on your mouse or touchpad. Pan around the scene if you need to by pressing Alt (PC) or Option (Mac) then clicking and dragging the Tilemap. Select the PlayerObject from the Hierarchy view to see its Box Collider. Then hold down Control (PC) or Cmd / ⌘ (Mac) and select the Layer_Trees_and_ Rocks TileMap, without deselecting the PlayerObject.

Both GameObjects should now be selected, and you should see a collider around the Player and another collider around the tile in the Tilemap. Depending on how you've painted your Tilemap, the exact Tiles will differ, but as you can see in Figure 4-33, the collider boxes show up as thin green lines for each object.

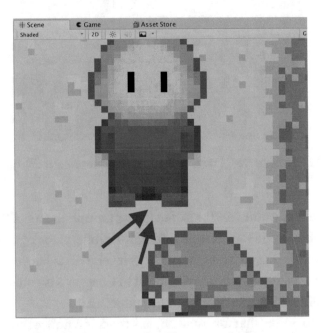

Figure 4-33. *The gap between the Player and objects around her are due to the collider boxes—the thin green box*

The colliders for the rock and the player have collided, preventing the player from moving any closer. Because the collider isn't hugging the rock very closely, there's a noticeable gap between where the player has stopped and the rock. We can fix this by editing the Physics Shape for each type of sprite.

Editing Physics Shapes

To edit the Physics Shape for sprites in a spritesheet, select the Outdoor Objects spritesheet in the Project view and open the Sprite Editor in the Inspector. Go to the Sprite Editor drop-down menu on the top-left and select Edit Physics shape, as seen in Figure 4-34.

Figure 4-34. *Select the Edit Physics Shape in the Sprite Editor*

Select a sprite that you want to edit and press the update button next to "Outline Tolerance" to see the physics shape outline around the sprite.

Drag the boxes to match the outline of your object however you wish (Figure 4-35). There's no need to get ultra-precise with the Physics Shape unless your game mechanics really depend on it. You can create additional points by clicking on the line itself and delete points by selecting a point and hitting Control (PC) or Cmd / ⌘ (Mac) + delete.

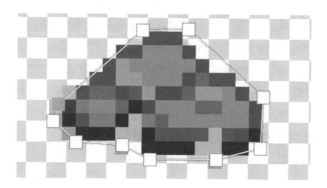

Figure 4-35. *Matching the Physics Shape to the sprite*

When you're satisfied with the Physics Shape, press the Apply button and close the Sprite Editor. To use this new Physics Outline in the scene, be sure the relevant Tilemap is selected and press the Reset button from the gear icon drop-down menu on the Tilemap Collider 2D component, as seen in Figure 4-36. This will force the Unity Editor to read the updated Physics Shape information.

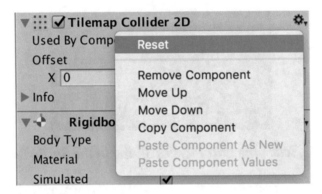

Figure 4-36. *Reset the Tilemap Collider 2D component to use the new Physics Shape*

Now press the play button and see how your new and improved colliders are working out.

Tip   Unity takes its best guess in terms of merging the colliders when it makes a Composite Collider so it's possible that if you left gaps around sprites when you adjusted their Physics Outlines in the Tile Editor, you won't see all the tiles merged into one giant collider. You can either adjust the Physics Outlines in the Tile Editor again or leave it if there aren't many gaps. Remember: if you adjust the Physics Outlines for objects, you'll need to reset the component each time to get the updated Physics Outline.

Because you're an expert on colliders now, you may also want to adjust the Box Collider 2D on our player to be a bit smaller, as seen in Figure 4-37.

Figure 4-37. *Adjust the collider size on our player for a better fit*

Now that we're familiar with Tilemap Colliders, let's use them to create a boundary around the land mass in our map so that the player can't walk into the water. Your game might have different requirements—it's possible that you'll want the player to walk into the water for some reason. But what follows is one of several different techniques to prevent the player from walking into areas you don't want them in.

Select your Layer_Ground and remove any tiles from the area that you don't want the player to walk into. In the sample map we've created, we'll remove the water tiles because we don't want the player walking into the water. We're removing these tiles because we're going to paint them onto a different layer. Now create a new Tilemap layer called, "Layer_Water". Make sure to set the Sorting Layer on the new layer to Ground, just to stay consistent.

Make sure to select the newly created layer as your Active Tilemap in the Tile Palette screen. Paint the area that you would like to keep the player out of, such as the water, as seen in Figure 4-38. Note that in Figure 4-38, we have the Focus On setting set to the Tilemap, so we can see only the tiles from the currently selected Tilemap layer.

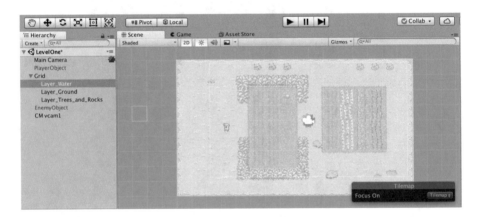

Figure 4-38. *Turn Focus On to see the new Tilemap Layer clearer*

We want to add a Tilemap Collider 2D and a Composite Collider 2D to the Layer_Water Tilemap. Adding the Composite Collider 2D will automatically add a Rigidbody 2D component as well. Set the Rigidbody 2D Body Type to Static, because we don't want the ocean tiles moving anywhere when they collide with the player. Last, check the "Used by Composite" box in the Tilemap Collider 2D to combine all the individual tile colliders into one efficient collider.

Press the Play button and notice how the player can no longer walk into the water. What we've done here with Colliders is really nothing new. You've done this sort of thing earlier in this chapter when we worked with Tilemap Colliders.

Summary

In this chapter we've covered some core concepts in making 2D games with Unity. We learned how to turn sprites into Tile Palettes and used them to paint Tilemaps. We've used colliders to prevent the player from walking through objects and how to tweak them for a better player experience. We learned how to configure the Camera to achieve a balance between scaling, art size, and resolution, which is very important in 2D pixel-art style games. One of the most valuable tools we covered in this chapter was Cinemachine—a powerful tool for automating camera movements. If you're interested in learning more about Cinemachine, `https://forum.unity.com` is a great place to ask questions and learn from the people who created it! In Chapter 5, you're going to see all of what we've learned so far come together and you'll start to feel as if you're really making a game.

CHAPTER 5

Assembling the Nuts and Bolts

We've learned a lot so far about the tools Unity provides to build games, and now we're going to start putting it all together. In this chapter, we'll build the C# class structure used for the Player, Enemies, and any other characters that might pop up in a game. We'll also create a few prefabs that the player can pick up, including coins and power-ups, and learn how to specify which object collisions our game logic cares about and which it doesn't. We'll review an important Unity-specific tool called Scriptable Objects, as well as cover techniques for leveraging them to build a clean, scalable game architecture.

Character Class

In this section, we're going to lay the groundwork for the class structure used for every character, enemy, or player in our game. There are certain traits that every "living" character in our game will have, such as the concept of health.

Health points or "hit-points" are used to measure how much damage a character can take before dying. Hit-points is a carry-over term from the old days of tabletop war gaming, but present-day games of every genre typically have a concept of hit-points or health points.

In Figure 5-1, a screenshot from the game *Castle Crashers*, developed by The Behemoth, demonstrates an example of how many games choose to visually represent a characters remaining hit-points. This screenshot shows a common technique: a red hit-point or health-bar, underneath each character name on the top of the screen.

Figure 5-1. *Hit-points are indicated as red bars of varying length on top of the screen*

For now, we're just going to keep track of hit-points, but eventually we'll build our own health bar to visually represent our player's remaining health.

Create a new folder under Scripts called MonoBehaviours. Because we'll be creating more MonoBehaviours, it makes sense to give them their own folder. Move the MovementController script into this folder, because it inherits from MonoBehaviour.

Inside the MonoBehaviours folder, create a new C# script called Character. Double-click the Character script to open it in our Editor.

We're going to build a generic Character class from which our Player and Enemy classes will inherit. This Character class will contain functionality and properties common to all character types in our game.

Enter the following code and don't forget to save when you're finished. As usual, don't type in the line comments.

```
using UnityEngine;

// 1
public abstract class Character : MonoBehaviour {

// 2
    public int hitPoints;
    public int maxHitPoints;
}
```

// 1

We'll use the Abstract modifier in C# to indicate that this class cannot be instantiated and must be inherited by a subclass.

// 2

Track the characters current hitPoints as well as the maximum number of hit-points. There is a limit to how "healthy" a character can get.

Make sure to save this script when you're finished.

Player Class

Next we're going to create the basic Player class. In our MonoBehaviours folder, create a new C# script called Player. This Player class will start out extremely simple, but we'll add functionality to it as we go along.

Enter the following code. We've removed the Start() and Update() functions.

```
using UnityEngine;

// 1
public class Player : Character
{
  // Empty, for now.
}
```

// 1

All we want to do for now is inherit from the Character class to gain properties like hitPoints.

Save the script then switch back to the Unity Editor.

Select the Player prefab. Drag and drop the Player script into the Player object and set its properties as seen in Figure 5-2. Give the player 5 hit-points and 10 maximum hit-points to start with.

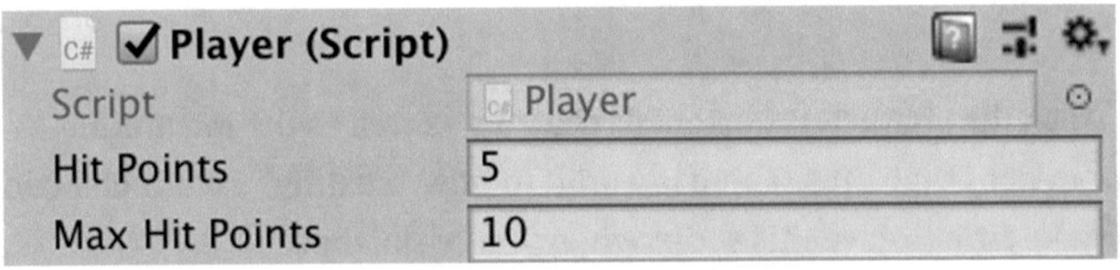

Figure 5-2. *Configure our Player script*

We're starting the player with less than their max hit-points because later in this chapter, we're going to build the functionality where the player can pick up heart power-ups to increase their health.

Focus on Prefabs

Life isn't all fun and games for our adventurer and even intrepid heroes need to make a living somehow. Let's create some coins in the scene for her to pick up.

From the downloaded game assets folder for this book, select the spritesheet titled, "hearts-and-coins32x32.png", which totally sounds like an 1980s glam-rock metal band, and drag it into the Assets ➤ Sprites ➤ Objects folder.

The Import Settings in the Inspector should be set to the following:

Texture Type: Sprite (2D and UI)

Sprite Mode: Multiple

Pixels Per Unit: 32

Filter Mode: Point (no filter)

Ensure the Default button is selected at the bottom
and set Compression to: None

Press the Apply button, and then open the Sprite Editor.

From the Slice menu, select Grid By Cell Size and set the Pixel Size to width: 32, height: 32. Press Apply and close the Sprite Editor.

Create a Coin Prefab

In this section, we're going to create the Coin prefab itself.

Create a new GameObject in the project view and rename it to CoinObject. Select the four individual coin sprites from the sliced heart-coin-fire spritesheet and drag them onto the CoinObject to create a new animation. Follow the same steps from Chapter 3 when we created the Player and Enemy animations. Rename the animation clip to "coin-spin" and save it to the Animations ➤ Animations folder. Rename the generated Controller, "CoinController" and move it to the Controllers folder.

In the Sprite Renderer component, click the little dot next to the "Sprite" form and select a Sprite to use when previewing this component in the Scene view.

Create a new Sorting Layer by selecting the Sorting Layer drop-down menu in the Sprite Renderer component, click "Add Sorting Layer", then add a new layer called, "Objects" between the Ground and Characters layers.

Select the CoinObject again and set its Sorting Layer to: Objects.

To allow the player to pick up coins, we need to configure two aspects of the CoinObject:

1. Some way to detect that the player has collided with the coin

2. A custom Tag on the coin that says it can be picked up

Set Up the Circle Collider 2D

Select the CoinObject again and add a Circle Collider 2D component to it. A Circle Collider 2D is a type of primitive collider that we'll use to detect when a player runs into the coin. Set the Radius of the Circle Collider 2D to: 0.17, so it's approximately the same size as the Sprite.

The script logic we're about to write requires the player to move through the coin to pick it up. To allow this, we'll use the Circle Collider 2D a bit differently than we've used other Colliders. If we simply added a Circle Collider 2D to the CoinObject, the player wouldn't be able to walk through it. We want the Circle Collider 2D on the CoinObject to act as a sort of "trigger" and detect when another Collider interacts with it. We don't want the Circle Collider 2D to stop the other Collider from moving through it.

To use the Circle Collider 2D as a trigger, we need to ensure the "Is Trigger" property is checked as seen in Figure 5-3.

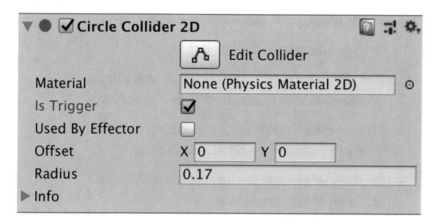

Figure 5-3. *Check the Is Trigger box on the Circle Collider*

Set Up a Custom Tag

We also want to add a Tag to the CoinObject that a script can use to detect if another object can be picked up.

Let's create a new tag from the Tags & Layers menu called, "CanBePickedUp":

1. Select the CoinObject from the Project view

2. On the top-left of the Inspector, select "Add Tag" from the Tags menu.

3. Create the CanBePickedUp tag

4. Select the CoinObject again and set its Tag to: CanBePickedUp

We're ready to create the prefab.

Create a prefab from the CoinObject by dragging it into the prefabs folder. You can delete the CoinObject from the Project view after you've created the prefab.

In summary, the steps to create an interactable prefab:

1. Create a GameObject and rename it.

2. Add sprites for the prefab animation. This will attach a Sprite Renderer Component to the GameObject.

3. Set the prefab's Sprite property. This sprite will be used to represent the prefab in the Scene.

4. Set the Sorting Layer so the prefab is visible and rendered in the correct order.

5. Add a Collider 2D component appropriate to the shape of the sprite.

6. Depending on type of prefab you're creating, set: Is Trigger on the Collider.

7. Create tag called CanBePickedUp and set tag of object to CanBePickedUp.

8. Change the Layer if needed.

9. Drag GameObject to prefabs folder to use as prefab.

10. Delete the original GameObject from the Hierarchy view.

Tip   Drag and Drop a Coin prefab into the scene then select it. Uncheck the Is Trigger box on the Coin prefabs for a second. Notice how the text "Is Trigger" turns a bold blue. This is Unity's way of reminding us that this value has only been changed on this instance of the prefab. If we want to save this setting for all instances of the prefab, press the Apply button at the top-right of the Inspector. Make sure to check Is Trigger when you're done, so the coin prefab behaves properly.

Layer-Based Collision Detection

We want to give the player in our RPG the ability to pick up coins by walking into them. Our game will also have enemies walking around the map, but we want the enemies to walk right through the coins without picking them up.

As we discussed in Chapter 3, Layers are used to define collections of GameObjects. Collider components that are attached to GameObjects on the same Layer will be aware of each other and can interact. We can create logic based off of these interactions to do things such as pick up objects.

There's also a technique to make Collider components on different layers aware of each other. This approach uses a Unity feature called **Layer-Based Collision Detection.**

We'll use this feature so that the player and coin colliders, despite being on different layers, are aware of each other. We'll also configure things so that the enemy colliders aren't aware of the coins because they can't pick them up. If two colliders aren't aware of each other, they won't interact. The enemy will walk right through the coins without picking them up.

To see this feature in action, first we need to create and assign Layers to the relevant GameObjects.

We learned how to create new Layers in Chapter 3, but if you need a refresher:

1. Select the CoinObject in the Hierarchy

2. In the Inspector, select the Layer drop-down menu

3. Select: "Add Layer"

4. Create a new Layer called: "Consumables"

5. Create another Layer called: "Enemies"

The Consumables layer will be used for items such as coins, hearts, and other objects that we want the player to consume. The Enemies layer will be used for: you guessed it—enemies.

After creating the two new Layers, the Inspector should look like Figure 5-4.

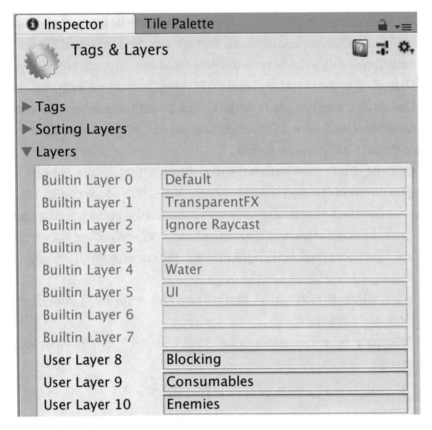

Figure 5-4. *Add an Enemies Layer*

Go to the Edit menu ➤ Project Settings ➤ Physics 2D. Look at the **Layer Collision Matrix** on the bottom of the Physics2DSettings view. This is where we'll configure the layers to allow the enemies to walk right through coins, power-ups, and whatever else we choose.

By checking and unchecking boxes in the intersection of a column and a row, we can configure which layers are aware of each other and will interact. Colliders on objects from different layers can interact if the box at the intersection of the two layers is checked.

We want to configure the player and coin objects so their colliders are aware of each other. We want the enemy colliders to be unaware of the coin colliders.

Uncheck the box at the intersection between Consumables and Enemies so it resembles Figure 5-5. Objects in the Enemies layer will no longer have an interaction triggered by colliding with an object on the Consumables layer. The two different layers are now unaware of each other. We haven't scripted the enemies to walk around the level yet—that comes later. But when we do, the enemies won't be aware of the coins because the two layers are not configured to interact.

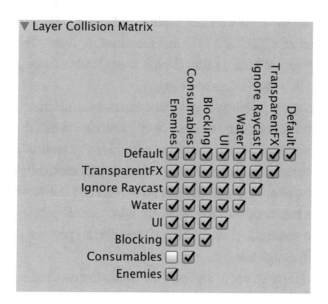

Figure 5-5. *The Layer Collision Matrix allows us to configure layer interactions*

Select the CoinObject prefab and change its layer to be: Consumables. While we're at it, select the EnemyObject prefab in the Prefabs folder and change its layer to be: Enemies.

Now drag a CoinObject prefab somewhere onto the scene.

Press play and walk the character over to the coin. You'll notice that the player can walk through the coin. The CoinObject is on the Consumables layer, and the Player is on the Blocking layer. Because we left the box for these layers checked in the Collision Matrix, the layers are aware of each other when their respective objects collide. We're going to use this awareness to script logic allowing the player to pick up coins.

Triggers and Scripting

As we touched on earlier, Colliders aren't used only to detect that two objects have run into one another. Colliders also can be used to define a range around an object and to detect that another GameObject has entered that range. When another GameObject is within range, scripted behaviors can be *triggered* accordingly.

The "Is Trigger" property is used to detect when another object has entered the range defined by the Collider. When the player's collider touches the coin's circle collider, the method: void OnTriggerEnter2D(Collider2D collision) is automatically called on both objects attached to the colliders. We can use this method to customize the behavior that should occur when two objects collide. Because we're setting Is Trigger, the colliders do not prevent the player from walking through the coin any more.

Open the Player.cs script and add the following method toward the bottom.

```
// 1
void OnTriggerEnter2D(Collider2D collision)
{
```

```
// 2
    if (collision.gameObject.CompareTag("CanBePickedUp"))
    {
// 3
        collision.gameObject.SetActive(false);
    }
}
```

Let's go through this method implementation.

// 1

OnTriggerEnter2D() is called whenever this object overlaps with a trigger collider.

// 2

Use the collision to retrieve the gameObject that the player has collided with. Examine the tag of the collided gameObject. If that tag is "CanBePickedUp" then continue execution inside the if-statement.

// 3

We know that the other GameObject can be picked up, so we'll create the impression that the object has been picked up and hide it in the scene. We're not actually scripting the functionality to pick the object up yet—that comes later.

Press Save in Visual Studio, then go back to the Unity Editor and press play. Walk the player over to the coin in your scene and watch as the coin disappears when the player touches it.

To summarize, when the player collides with the coin, the Colliders detect the interaction, the script logic determines if this object can be picked up, and if so, we set the coin to be inactive. Pretty neat!

Tip   Make sure to press Save whenever you make changes to a script, or the changes won't be compiled in the Unity Editor and won't be reflected in your game. It's very common to make a quick change then flip back to Unity and wonder why you don't see anything different happening.

Scriptable Objects

Scriptable Objects are an important concept to learn for any Unity game developer looking to build a clean game architecture. Scriptable Objects can be thought of reusable data containers that are defined via C# script, generated via the Asset menu, and saved in a Unity project as Assets.

There are two primary use cases for Scriptable Objects:

- Reducing memory usage by storing a reference to a single instance of the Scriptable Object asset. This is done instead of making a copy of all the values of each object every time you use it and thereby increasing the memory usage.

- Predefined pluggable data sets.

To explain the first use case, let's think about a contrived example: Imagine that we created a prefab with a string property containing the entire text of this book. Each time we created another instance of that prefab, we would also create a new copy of the entire text of this book. As you can imagine, this approach would start to use up memory in your game rather quickly.

If we used a Scriptable Object inside that prefab to hold the entire text of this book, then each time we created a new instance of the prefab, it would in turn reference the same exact copy of this book text. We could spawn as many copies of the prefab as we'd like, and the memory used by the book text would remain the same.

Regarding the first use case, an important item to remember when using Scriptable Objects is that each time we reference a Scriptable Object asset, we are referring to the same Scriptable Object in memory. A consequence of this approach is that if we change any data in this Scriptable Object reference, we would change the data in the Scriptable Object asset itself, and those changes would remain when we stopped running our game. If we wanted to change any values on the Scriptable Object asset during runtime without permanently changing the original data, then we should make a copy of it in memory first.

Unity developers also frequently use Scriptable Objects in their game architecture to define pluggable data sets. Data sets can be defined to describe items that a player may find in a store or inventory system. Scriptable Objects also can be used to define properties such as attack and defense levels in a digital version of a card game.

Scriptable Objects inherit from the `ScriptableObject` class, (which in turn inherits from `Object`), not `MonoBehaviour`, so we don't have access to the `Start()` and `Update()` methods. These methods wouldn't really make sense to use anyway because Scriptable Objects are used to store data. Because Scriptable Objects don't inherit from `MonoBehaviour`, they can't be attached to GameObjects. Instead of attaching to GameObjects, a common way to use Scriptable Objects is to create a reference to them from inside Unity scripts that do inherit from `MonoBehaviour`.

Creating a Scriptable Object

We're going to create a Scriptable Object called "Item" to hold data about objects that the player can consume or pick up. We'll reference this Scriptable Object in a script that derives from `MonoBehaviour` and attach that script to the Item's prefab. When a player collides with the prefab, we'll grab a reference to the Scriptable Object and give the impression that the item has been picked up by deactivating it. Eventually we will add these objects to an Inventory we'll build.

Create a folder in the Scripts directory called, "Scriptable Objects". Then right-click and create a new script called Item.

Type the following into Item.cs, and don't forget to save when you're done. As usual, we'll explain what the code does in detail.

```
using UnityEngine;

// 1
[CreateAssetMenu(menuName = "Item")]

// 2
public class Item : ScriptableObject {

// 3
    public string objectName;

// 4
    public Sprite sprite;

// 5
    public int quantity;

// 6
    public bool stackable;

// 7
    public enum ItemType
    {
        COIN,
        HEALTH
    }
```

```
// 8
    public ItemType itemType;
}
```

Let's go through the Item script:

```
// 1
```

CreateAssetMenu creates an entry in the Create submenu, as seen in Figure 5-6. This allows us to easily create instances of the Item Scriptable Object.

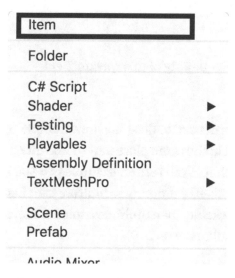

Figure 5-6. Instantiate instances of Item from the Create Submenu

These Scriptable Object instances are actually stored in the project as separate asset files and their properties can be modified on the object itself via the Inspector.

// 2

Inherit from `ScriptableObject`, not `Monobehaviour`.

// 3

The field: `objectName`, can serve a few different purposes. It will certainly come in handy for debugging, and perhaps your game will display the name of an Item in a storefront, or another game character will mention it.

// 4

Store a reference to the Item's Sprite, so we can display it in the game.

// 5

Keep track of the quantity of this specific Item.

// 6

Stackable is a term used to describe how multiple copies of identical items can be stored in the same place and can be interacted with by the player at the same time. Coins are an example of a Stackable item. We set the Boolean `Stackable` property to indicate if an item is Stackable. If an item is not Stackable, then multiple copies of that item cannot be interacted with simultaneously.

// 7

Define an enum used to indicate the type of an item. Although `objectName` may be displayed to the player at points within the game, properties of `ItemType` will never be shown to the player and will only be used by game logic to internally identify the object. Continuing with our Coin item example, your game may have different types of coins, but they will all be classified as the `ItemType`: Coin.

// 8

Create a property called `itemType` using the `ItemType` enum.

Build the Consumable Script

Scriptable Objects don't inherit from MonoBehaviour so they can't be attached to GameObjects. We're going to write a small script that inherits from MonoBehaviour with a property holding a reference to Item. Because this script will inherit from MonoBehaviour, it can be attached to a GameObject. In the MonoBehaviours folder, right-click and create a new C# script called, "Consumable".

```
using UnityEngine;

// 1
public class Consumable : MonoBehaviour {

//2
    public Item item;
}
```

// 1

Inherit from MonoBehaviour so we can attach this script to a GameObject.

// 2

When the Consumable script is added to a GameObject, we'll assign an Item to the item property. This will store a reference to the Scriptable Object asset in the Consumable script. Because we've declared it public, it's still accessible from other scripts.

As mentioned earlier, if we change any data in this Scriptable Object reference, we would change the data in the Scriptable Object asset itself, and those changes would remain when we stopped running our game. If we wanted to change any values on the Scriptable Object during runtime without changing the original data, then we should make a copy of it first.

Save the Consumable script and switch back to the Unity Editor.

Assembling Our Item

Select the CoinObject prefab and drag the Consumable script onto it. We need to set the Consumable Item property seen in Figure 5-7 to an Item Scriptable Object. We're going to create an Item Scriptable Object to attach.

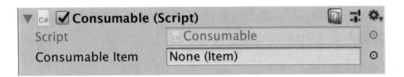

Figure 5-7. *Consumable Item is of type Item, which is a Scriptable Object*

In the Scriptable Objects folder, right-click and Select Create ➤ Item, at the very top of the Asset menu to create an Item Scriptable Object. If you'd prefer to use the menu bar at the top of the Unity Editor, you can select Assets ➤ Create ➤ Item.

Rename the Scriptable Object, "Item". Ensure the Item Scriptable Object is selected, and then examine the Unity Inspector. Change the settings for the Item to Figure 5-8. Name the object, "coin", check off Stackable and select COIN from the Item Type drop down.

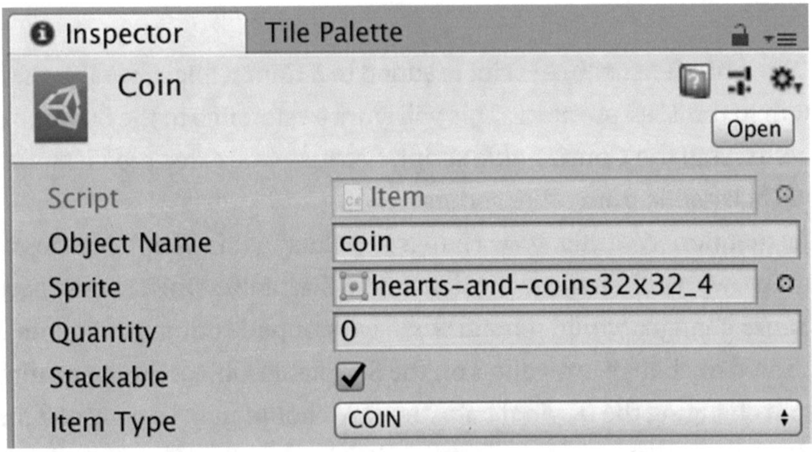

Figure 5-8. *Set the properties of the Coin Item*

Set the sprite property to the sprite named: "hearts-and-coins32x32_4",
as seen in Figures 5-8 and 5-9. This sprite is a clear representation of the
Item and will be used when we want to show the Item in a static context,
such as in an inventory toolbar. This is different from how we've been
displaying animated sprites when they appear in a Scene.

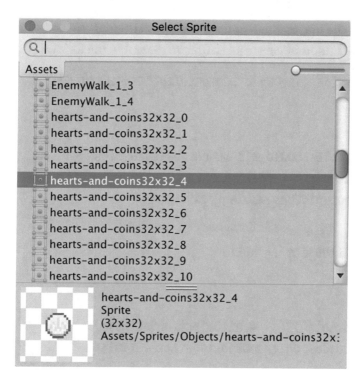

Figure 5-9. *Select a sprite to represent the Coin Item*

Go back to the Consumable script in the Coin prefab, and set
Consumable Item to our Coin Item, as seen in Figure 5-10.

▼ c# ✔ Consumable (Script)		⬚ ⛬ ✿,
Script	c# Consumable	⊙
Consumable Item	▣ Coin (Item)	⊙

Figure 5-10. *Set Consumable Item to our new Coin Item*

Player Collisions

Our Player class already has logic for detecting a collision with a Coin prefab, but now we want to grab a reference to the Scriptable object, so we can hide it when the player runs into it. This will serve as the effect of adding the Coin to the player's inventory.

Inside the Player class, in the OnTriggerEnter2D method, change the existing if-statement we wrote earlier, to resemble the following:

```
if (collision.gameObject.CompareTag("CanBePickedUp"))
{

// 1
// Note: This should all be on a single line
  Item hitObject = collision.gameObject.
  GetComponent<Consumable>().item;

// 2
    if (hitObject != null)
    {

// 3
        print("it: " + hitObject.objectName);
        collision.gameObject.SetActive(false);
    }
}
```

There's a lot going on here, so we'll cover it piece by piece. Overall, our goal is to retrieve a reference to the Item (a Scriptable Object) inside the Consumable class and assign it to hitObject.

// 1

First we grab a reference to the gameObject attached to the collision. Remember that every collision will have a GameObject that it collided with attached to the `collision`. At this point in our game, the `gameObject` will be a coin, but later on it might be any type of GameObject with the tag, "`CanBePickedUp`".

We call `GetComponent()` on the `gameObject` and pass in the Script name, "Consumable" to retrieve the attached `Consumable` script component. We attached the `Consumable` script earlier. Finally we retrieve the property called `item` from the `Consumable` component and assign it to `hitObject`.

// 2

Check to see if the `hitObject` is null. If the `hitObject` is not `null`, then we've managed to successfully retrieve the `hitObject`. If the `hitObject` is `null`, do nothing. Safety checks like this help to avoid bugs down the road.

// 3

To ensure that we've retrieved the `item`, print out the `objectName` property, which we set earlier in the Inspector.

Save the script and switch back to the Unity Editor. Press the play button and walk the player into a coin. You should see the text in Figure 5-11 print out in the console.

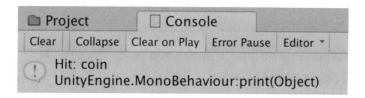

Figure 5-11. *The collision with the coin has been properly detected*

Creating a Heart Power-Up

Now that we know how to create Scriptable Objects, let's create another object that the player can pick up: a heart power-up. Use the sprites that we sliced earlier from the "hearts-and-coins32x32.png" sprite-sheet.

Let's review the steps to create a prefab.

1. Create a GameObject and rename it to "HeartObject".

2. Add sprites for the prefab animation. Use the sprites titled: "hearts-and-coins32x32" ending in 0, 1, 2, and 3. Name the newly created animation, "heart-spin" and save it to the Animations ➤ Animations folder.

3. Create a prefab out of the HeartObject by dragging it into the prefabs folder, then deleting the original object out of the Hierarchy.

4. Select the Heart prefab in the folder and set the prefab's Sprite property. This property is used when previewing in the Scene.

5. On the Sprite Renderer component, set the Sorting Layer to Objects so the prefab is visible.

6. Add a Collider 2D component. We can use a Circle Collider, Box, or Polygon 2D, but for the heart shaped sprite, a Polygon 2D will work best. Edit the collider shape if needed.

7. Depending on type of prefab you're creating, set: Is Trigger on the Collider.

8. Set the Tag on the GameObject. We'll use: CanBePickedUp, for this prefab.

9. Change Layer to, "Consumables."

10. Drag GameObject to prefabs folder to use as prefab.

11. Delete the original GameObject from the Hierarchy view.

Tip If you select multiple sprites for an animation at the same time, you can preview them in the Inspector. We've selected all four heart sprites at the same time in Figure 5-12.

Figure 5-12. *Preview multiple sprites at a time in the Inspector*

Click and drag a heart prefab somewhere onto the scene (Figure 5-13).

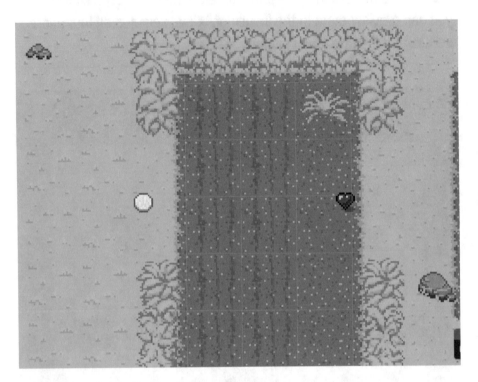

Figure 5-13. *A heart prefab, waiting to be picked up*

We're going to set up the Heart prefab so that it contains a reference to a Scriptable Object the same way the Coin prefab does. Add the Consumable script to the Heart prefab by selecting the prefab, then pressing the "Add Component" button and typing, "Consumable".

Now we need to create a new instance of the Item Scriptable Object. This new instance will be its own asset, to be stored in the Project view, along with all the other assets in our project.

Open the Scriptable Objects folder in the Project view. Right-click, then select Create ➤ Item, and then rename the created Item, "Heart". Select the Heart Item and change the settings to what we have in Figure 5-14.

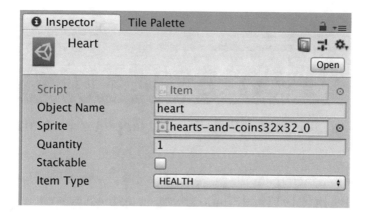

Figure 5-14. *Settings for the Heart Scriptable Object*

We've named the new Heart Item, "heart", given it a sprite that we'll use when displaying in the inventory later on, and set its quantity to 1. This value will be used to increment the player's hit-points when the player picks up the heart. We're also setting the Item Type to HEALTH. Don't click Stackable, because hearts won't be stored in the player's inventory and will instead be immediately consumed.

Because we have the Consumable Script on the Heart prefab, we can press the circle next to the Consumable Item property and add our new Heart Item, as seen in Figure 5-15.

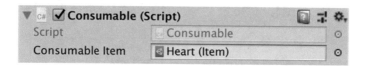

Figure 5-15. *Assign the Heart Item to the Consumable Item property*

That's it! If you press play and walk the player into the heart prefab on screen, you should see the text in Figure 5-16 print out in the console.

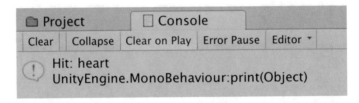

Figure 5-16. *Logging confirmation that the player ran into the heart prefab*

We want to increment the player's `hitPoints` every time she picks up a heart. Switch back to Visual Studio and open up the Player class.

Change the `OnTriggerEnter2D()` method to the following. Some of this code has been discussed earlier in this chapter, so we won't cover it again.

```
void OnTriggerEnter2D(Collider2D collision)
    {
        if (collision.gameObject.CompareTag("CanBePickedUp"))
        {

    Item hitObject = collision.gameObject.
    GetComponent<Consumable>().item;

            if (hitObject != null)
            {
                print("Hit: " + hitObject.objectName);

// 1

                switch (hitObject.itemType)
                {

// 2

                    case Item.ItemType.COIN:
                        break;

// 3

                    case Item.ItemType.HEALTH:
```

```
                    AdjustHitPoints(hitObject.quantity);
                    break;
                default:
                    break;
            }

            collision.gameObject.SetActive(false);
        }
    }
}
// 4
    public void AdjustHitPoints(int amount)
    {
// 5
        hitPoints = hitPoints + amount;
        print("Adjusted hitpoints by: " + amount + ". New
        value: " + hitPoints);
    }
```

Let's go through this code.

// 1

Use a switch statement to pattern match the hitObject property: itemType, with the ItemType enum defined in the Item class. This allows us script specific behaviors when colliding with each ItemType.

// 2

In the case where the hitObject is of type COIN, don't do anything just yet. We're going to learn how to pick up coins when we build an Inventory.

// 3

In the case where the player runs into an item of type HEALTH, call the method AdjustHitPoints(int amount) that we're about to write. This method takes a parameter of type int, which we'll get from the hitObject property quantity.

// 4

This method will adjust the player's hit-points by the amount in the parameter. There are two main advantages in putting the hit-point adjustment logic into a separate function, rather than placing the logic inside the switch statement.

The first advantage is clarity. Clear code is easier to read and understand, and thus tends to be less buggy. We want to keep the intention and organization of our code as clear as possible at all times.

The second advantage is that by putting the logic into a function, we can easily invoke it from other places. In theory there may be situations when a player's hit-points are adjusted by things other than running into a HEALTH Item.

// 5

Add the amount parameter to the existing hit-point count, and then assign the result to hitPoints. This method also can be used to decrement hitPoints by passing in a negative number for the amount parameter. We'll use this when the Player takes damage.

Save the Player script and switch back to the Unity Editor.

Press Play and make the Player run into the Heart prefab. You should see the message in Figure 5-17 output in the console.

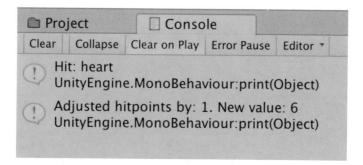

Figure 5-17. *Adjust the Player's hitPoints*

Summary

In this chapter, we've started to assemble the various Unity elements into working game mechanics. We've built the foundational C# scripts that will be used for all character types in our game, as well as created several types of prefabs that the player can interact with. Collision detection is a fundamental aspect of game development, and we've learned about the tools the Unity Engine provides to detect and customize collision detection. We've also learned about Scriptable Objects, which are reusable data containers that make our game architecture cleaner.

CHAPTER 6

Health and Inventory

This chapter is a big one. We'll tie everything we've learned so far together to build a health bar to track the players' hit-points. Besides leveraging Game Objects, Scriptable Objects, and Prefabs, we'll learn about some new Unity component types, such as the Canvas and UI Elements.

No RPG would be complete without an inventory system, so we'll build one, along with an on-screen inventory bar that will display all the objects the player is holding. This will be an intense chapter, with lots of scripting and prefabs, but by the end of it you'll feel much more confident in building out your own game components.

Creating a Health Bar

As we discussed in the Character Class section of Chapter 5, many video games have the concept of character hit-points and a health bar to track health. We're going build a health bar to track the health levels of our intrepid player.

Canvas Objects

Our health bar will use something called a Canvas as the main Game Object. What is a Canvas? A Canvas is specific type of Unity Object responsible for rendering user-interface, or "UI" Elements in a Unity Scene. Every UI Element in a Unity scene needs to be the child object of a

© Jared Halpern 2019
J. Halpern, *Developing 2D Games with Unity*, https://doi.org/10.1007/978-1-4842-3772-4_6

Canvas object. A scene may have multiple Canvas objects, and if a Canvas does not exist when a new UI Element is created, then one will be created and the new UI Element will be added as a child of that Canvas.

UI Elements

UI Elements are game objects that encapsulate specific, commonly needed user-interface functionality such as buttons, sliders, labels, a scroll bar, or input field. Unity allows developers to build out custom user-interfaces quickly by offering premade UI Elements instead of requiring that the developer create them from scratch.

One thing to note about UI Elements is that they use a Rect Transform instead of a regular Transform component. Rect Transforms are identical to regular Transforms except that in addition to position, rotation, and scale, they also have width and height. Width and Height are used to specify the dimensions of the rectangle.

Building the Health Bar

Right-click anywhere in the Hierarchy view and select UI ➤ Canvas. This creates two objects automatically: a Canvas and an EventSystem. Rename the Canvas object, "HealthBarObject".

The EventSystem is a way for the user to interact directly with Objects using the Mouse or other input devices. We don't need it at the moment, so you can delete it.

Select the HealthBarObject and look for the Canvas component. Be sure that Render Mode is set to Screen Space Overlay and check the box that says Pixel Perfect.

Setting Render Mode to Screen Space Overlay ensures that Unity renders UI Elements on top of the scene. If the screen is resized, the Canvas containing the UI Elements will automatically resize itself. The Canvas component sets its own Rect Transform settings and cannot be changed. If you need a UI Element to be smaller, you resize the element itself, not the Canvas.

Now that we've created a Canvas object, let's make sure that all the UI Elements, such as the health bar we're building, always have the same relative size on the screen.

Select the HealthBarObject and look for the Canvas Scaler component. Set the UI Scale Mode to: Scale With Screen Size, as seen in Figure 6-1 and set the Reference Pixels Per Unit to 32.

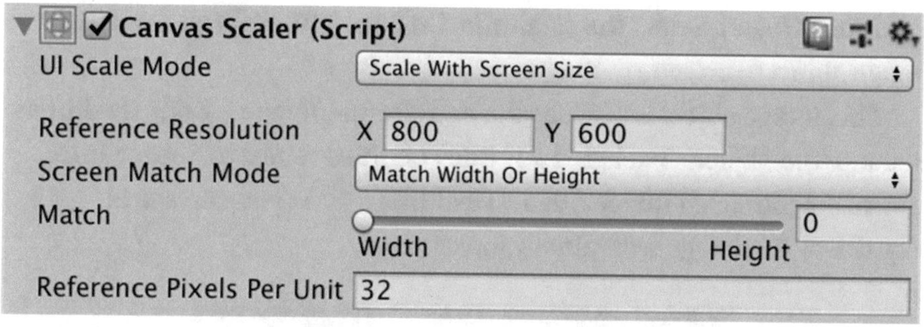

Figure 6-1. *Setting UI Scale Mode*

This ensures that the Canvas size scales appropriately with the screen size.

It's time to import the sprites that we'll use for the Health Bar. Create a new subfolder in the Sprites folder called, "Health Bar". We'll put all of our Health Bar related sprites in this folder. Now drag the spritesheet called, "HealthBar.png" into the folder we just created.

Select the HealthBar spritesheet and use the following import settings in the Inspector:

Texture Type: Sprite (2D and UI)

Sprite Mode: Multiple

Pixels Per Unit: 32

Filter Mode: Point (no filter)

Ensure the Default button is selected at the bottom
and set Compression to: None

Press the Apply button, and then open the Sprite Editor.

From the Slice menu, be sure that "Type" is set to: Automatic. We're
going to let the Unity Editor detect the boundaries of these sprites.

Press Apply to slice the sprites, and then close the Sprite Editor.

Next we're going to add an Image object, which is a UI Element, to the
HealthBarObject. Select the HealthBarObject, right-click, and go to UI ➤
Image object to create an Image.

This Image object will act as the background Image for our HealthBar.
Rename the object, "Background". Click on the dot next to Source Image
and select the sliced image titled, "HealthBar_4". As you can see in
Figure 6-2, the image will initially look square.

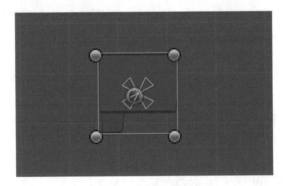

Figure 6-2. *The Background image before adjusting the size*

With the Background object selected, change the Rect Transform
Width to: 250 and Height to: 50.

Press "W" to use the Toolbar shortcut for the Move tool. Using the
handles, move the Background object to the top-right corner of the Canvas
as seen in Figure 6-3.

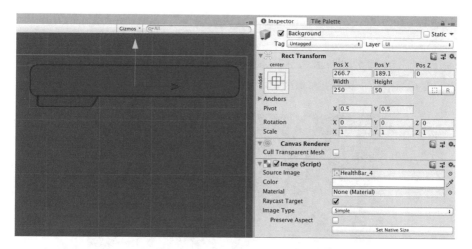

Figure 6-3. *After resizing and moving the health bar*

Anchors

You may have noticed the star-like symbol in the center of Figure 6-2 and in Figure 6-4. This symbol is made up of four small triangular handles representative of a property specific to UI Elements called the Anchor Points.

Figure 6-4. *The Anchor Points for the selected UI Element*

As designated by the blue lines in Figure 6-5, each diamond in the Anchor Points corresponds to a corner of the Rect Transform of the UI Element. The top-left Anchor Point diamond corresponds to the top-left corner of the UI Element, and so forth.

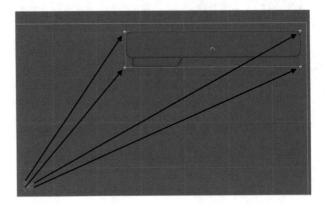

Figure 6-5. *The four Anchor Points correspond to the four corners of the UI Element*

Each corner of a UI Element will always be rendered with the same distance relative to its respective Anchor Point. This ensures that UI Elements are always in the same location, scene to scene. The ability to set a consistent distance between Anchor Points and UI Elements becomes especially helpful when the size of the Canvas scales along with the size of the screen.

By adjusting the location of the Anchor Points, we can be sure that the health bar always appears in the top-right corner of the screen. We'll position the Anchor Points to show a small margin between the screen edges and the health bar, irrespective of how big the screen is.

Adjusting the Anchor Points

Select the Background object. In the Rect Transform component, press on the Anchor Presets icon highlighted in Figure 6-6.

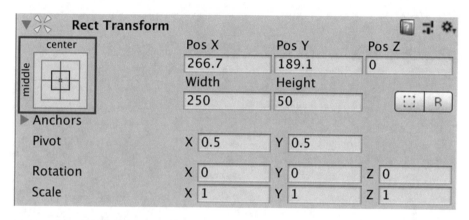

Figure 6-6. *The Anchor Presets button*

Pressing on the icon should give you a menu of Anchor Presets, as seen in Figure 6-7. By default, the middle-center is selected. This explains why the Background object's Anchors appear in the middle of the Canvas.

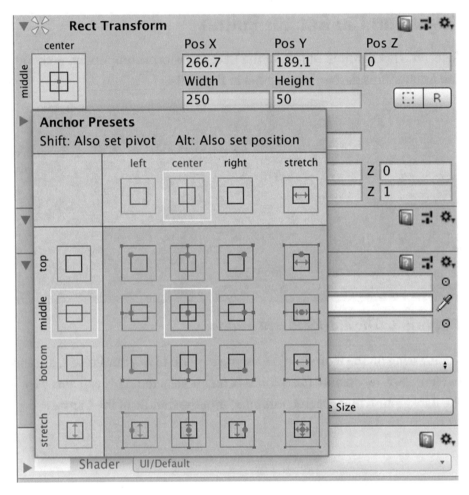

Figure 6-7. *The default Anchor Presets are: middle-center*

We want to anchor the Health Bar relative to the top-right corner of the screen at all times. Select the Anchor Preset setting in the column titled, "right" and the row titled, "top". You'll see a white box surrounding the selected Anchor Preset, as seen in Figure 6-8.

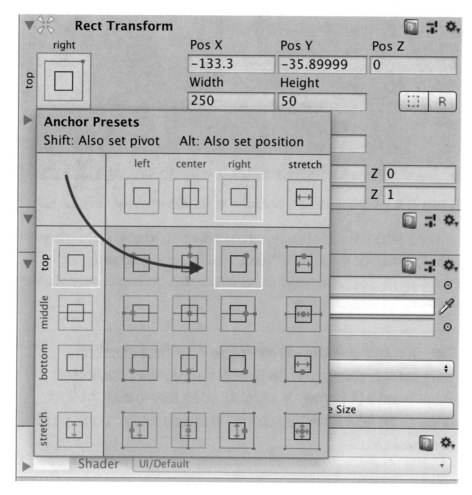

Figure 6-8. *Select top-right Anchor Presets*

Press the Anchor Preset icon to close it and notice how the Anchor
Points have now moved to the top-right corner of the Canvas (Figure 6-9).

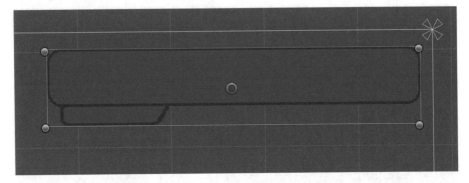

Figure 6-9. *Anchor Presets are now in the top-right of the Canvas*

We've left a little bit of space between the health bar and the corner of the Canvas, and the Anchor Points are all collected in the top-right. Regardless of how much we scale the screen size, the health bar will always be situated in that exact spot.

Tip   The Anchor Points will not appear if the Rect Transform component is collapsed in the Inspector. If you don't see Anchor Points when a UI Element is selected, make sure to click the little arrow to the left of "Rect Transform" to expand the component if it's collapsed.

UI Image Masks

Right-click on the Background object and create another Image object. Because we're creating this Image object while selecting the Background object, it will be created as a "child" object. It's the same *type* of object as the Background Image object, but we'll be using it a bit differently. The child Image object will act as a mask. This mask works a bit differently than a mask you might wear on Halloween. In fact, it works exactly the opposite of a Halloween mask. Instead of hiding what's underneath it, this mask will only show portions of any underlying child images that fit the shape of the mask. The underlying image in this case will be the health meter and will be added as a child object.

Select the Image object and rename it, "BarMask". Set the Source Image to: HealthBar_3. It should look like Figure 6-10.

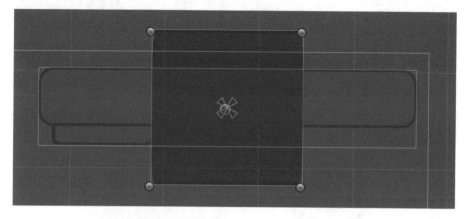

Figure 6-10. *After setting the Source Image for the HealthBar Mask*

As you can see in Figure 6-10, child objects that are UI Elements also have Anchor Points, but these Anchor Points are relative to their parent object. The Anchor Points of the BarMask are centered by default with respect to the Background object.

With the BarMask object selected, resize the Rect Transform to Width: 240 and Height: 30. We want to make the BarMask a bit smaller than the health bar dimensions to show a margin around the actual health meter.

Press "W" to use the Toolbar shortcut for the Move tool. Move the BarMask into position as seen in Figure 6-11. If you prefer to enter the location manually on the Rect Transform, you can set Pos X: 0, Pos Y: 6.

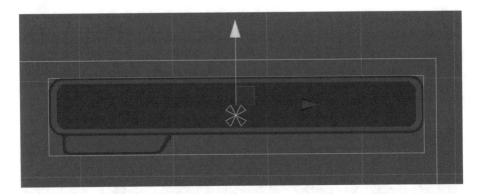

Figure 6-11. *Move the BarMask into position*

With the BarMask object still selected, click the Add Component button in the Inspector and add a "Mask" component, as seen in Figure 6-12.

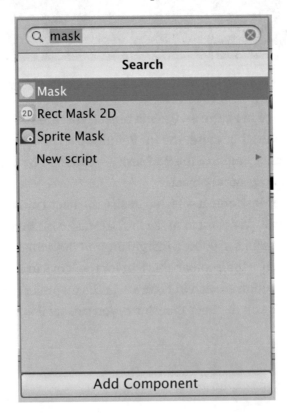

Figure 6-12. *Add a Mask component to the BarMask object*

186

This is the component that will do the actual masking. Any child object of a parent containing a Mask will be masked automatically.

Right-click on BarMask and add a child UI Element of type: Image. This is the same process we followed earlier when we created the BarMask. Call this child Image Object: "Meter". Set its Source Image to: HealthBar_0 as seen in Figure 6-13 and change the Width to: 240 and Height to: 30.

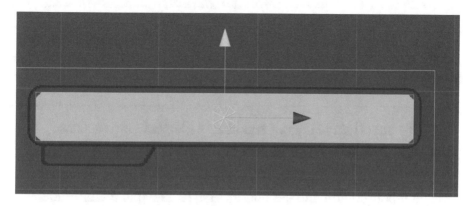

Figure 6-13. *Set the dimensions for the Meter Image object*

Because Meter is the same size as BarMask and was created as a child object, you won't have to reposition it.

The spritesheet images included with the assets for this book include several alternate meter images. We're using the solid green meter in this example, but feel free to choose your favorite.

Select the Meter object and on the Image component, change the Image Type to: Filled. Then change the Fill Method to: Horizontal, and the Fill Origin to: Left. These settings will ensure that the health bar *fills* from the left to the right, horizontally.

With the Meter object selected, slide the Fill Amount slider to the left slowly. As seen in Figure 6-14, you should see the meter slowly shrink in size, indicating that the player is losing hit-points.

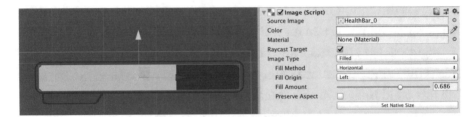

Figure 6-14. *Move the Fill Amount to the left to simulate that the Player is losing hit-points*

We will write code to update the Meter's Fill Amount programmatically to indicate the remaining number of hit-points.

Tip   It's important to understand how UI Elements are rendered. The order in which objects appear in the Hierarchy view is the order in which they'll be rendered. The top-most objects in the Hierarchy will be rendered first and the bottom last, resulting in the top-most objects appearing in the background.

Importing Custom Fonts

It's very likely that you'll want to use custom fonts in your project. Luckily, it's very simple to import and use custom fonts in Unity. This project includes a freely available custom font with a retro style called Silkscreen. Silkscreen is a typeface created by Jason Kottke.

Right-click on the Assets folder in the Project view and create a new folder called, "Fonts".

Open the directory on your local computer where you saved the Assets files for this chapter and look in the Fonts folder. Locate the .zip file titled, "silkscreen.zip" and double-click it to unzip it. Unzipping it will have created another folder called, "silkscreen" and inside that folder, you'll see a file called, "slkscr.ttf".

Drag and drop that font file, "slkscr.ttf", into the Fonts folder in your Unity project to import it. Unity will detect the file type and make the font available in any relevant Unity components.

Adding Hit-Points Text

Right-click on the Background object and select from the menu: UI ➤ Text, to add a Text UI Element as a child of the Background. Rename the object to, "HPText". This Text object will show the number of remaining hit-points.

On the Rect Transform component of HPText, set the Width to: 70, and Height to: 16. On the Text component of HPText, change the Font Size to 16, and the Color to white. Change the Font to "slkscr", which is the custom silkscreen font we just imported. Set the Paragraph Horizontal and Vertical Alignment to left and center, respectively, as seen in Figure 6-15.

▼ T ☑ Text (Script)

Text

HP:100

Character

Font	A slkscr	⊙
Font Style	Normal	↕
Font Size	16	
Line Spacing	1	
Rich Text	☑	

Paragraph

Alignment

Figure 6-15. *Configuring the Text component*

The health bar image has a little tray on the bottom that provides a backdrop and improves the visibility of the text. Move the HPText object onto the tray so that it resembles Figure 6-16.

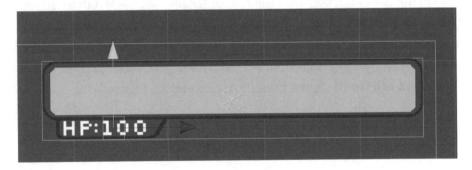

Figure 6-16. *Move the HPText object into the tray*

Change the HPText Anchor Points to be bottom-left, as seen in Figure 6-17.

190

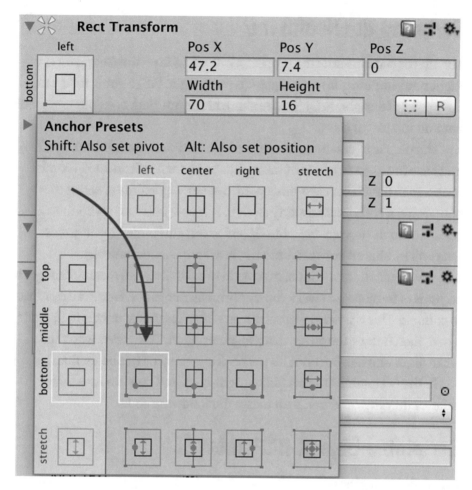

Figure 6-17. *Set the HPText Anchor Points to bottom-left*

We want to make sure the HPText remains the same distance from the left and bottom of its parent object.

Drag the HealthBarObject into the prefabs folder to create a prefab and rename the prefab: HealthBarObject. Do not delete the HealthBarObject from the Hierarchy view—we'll be working with it later.

Eventually we're going to create a reference to the HealthBarObject prefab inside the Player object, so that the Player script can easily find it. But first we have to build the Health Bar Script.

Scripting the Health Bar

The Player class inherits the property: hitPoints, from the Character class. Right now, hitPoints is just a regular type: integer. We're going to leverage the power of Scriptable Objects to share hit-points data between the health bar and the player class.

The plan is to create an instance of this HitPoints Scriptable Object and save the asset to the ScriptableObjects folder. We'll add a HitPoints property to the Player class and create a separate HealthBar script containing a HitPoints property as well. Because both scripts contain a reference to the same Scriptable Object asset: HitPoints, the hit-points data will be shared between both of these scripts automatically.

As we build this functionality, keep in mind that we are making changes to sections of the code that will temporarily break things and cause the game not to compile. This is normal—think of it as taking apart a car engine to upgrade a part, then putting the engine back together again. The engine won't run while disassembled, but once it's put back together, it'll run better than before.

In the Scriptable Objects folder, right-click and create a new script called, HitPoints, and update it to use the following code.

Scriptable Object: HitPoints

```
using UnityEngine;

// 1
[CreateAssetMenu(menuName = "HitPoints")]
public class HitPoints : ScriptableObject
{

// 2
    public float value;
}

// 1
```

We used the same technique in Chapter 5. `CreateAssetMenu` creates an entry in the Create submenu, which allows us to easily create instances of the HitPoints Scriptable Object. These instances are saved as assets in the Unity Project.

`// 2`

Use a float to hold the hit-points. We'll need to assign a float to the Image object property: Fill Amount, in the Meter object of our health bar, so it makes our lives a bit easier to start with a float.

Update the Character Script

We need to make a small change to the Character script to utilize the HitPoints script that we just created. In the Character script, change the line:

```
public int hitPoints;
```

To:

```
public HitPoints hitPoints;
```

We've changed the type from: `int`, to our newly created Scriptable Object: `HitPoints`.

And change the type of `maxHitPoints` from `int` to `float`:

```
public float maxHitPoints;
```

Because we're using a `float` inside the HitPoints object to store the current value, we've changed `maxHitPoints` in the Character script to `float` as well.

Add the following additional property:

```
public float startingHitPoints;
```

We'll use this property to set the number of hit-points a character starts with.

Update the Player Script

Add the following two properties anywhere above the Start() method.

```
// 1
public HealthBar healthBarPrefab;
```

```
// 2
HealthBar healthBar;
```

// 1

Used to store a reference to the HealthBar prefab. We'll use this reference as a parameter to Instantiate() we instantiate a copy of the HealthBar prefab.

// 2

Used to store a reference to the instantiated HealthBar.

Inside the existing Start() method, add the following lines:

```
// 1
hitPoints.value = startingHitPoints;
```

```
// 2
healthBar = Instantiate(healthBarPrefab);
```

// 1

The Start() method will only be called once—when the script is enabled. We want to start the player off with startingHitPoints, so we assign it to the current hitPoints.value.

// 2

Instantiate a copy of the Health Bar prefab and store a reference to it in memory.

There's one important thing that we didn't do when we scripted the logic to pick up hearts and increment a player's hit-points. The player's current hit-points should never exceed their maximum allowable hit-points. We'll add that logic now.

Change the OnTriggerEnter2D() method to:

```
void OnTriggerEnter2D(Collider2D collision)
{
    if (collision.gameObject.CompareTag("CanBePickedUp"))
    {
        Item hitObject = collision.gameObject.
        GetComponent<Consumable>().item;

        if (hitObject != null)
        {
// 1
            bool shouldDisappear = false;

            switch (hitObject.itemType)
            {
                case Item.ItemType.COIN:
// 2
                    shouldDisappear = true;
                    break;
                case Item.ItemType.HEALTH:
// 3
                    shouldDisappear =
                    AdjustHitPoints(hitObject.quantity);
                    break;
                default:
                    break;
            }
// 4
```

```
            if (shouldDisappear)
            {
                collision.gameObject.SetActive(false);
            }
        }
    }
}

// 5
public bool AdjustHitPoints(int amount)
{

// 6
    if (hitPoints.value < maxHitPoints)
    {

// 7
        hitPoints.value = hitPoints.value + amount;

// 8
        print("Adjusted HP by: " + amount + ". New value: " +
        hitPoints.value);

// 9
        return true;
    }

// 10
    return false;
}

// 1
```

This value will be set to indicate that the object in the collision should
disappear.

```
// 2
```

Any coins the player collides with should disappear by default, to give the illusion that they've been picked up and added to a player's inventory. We'll be creating a player inventory in the next section so this line will suffice for now.

// 3

We're about to add additional logic to "cap" the hit-point quantity at: maximumHitPoints—a property that the Player class inherits from Character class. The AdjustHitPoints() method, referred to in the following, will return true if the hit-points were adjusted, and false if they were not.

Although a player's health bar is full, AdjustHitPoints() will return false and any hearts that they've run into won't be "picked up" and will remain active in the Scene.

// 4

If AdjustHitPoints() returned true, then the prefab object should disappear. The way that we've designed this logic, any new items that we add to the switch statement in the future can also set the shouldDisappear value to make the object disappear.

// 5

The AdjustHitPoints() method will return type: bool, indicating if hitPoints was successfully adjusted.

// 6

Check if the current hit-points are less than the maximum allowed hit-points.

// 7

Adjust the player's current hitPoints by amount. This approach will also allow for negative adjustments.

```
// 8
```

Print out a method to help in debugging. This is optional.

```
// 9
```

Return `true` to indicate that the hit-points were adjusted.

```
// 10
```

Return `false` to indicate that the player's hit-points were not adjusted.

Create the HealthBar Script

Right-click in the MonoBehaviours folder HealthBar:script, creation and create a new C# called HealthBar. Use the following code to create the health bar script.

```
using UnityEngine;

// 1
using UnityEngine.UI;

public class HealthBar : MonoBehaviour
{
// 2
    public HitPoints hitPoints;

// 3
    [HideInInspector]
    public Player character;

// 4
    public Image meterImage;
```

```
// 5
    public Text hpText;
// 6
    float maxHitPoints;

    void Start()
    {
// 7
        maxHitPoints = character.maxHitPoints;
    }

    void Update()
    {
// 8
        if (character != null)
        {
// 9
            meterImage.fillAmount = hitPoints.value /
            maxHitPoints;
// 10
            hpText.text = "HP:" + (meterImage.fillAmount * 100);
        }
    }
}
// 1
```

Importing the UnityEngine.UI namespace is required to work with UI Elements.

```
// 2
```

A reference to the same HitPoints asset (a Scriptable Object) that the player prefab refers to. This data container allows us to share data between the two objects automatically.

// 3

We'll need a reference to the current Player object to retrieve the maxHitPoints. This reference will be set programmatically instead of via the Unity Editor, so it makes sense to hide it in the Inspector to eliminate confusion.

We use [HideInInspector] to hide this public property in the Inspector. The brackets syntax for [HideInInspector] indicates that it's an **Attribute**. Attributes allow additional behaviors to methods and variables.

// 4

We created this property for convenience and simplicity, so that we don't have to search through various child objects to find the Meter Image object. We'll set this in the Unity Editor by dragging and dropping the Meter object into this property, once the HealthBar script is attached.

// 5

This is another property created for convenience and simplicity. We'll set this in the Unity Editor by dragging and dropping the HPText object into this field.

// 6

Because the maximum number of hit-points won't be changing in our current game design, we'll cache it in a local variable.

// 7

Retrieve and store the maximum hit-points for the Character.

// 8

Check to make sure the reference to character is not null before we try to do anything with it.

// 9

The Fill Amount property of the Image requires that the value be between 0 and 1. We convert the current hit-points into a percentage by dividing the current hit-points by the maximum hit-points, and then assign the result to the Meter's Fill Amount property.

// 10

Modify the HPText Text property to show the hit-points remaining as a whole number. Multiply the fillAmount by 100 (e.g., .40 = HP: 40, or .80 = HP: 80).

Tip   As you're building out the architecture for your game, think about whether a public variable needs to be visible in the Unity Editor, or if it will be set programmatically. If it will be set programmatically, use the [HideInInspector] attribute to save yourself some confusion down the road when you inspect a prefab and can't recall if a property needs to be set.

There's one last bit we need to add. Go back to the Player script and inside the existing Start() method, add the following line:

```
healthBar.character = this;
```

This line sets the `Player character` property inside `healthBar` to the instantiated Player. We've saved this for last so that you can see the connection between the code we just added to HealthBar and the Player script. The HealthBar script uses this player object to retrieve the `maxHitPoints` property.

Configure the Health Bar Component

Switch back to the Unity Editor and select the HealthBarObject from the Prefabs folder in the Project view. Add the Health Bar script to the HealthBar object.

The properties we've just created should be blank, as shown in Figure 6-18.

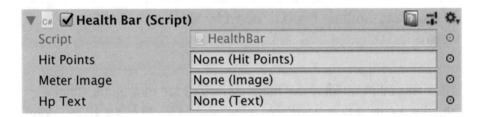

Figure 6-18. *Health Bar script before setting the properties*

In the Scriptable Objects folder, right-click and use the menu option we created: Create ➤ HitPoints to create a new instance of the HitPoints object. Rename it: "HitPoints", as shown in Figure 6-19. This HitPoints object is an actual asset, saved in the project folder.

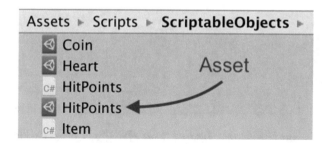

Figure 6-19. Creating a HitPoints asset from a Scriptable Object

With the HealthBarObject selected, drag the HitPoints object onto the Hit Points property, as shown in Figure 6-20.

▼ c# ☑ Health Bar (Script)		🔲 📑 ⚙,
Script	HealthBar	⊙
Hit Points	⬦ HitPoints (HitPoints)	⊙
Meter Image	None (Image)	⊙
Hp Text	None (Text)	⊙

Figure 6-20. Drag the HitPoints object to the property

As you can see, the HitPoints property is now **bold**. As we discussed earlier, this is the Unity Editor's way of reminding us that we've only changed this specific instance of a prefab. If we want to apply the change to all instances of the prefab, we must press the Apply button on the upper right of the Inspector. Keep in mind that there may be circumstances in the future, in which you wouldn't want to apply a change to every existing prefab.

We're about to set the properties we created in the Health Bar script, which was added to HealthBarObject. The properties such as HitPoints hitPoints and Text hpText in the script will actually be set to reference some of the child objects of HealthBarObject.

Select the HealthBarObject and click the little dots next to each of the properties in the Health Bar script. Select the appropriate value for each property, as seen in Figure 6-21. When you're done, press the Apply button in the Inspector.

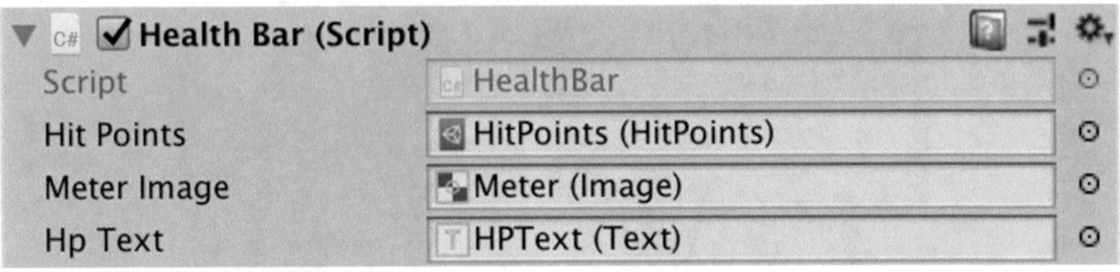

CHAPTER 6   HEALTH AND INVENTORY

Figure 6-21. Set the Meter Image and Hp Text using the respective objects on the health bar

Select the PlayerObject prefab in the Prefabs folder. Drag the HitPoints Scriptable Object that we created into the Hit Points property on the Player script. Remember that we're using this same HitPoints object in the Health Bar object. Hit-points data is being shared between two separate objects like magic.

Set the properties in the Player script as follows: Starting Hit Points to 6, Max Hit Points to 10, and drag the HealthBarObject to set the Health Bar Prefab property as shown in Figure 6-22.

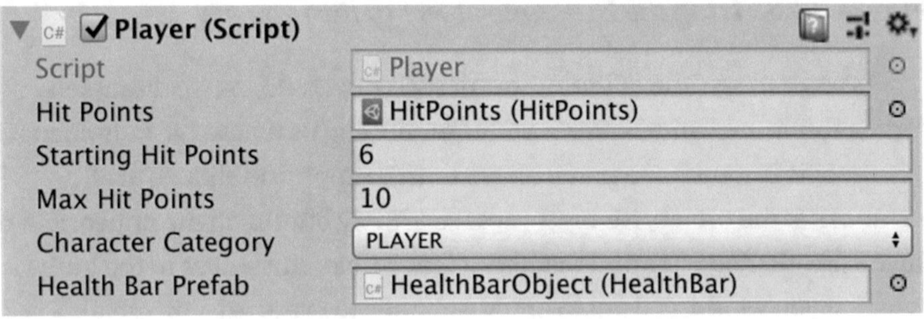

Figure 6-22. Setting the Health Bar Prefab property to the HealthBarObject prefab

Let's summarize what we've just built.

- When the player collides with a heart, AdjustHitPoints() increments the value inside the HitPoints object.

204

- The HealthBar script also has a property called
  hitPoints that references the same HitPoints object
  as the Player. HealthBar inherits from MonoBehaviour,
  which means it calls the Update() method with every
  frame.

- In the Update() method of the HealthBar script, we
  check the current value inside HitPoints and set the
  Fill Amount on the Meter Image. This adjusts the visual
  appearance of the health meter.

It's time to test out the Health Bar. Make sure you've saved all of
the Unity Scripts, and press apply on the HealthBarObject to apply the
changes. Delete the HealthBarObject to delete it from the Hierarchy.

Press Play and walk the player around to pick up hearts. The health bar
should add up 10 points each time the player picks up a heart, as seen in
Figure 6-23.

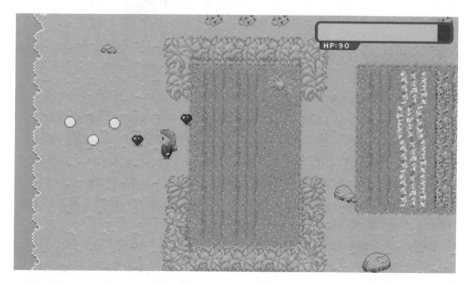

Figure 6-23. *The health bar will add points every time the player
collects a heart*

205

Congratulations! You've built a health bar!

Tip   If you need to work with an object in the Hierarchy or Project view but want to keep a different object visible in the Inspector, click the lock icon as seen in Figure 6-24 to keep the original object visible. Locking an object makes it a bit easier to work when you need to drag and set other objects as properties. To unlock the object, simply press the lock icon again.

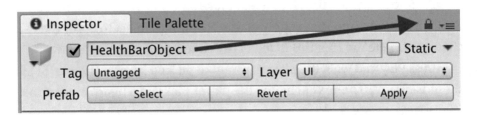

Figure 6-24. *Use the lock button to keep the object open in the Inspector*

Inventory

Many video games have the concept of an inventory—a place to store things that the player picks up. In this section, we're going to create an Inventory Bar containing several Item Slots to hold items. A script will be attached to the Inventory Bar that will manage the players' inventory as well as the appearance of the Inventory Bar itself. We'll turn the Inventory Bar into a prefab and store a reference to it in the Player object, just as we did with the Health Bar.

Right-click anywhere in the Hierarchy view and select UI ➤ Canvas; this will create two objects: a Canvas and an EventSystem. Rename the Canvas object, "InventoryObject" and delete the EventSystem.

With InventoryObject selected, check: Pixel Perfect in the Canvas component, and set the UI Scale Mode property to: Scale with Screen Size, just as we did earlier for the Health Bar.

Right-click InventoryObject again and select Create Empty. This will create an empty UI Element. Rename the empty Element: "InventoryBackground".

Tip   If you can't see the object you're working with, double-click it in the Hierarchy view to center it in the Scene. Double-click the InventoryBackground object to center it.

Be sure InventoryBackground is selected and press the Add Component button. Search for and add the Horizontal Layout Group, as seen in Figure 6-25.

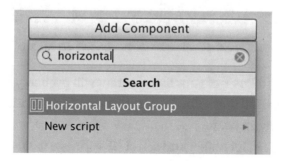

Figure 6-25.   *Add a Horizontal Layout Group*

The Horizontal Layout Group component will automatically arrange for all of its subviews to be placed alongside each other horizontally.

With InventoryObject selected, create an empty GameObject child and rename it: "Slot".

A Slot object will display a single Item, or a quantity of "Stackable" Items. When our game is running, we're going to programmatically instantiate five copies of the Slot prefab.

Each Slot parent object will contain four child objects: a background Image, a tray Image, an item Image, and a Text object.

Select the Slot object and set its Width and Height in the Rect Transform component to 80 and 80 as seen in Figure 6-26.

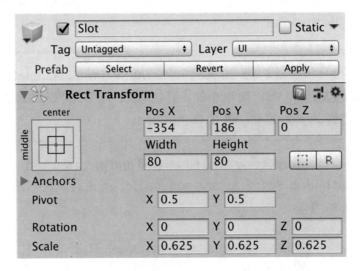

Figure 6-26. *Set the Slot element dimensions to 80 × 80*

The Pos X and Pos Y of your Slot element will probably differ from Figure 6-26 and that's fine because we'll be instantiating these programmatically anyway.

Right-click the Slot object and select UI ➤ Image to create an Image child object. Rename the child object: "Background". Right-click the Slot object and create another Image named: "ItemImage". Background and ItemImage should both be children of Slot.

Now we are going to add a little "tray" in which we'll place the Stackable items quantity text. Select the Background object and create an Image child object. Rename the Image object: "Tray". Right-click on Tray and select UI ➤ Text to create a Text child object, rename this object: "QtyText".

When you're done, the Slot structure should look like Figure 6-27.

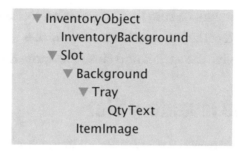

Figure 6-27. *Setting up the Tray and QtyText children*

It's important that all of these objects are in the correct order in the Hierarchy. Ordering them as we see Figure 6-27 will ensure that the background renders first, and the ItemImage, Tray, and QtyText render on top of it. If you've accidentally created an object with the wrong parent object, just click and drag it onto the correct parent.

Import the Inventory Slot Image

Create a new folder under Sprites called, "Inventory". In the local directory where you downloaded the assets for this chapter, select the spritesheet called, "InventorySlot.png" from the Spritesheets folder. Drag it into the Sprites/Inventory folder in the Project view.

Select the InventorySlot spritesheet and use the following import settings in the Inspector:

Texture Type: Sprite (2D and UI)

Sprite Mode: Multiple

Pixels Per Unit: 32

Filter Mode: Point (no filter)

Ensure the Default button is selected at the bottom and set Compression to: None

Press the Apply button, and then open the Sprite Editor.

From the Slice menu, be sure that "Type" is set to: Automatic. We'll let the Unity Editor detect the boundaries of these sprites.

Press Apply to slice the sprites and close the Sprite Editor.

Configure the Inventory Slot

The Inventory Slot consists of a few different items, each with their own configuration. Once configured, we'll turn the Inventory Slot into its own prefab and detach it from the main InventoryObject.

Configure the ItemImage

Select the ItemImage object in the Slot. In the Rect Transform component, change the Width and Height to 80.

Disable the Image by checking the box in the upper-left of the component in the Inspector. We're going to enable it once we place an image in the slot. The Image component of ItemImage should resemble Figure 6-28.

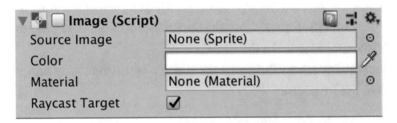

Figure 6-28. *Disable the Image component of ItemImage*

We disable the image because if no source image is provided to an Image component, the Image component will default to the default color. We don't want to show a giant empty white box, so instead we disable the Image component until we have a Source Image to show.

Configure the Background

Select the Background object and ensure the Image component settings are set up as seen in Figure 6-29. Use "InventorySlot_0" as the Source Image and make sure Image Type is set to Simple.

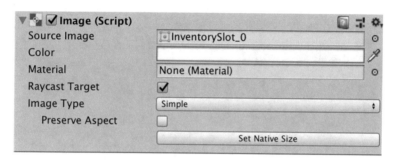

Figure 6-29. *Configure the Slot's Background*

Set the Width and Height of the Background's Rect Transform component to 80 and 80, as seen in Figure 6-30.

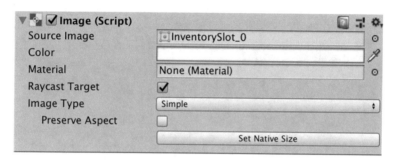

Figure 6-30. *Setting the Width and Height of the Background*

Configure the Tray

Select the Tray object and change its Width and Height to 48 × 32. Set the Image component's Source Image to: "InventorySlot_1" as seen in Figure 6-31.

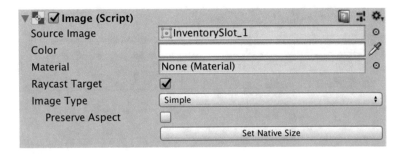

Figure 6-31. *Setting the Tray image*

Because the Tray was added as a child object of Background, it was automatically set to a Pos X and Pos Y of 0 and 0, as seen in Figure 6-32.

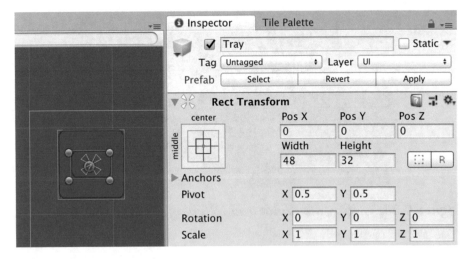

Figure 6-32. *Default placement of the Tray*

Set the Tray's Anchor Points to bottom-right, then change the Pos X and Pos Y to 0 and 0 again. This should result in the Tray's center being moved to the bottom-right corner of its parent object, as seen in Figure 6-33.

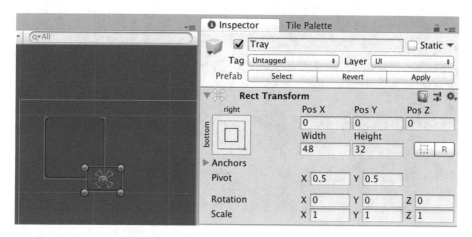

Figure 6-33. *Anchor Points set to bottom-right, and Pos X, Y to: 0, 0*

Configure QtyText—the Quantity Text

Text objects are used to display noninteractable text to the user. They're helpful for displaying text in-game, debugging, and designing custom GUI controls. The Text object in our Inventory will be used to display the quantity of Stackable Items, such as coins, in a Slot.

Select the Text component and change its Width to 25 and Height to 20. In the Text (Script) component, change the text to "00". We're changing the text to 00 to help us see the location of the text. Set the font to "slkscr" (our custom Silkscreen font) and leave the Font Style as Normal. Change the Font Size to 16, the color to White, and the alignment to what we see in Figure 6-34.

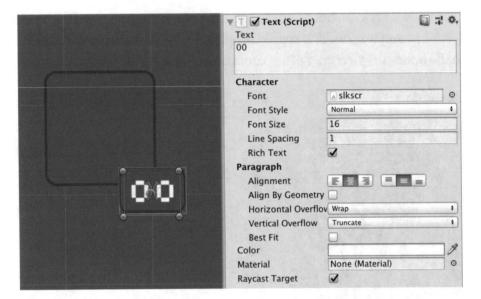

Figure 6-34. Configuring the Text component inside the Text object

Because the QtyText object is a child of Tray, we'll leave the Anchor Points at their default: middle-center. There's no need to move them.

Once you're satisfied with the placement of the Text, disable the Text component by unchecking the box in the top-left of the Text component on the Text object. We're disabling the Text because we don't want to show a quantity until we have multiple stackable items occupying the same Slot. We'll enable the component programmatically.

Create the Prefabs

Now that all the child elements are in place, we're going to make a prefab out of just the Slot. We'll programmatically instantiate copies of this prefab and use them to populate the Inventory Bar.

Select the highlighted item: Slot, as seen in Figure 6-35 and drag that into the prefabs folder to create a Slot prefab. Make sure you don't select the entire InventoryObject—we just want to create a prefab out of the Slot. We'll come back and use this prefab in just a little while.

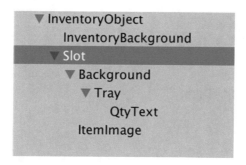

▼ InventoryObject
    InventoryBackground
    ▼ Slot
      ▼ Background
        ▼ Tray
          QtyText
      ItemImage

Figure 6-35. *Select and drag Slot into the prefabs folder to create a prefab*

Once you've created a prefab out of the Slot, delete the Slot from the Hierarchy view, so that only the InventoryObject and InventoryBackground remain. It should resemble Figure 6-36.

▼ InventoryObject
    InventoryBackground

Figure 6-36. *After creating a Slot prefab and removing the Slot from its parent*

Last but not least, click and drag the InventoryObject into the prefabs folder to create a prefab, and then delete it from the Hierarchy.

Build the Slot Script

We're going to build a simple script to hold a reference to the Text object inside the Slot. This script will be attached to each Slot object.

Select the Slot prefab in the Project view and add a new script to it called: "Slot". Use the following code in the script:

```
using UnityEngine;
using UnityEngine.UI;
```

```
// 1
public class Slot : MonoBehaviour {

// 2
    public Text qtyText;
}
```

`// 1`

Inherit from MonoBehaviour so that we can attach this script to the Slot object.

`// 2`

A reference to the Text object inside the Slot. We'll set this in the Unity Editor.

Save this script and switch back to the Unity Editor. We want to set the Qty Text property that we just created on the Slot script. The problem is, if we select the Slot prefab in the Project view, we can only see the Background and ItemImage children, as seen in Figure 6-37.

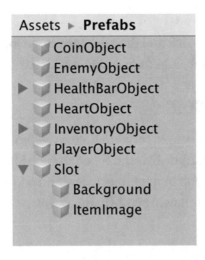

Figure 6-37. *We cannot see the Tray or QtyText child objects when selected in the Project view*

This limitation was deliberately put in place by the Unity designers to discourage a developer from making references to objects deep inside the nested parent–child hierarchy.

To see all of the child objects of a prefab in the Unity Editor, we need to temporarily instantiate a copy. Drag the Slot prefab onto the Hierarchy view or into the Scene to create an instance of the Slot temporarily.

If we select the newly instantiated copy in the Project view, we can see all of the Slot's child objects once again as seen in Figure 6-38.

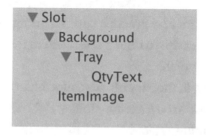

Figure 6-38. *View of all of the Slot prefabs children*

You won't be able to actually view the Slot prefab in the Scene because it's not the child of a Canvas object at the moment. That's okay—all we need right now is to be able to access the QtyText object

Set the Qty Text property on the Slot script by clicking the little dot next to it, as seen in Figure 6-39.

Figure 6-39. *Setting the Qty Text property of the Slot script*

Having a reference to the QtyText object in the script makes it much easier to find later without having to keep track of indexes. Referencing an object by a specific index is also a somewhat fragile way of doing things. If the order was to change, or an additional component was added, the index would change and the script would no longer work properly.

Press the Apply button in the top-right corner of the Inspector to apply the changes to the Slot prefab, then delete the prefab from the Hierarchy view.

Create the Inventory Script

The next step is to write a script to manage the player's inventory, as well as the appearance of the Inventory Bar. This script will be attached to the InventoryObject. The Inventory script is going to be more complex than any of the classes we've worked on so far but think of this as an opportunity to learn a lot and practice your scripting skills.

We'll also create a script to hold a reference to the QtyText and attach that script to the Slot prefab.

In the Project view, in the MonoBehaviours folder, create a new subfolder called, "Inventory". Inside the Inventory folder, right-click and create a new C# Script called, "Inventory". Double-click to open in Visual Studio.

Replace the default code inside Inventory with the following.

Set-Up Properties

First, we want to set up the properties for the Inventory class.

```
using UnityEngine;
using UnityEngine.UI;

public class Inventory : MonoBehaviour
{
// 1
    public GameObject slotPrefab;

// 2
    public const int numSlots = 5;

// 3
    Image[] itemImages = new Image[numSlots];
```

```
// 4
    Item[] items = new Item[numSlots];
// 5
    GameObject[] slots = new GameObject[numSlots];

    public void Start()
    {
      // Empty for now
    }
}
// 1
```

Store a reference to the Slot prefab, which we'll attach in the Unity Editor. Our Inventory script will instantiate multiple copies of this prefab to use as the Inventory Slots.

// 2

The Inventory Bar will contain five slots. We use the const keyword because we should not dynamically modify this number at runtime because several instance variables in the script rely on it.

// 3

Instantiate an array called itemImages of size numSlots (5). This array will hold Image components. Each Image component has a Sprite property. When the player adds an Item to their Inventory, we set this Sprite property to the Sprite referenced in the Item. The Sprite will be displayed in the Slot in the Inventory Bar. Remember that Items in our game are really just Scriptable Objects, or data containers, bundling together information.

// 4

The items array will hold references to the actual Item, of type Scriptable Objects, that the player has picked up.

// 5

Each index in the slots array will reference a single Slot prefab. These Slot prefabs were dynamically instantiated at runtime. We'll use these references to find the Text object inside a Slot.

Instantiate the Slot Prefabs

Add the following method to the Inventory class. This method is responsible for dynamically creating the Slot objects from the prefab.

```
public void CreateSlots()
{
// 1
    if (slotPrefab != null)
    {
// 2
        for (int i = 0; i < numSlots; i++)
        {
// 3
            GameObject newSlot = Instantiate(slotPrefab);
            newSlot.name = "ItemSlot_" + i;
// 4
            newSlot.transform.SetParent(gameObject.transform.
            GetChild(0).transform);
// 5
            slots[i] = newSlot;
```

```
// 6
        itemImages[i] = newSlot.transform.GetChild(1).
        GetComponent<Image>();
    }
  }
}
```

// 1

Check to make sure that we've set the Slot prefab via the Unity Editor, before we try to use it programmatically.

// 2

Loop through the number of slots.

// 3

Instantiate a copy of the Slot prefab and assign it to newSlot. Change the name of the instantiated GameObject to "ItemSlot_" and append the index number to the end. Name is a property intrinsic to every GameObject.

// 4

This script will be attached to InventoryObject. The InventoryObject prefab has a single child object: Inventory.

Set the Parent of the instantiated Slot to the child object at index 0 of InventoryObject. The child object at index 0 is: Inventory, as seen in Figure 6-40.

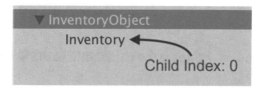

Figure 6-40. *Inventory is a child object of InventoryObject at index: 0*

// 5

Assign this new Slot object to the slots array at the current index.

// 6

The child object at index 1 of the Slot is an ItemImage. We retrieve the Image component from that ItemImage child and assign it to the itemImages array. The Source Image of this Image component is what will appear in the Inventory Slot when the player picks up the item. Figure 6-41 illustrates how ItemImage is at index: 1.

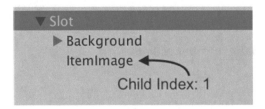

Figure 6-41. *ItemImage is a child object of Slot at index: 1*

Fill in the Start() Method

Let's fill in the Start() method. This is a short one.

```
public void Start()
{
// 1
    CreateSlots();
}
```

// 1

Call the method we wrote earlier to instantiate the Slot prefabs and set up the Inventory Bar.

The AddItem Method

Next we'll build out the method to actually add an item to the Inventory.

```
// 1
public bool AddItem(Item itemToAdd)
{
// 2
    for (int i = 0; i < items.Length; i++)
    {
// 3
        if (items[i] != null && items[i].itemType == itemToAdd.
        itemType && itemToAdd.stackable == true)
        {
            // Adding to existing slot
// 4
            items[i].quantity = items[i].quantity + 1;
// 5
            Slot slotScript = slots[i].gameObject.
            GetComponent<Slot>();
// 6
            Text quantityText = slotScript.qtyText;
// 7
            quantityText.enabled = true;
// 8
            quantityText.text = items[i].quantity.ToString();
// 9
            return true;
        }
```

```
// 10
        if (items[i] == null)
        {
            // Adding to empty slot
// Copy item & add to inventory. copying so we don't change
original Scriptable Object

// 11
            items[i] = Instantiate(itemToAdd);

// 12
            items[i].quantity = 1;

// 13
            itemImages[i].sprite = itemToAdd.sprite;

// 14
            itemImages[i].enabled = true;
            return true;
        }
    }

// 15
    return false;
}
```

Because this is a longer method, the individual lines of code are included above each explanation, so you don't have to keep flipping pages back and forth.

```
// 1
public bool AddItem(Item itemToAdd)
```

The method AddItem will take a single parameter of type Item. This is the item to be added to the Inventory. This method also returns a bool indicating if the item was successfully added to the Inventory.

```
// 2
for (int i = 0; i < items.Length; i++)
```

Loop through all the indexes in the items array.

```
// 3
```

These three conditions pertain to Stackable Items. Let's go through this if-statement:

```
items[i] != null
```

Check if the current index is not null.

```
items[i].itemType == itemToAdd.itemType
```

Check if the itemType of the Item is equal to the itemType of the Item we want to add to the Inventory.

```
itemToAdd.stackable == true
```

Check if the item to add is Stackable.

These three conditions combined will have the effect of checking to see if the current item in the index, if one exists, is of the same type the player wants to add. If it is the same type, and it's a Stackable item, then we want to add the new item to the stack of existing items.

```
// 4
items[i].quantity = items[i].quantity + 1;
```

Because we are stacking this Item, increment the quantity at the current index in the items array.

```
// 5
Slot slotScript = slots[i].GetComponent<Slot>();
```

When we instantiate a Slot prefab, what we're really doing is creating a GameObject with the Slot script attached to it. This line will grab a reference to the Slot script. The Slot script contains a reference to the QtyText child Text object.

```
// 6
Text quantityText = slotScript.qtyText;
```

Grab a reference to the Text object.

```
// 7
quantityText.enabled = true;
```

Because we're adding a stackable object to a slot already containing a stackable object, we now have multiple objects in a Slot. Enable the Text object that we'll use to display the quantity.

```
// 8
quantityText.text = items[i].quantity.ToString();
```

Each Item object has a quantity property of type int. ToString() will convert the type: int, into the type: String, so that it can be used to set the text property of the Text object.

```
// 9
return true;
```

Because we were able to add an object to the inventory, return true to indicate success.

```
// 10
if (items[i] == null)
```

Check if the current index of the items array contains an item. If it's null, then we're going to add newItem to this slot.

Because we're looping through the items array linearly each time, once we hit an index with a null item, that means we've looped through all the already held items. So we're either adding the first item of a particular itemType, or the item we're trying to add isn't Stackable.

Note that if we want to add the functionality to drop objects in the future, we'll have to modify this logic slightly. We would add the logic that says: when removing object from a Slot, shift all remaining objects left and leave no null Slots.

```
// 11
items[i] = Instantiate(itemToAdd);
```

Instantiate a copy of the itemToAdd and assign it to the items array.

```
// 12
items[i].quantity = 1;
```

Set the quantity on the Item object to 1.

```
// 13
itemImages[i].sprite = itemToAdd.sprite;
```

Assign the Sprite from the itemToAdd, to the Image object in the itemImages array. Note that this is the sprite we assigned earlier with the following line, when we set up the slots in CreateSlots(): itemImages[i] = newSlot.transform.GetChild(1).GetComponent<Image>();

```
// 14
itemImages[i].enabled = true;
return true;
```

Enable the itemImage and return true to indicate the itemToAdd was successfully added. Recall that we had originally disabled the image because if no source image is provided to an Image component, the Image component will default to the default color. Because we have assigned a Sprite, we enabled the Image component.

```
// 15
return false;
```

If neither of the two if-statements resulted in adding the itemToAdd to the Inventory, then the Inventory must be full. Return false to indicate the itemToAdd was not added.

Save the Inventory script and go back to the Unity Editor.

Select the InventoryObject and attach the Inventory Script to it via the Inspector. Drag the Slot prefab into the Slot Prefab property in the Inventory Script. There's no need to press the Apply button because we're modifying the InventoryObject prefab directly, instead of an instance of the prefab.

Update the Player Script

We've built this great inventory system but the player object is completely unaware that it exists. Open the Player script and add the following properties: inventoryPrefab and inventory, then add the Instantiate(inventoryPrefab) line anywhere inside the existing Start() method:

```
// 1
public Inventory inventoryPrefab;
```

```
// 2
Inventory inventory;

public void Start()
{
```

```
// 3
    inventory = Instantiate(inventoryPrefab);

    hitPoints.value = startingHitPoints;
    healthBar = Instantiate(healthBarPrefab);
    healthBar.character = this;
}
```

// 1

Store a reference to the Inventory prefab. We're going to use this in the Unity Editor in just a moment.

// 2

Used to store a reference to the Inventory once it's instantiated.

// 3

Instantiate the Inventory prefab. This line will store a reference to the prefab in the inventory variable. We store this reference so that we don't have to search for the Inventory each time we want to use it.

One Last Thing ...

Inside the existing OnTriggerEnter2D(Collider2D collision) method, change the switch statement to look like the following:

```
switch (hitObject.itemType)
{
    case Item.ItemType.COIN:
```

// 1

```
        shouldDisappear = inventory.AddItem(hitObject);
```

// 2

```
        shouldDisappear = true;
            break;
        case Item.ItemType.HEALTH:
        shouldDisappear = AdjustHitPoints(hitObject.quantity);
            break;
            default:
        break;
}
```

`// 1`

Call the `AddItem()` method on the local inventory instance and pass it `hitObject` as a parameter. Assign the result to `shouldDisappear`. If you recall back when we updated the Player script while building the Health Bar, if `shouldDisappear` is `true`, then the gameObject the player collided with will be set to inactive. Thus, if the object was added to the inventory, then the original object will disappear from the Scene.

`// 2`

Remove this line, as we no longer need it.

Save the Player script and switch back to the Unity Editor.

Select the Player prefab and drag the newly created InventoryObject prefab into the Inventory Prefab property of the Player script. It should look like Figure 6-42.

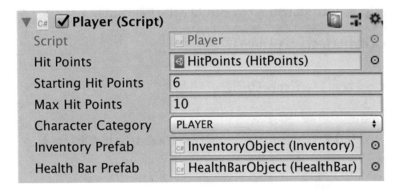

Figure 6-42. *Assign the InventoryObject to the Inventory Prefab property*

Add a few more Coins for the player to pick up by dragging and dropping the CoinObject prefab onto the Scene.

Now press the play button. Walk the player around the map and pick up coins. Notice how the quantity counter text appears when you're holding more than one coin, as seen in Figure 6-43.

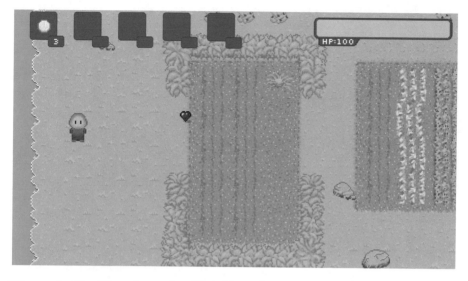

Figure 6-43. *The player is officially rich ... so very rich*

Summary

Whew! Well that was quite a lot to take in but think about how much we've accomplished. We've put Scriptable Objects and prefabs to use, and even learned about the Canvas and UI Elements. This chapter had us writing more C# than ever, and we learned a few tricks to keep our game architecture clean. We have a functioning Inventory and Health Bar, and our game is starting to look like a proper RPG.

CHAPTER 7

Characters, Coroutines, and Spawn Points

This chapter will see us building some central components important to any video game. We'll build a Game Manager responsible for coordinating and running the game logic, such as spawning the player when she dies. We'll also build a Camera Manager to ensure the camera is always set up properly. We'll be getting deeper into Unity and learning how to do things programmatically instead of relying on the Unity Editor. Doing things programmatically can make your game architecture more flexible and save you time in the long run. Throughout this chapter, you'll also learn some useful features of C# and the Unity Editor that will make your life easier and your code cleaner.

Create a Game Manager

Up until this point we've been creating bits and pieces of the game without any coordinating logic between these pieces. We're going to create a Game Manager script or "class" that will be responsible for running the game logic such as spawning the player if she is killed by her enemies.

© Jared Halpern 2019
J. Halpern, *Developing 2D Games with Unity*, https://doi.org/10.1007/978-1-4842-3772-4_7

Singletons

Before we start writing the RPGGameManager script, let's learn about a software design pattern called the Singleton. Singletons are used in situations where your application needs one and only one instance of a particular class to be created for the lifetime of the application. Singletons can be helpful when you have a single class that provides functionality used by several other classes in your game, such as coordinating game logic in a Game Manager class. Singletons can provide a public unified point of access to this class and its functionality. They also offer lazy instantiation, meaning they are created the first time they are accessed.

Before we start thinking about Singletons as the savior to our game development architecture, let's touch on some of the downsides of Singletons.

Although Singletons can provide a unified access point to functionality, this also means that the Singleton holds globally accessible values with indeterminate state. Any piece of code in your entire game can access and set the data inside the Singleton. Although this might seem like a good thing, imagine trying to figure out which one of the 20 different classes accessing a Singleton was setting a specific property to an incorrect value. That's the stuff of nightmares.

Another downside to using a Singleton is that we have far less control over the precise timing of the Singletons instantiation. For example imagine that our game is in the middle of a very graphically oriented section of code, when all of a sudden a Singleton that we'd hoped was created earlier in the game, is instantiated. The game stutters, affecting the end-users experience.

There are several other well-argued pros and cons for Singletons, and you should read up on them and make your own decisions about when to use them. When used sparingly, a Singleton can certainly make your life easier.

It makes sense to implement our RPGGameManager class as a Singleton because at any point in time, we'll only want one class coordinating the game logic. We won't have any performance issues because we're accessing and initializing the RPGGameManager when the Scene loads.

Every Singleton contains logic to prevent other instances of the Singleton from being created, thus maintaining its status as a single unique instance. We'll review some of that logic later when we create the RPGGameManager class.

Creating the Singleton

Create a new GameObject in the Hierarchy and rename it: "RPGGameManager". Then create a new folder under Scripts called: "Managers".

Create a new C# script called "RPGGameManager" and move it to the Managers folder. Add the script to the RPGGameManager object.

Open the RPGGameManager script in Visual Studio and use the following code to build out the RPGGameManager class:

```
using System.Collections;
using System.Collections.Generic;
using UnityEngine;

public class RPGGameManager : MonoBehaviour
{
// 1
    public static RPGGameManager sharedInstance = null;

    void Awake()
    {
```

```
// 2
        if (sharedInstance != null && sharedInstance != this)
        {
// 3
            Destroy(gameObject);
        }
        else
        {
// 4
            sharedInstance = this;
        }
    }

    void Start()
    {
// 5
        SetupScene();
    }

// 6
    public void SetupScene()
    {
        // empty, for now
    }
}
```

// 1

A static variable: sharedInstance is used to access the Singleton object. The singleton should *only* be accessed through this property.

It's important to understand that static variables belong to the *class itself* (RPGGameManager), not a specific instance of the class. A consequence of belonging to the Class itself is that only one copy of RPGGameManager.sharedInstance exists in memory.

If we create two RPGGameManager objects in the Hierarchy view, the second one to be initialized would share the same sharedInstance with the first RPGGameManager. This scenario would be inherently confusing, so we'll take steps to prevent it from happening.

The syntax for retrieving a reference to sharedInstance:

```
RPGGameManager gameManager = RPGGameManager.sharedInstance;
```

// 2

We only ever want one instance of the RPGGameManager to exist at a time. Check if sharedInstance is already initialized and not equal to this current instance. It's possible for this scenario to occur if you somehow create multiple copies of the RPGGameManager in the Hierarchy, or if you programmatically instantiate copies of the RPGGameManager prefab.

// 3

If sharedInstance is initialized and not equal to the current instance, then destroy it. There should be only one instance of RPGGameManager.

// 4

If this is the only instance, then assign the sharedInstance variable to the current object.

// 5

Consolidate all the logic to setup a scene inside a single method. This makes it easier to call again in the future from places other than the Start() method.

// 6

The SetupScene() method is empty for the time being, but that will soon change.

Build a GameManager Prefab

Let's create a RPGGameManager prefab. Follow the same process we've always used to create prefabs out of GameObjects:

1. Drag the RPGGameManager GameObject from the Hierarchy view into the prefabs folder in the Project view, to create a prefab.

2. Normally we would delete the original RPGGameManager object from the Hierarchy View. This time, keep it in the Hierarchy view because we're not finished working with it.

We've created a centralized management class responsible for running the game. Because it's a singleton, there will only be one instance of the RPGGameManager class in existence at a time.

Spawn Points

We want to be able to create or "spawn" characters—a player, or an enemy, at a specific location in the scene. If we're spawning enemies, then we may also want to spawn them at a regular interval as well. To accomplish this, we're going to create a Spawn Point prefab and attach a script to it with the spawning logic.

Right-click in the Hierarchy view, create an empty GameObject, and rename it: "SpawnPoint".

Add a new C# script to the SpawnPoint object we just created called: "SpawnPoint". Move the script to the MonoBehaviours folder.

Open the SpawnPoint script in Visual Studio and use the following code:

```
using UnityEngine;
public class SpawnPoint : MonoBehaviour
{
// 1
    public GameObject prefabToSpawn;
// 2
    public float repeatInterval;

    public void Start()
    {
// 3
        if (repeatInterval > 0)
        {
// 4
            InvokeRepeating("SpawnObject", 0.0f, repeatInterval);
        }
    }
// 5
    public GameObject SpawnObject()
    {
// 6
        if (prefabToSpawn != null)
        {
// 7
            return Instantiate(prefabToSpawn, transform.
            position, Quaternion.identity);
        }
```

```
// 8
      return null;
   }
}
```

// 1

This could be any prefab that we want to spawn once or at a consistent interval. We'll set this to be the player or enemy prefab in the Unity Editor.

// 2

If we want to spawn the prefab at a regular interval, we'll set this property in the Unity Editor.

// 3

If the repeatInterval is greater than 0 then we're indicating that the object should be spawned repeatedly at some preset interval.

// 4

Because the repeatInterval is greater than 0, we use InvokeRepeating() to spawn the object at regular, repeated intervals. The method signature for InvokeRepeating() takes three parameters: the method to call, the time to wait before invoking the first time, and the time interval to wait between invocations.

// 5

SpawnObject() is responsible for actually instantiating the prefab and "spawning" the object. The method signature indicates that it will return a result of type: GameObject, which will be an instance of the spawned object. We set the access modifier of this method to: public, so that it can be called externally.

// 6

Check to make sure we've set the prefab in the Unity Editor before we instantiate a copy to avoid errors.

// 7

Instantiate the prefab at the location of the current SpawnPoint object. There are a few different types of `Instantiate` methods used to instantiate prefabs. The specific method we're using takes a prefab, a `Vector3` indicating the position, and a special type of data structure called a Quaternion. Quaternions are used to represent rotations, and `Quaternion.identity` represents "no rotation." So we instantiate the prefab at the position of the SpawnPoint and without a rotation. We won't be getting into Quaternions as they can get pretty complex and are beyond the scope of this book.

Return a reference to the new instance of the prefab.

// 8

If the `prefabToSpawn` is null, then this Spawn Point was probably not configured properly in the editor. Return `null`;

Build a Spawn Point Prefab

Here's the plan: we'll set up a SpawnPoint for the player first, just to see how all the pieces fit together, and then we'll set up a SpawnPoint for enemies. To build a generic SpawnPoint, add the script we just wrote to the SpawnPoint GameObject, and then create a prefab out of it.

Follow the following process to create a prefab out of the SpawnPoint GameObject:

1. Drag the SpawnPoint GameObject from the Hierarchy view into the prefabs folder in the Project view, to create a prefab.

2. Delete the original SpawnPoint object from the Hierarchy View.

Drag the SpawnPoint prefab onto the Scene where you'd like the Player to appear. Rename the new instance of Spawn Point, "PlayerSpawnPoint" as seen in Figure 7-1. Do not press the Apply button, as we don't want to apply this change to the prefab itself—only this instance.

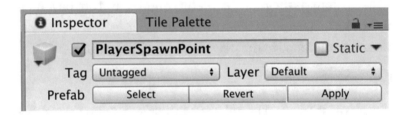

Figure 7-1. *Rename the Spawn Point*

As you can see in Figure 7-2, the location of the Spawn Point is barely visible in the Scene. Because there is no Sprite attached to the GameObject instance, it's difficult to see.

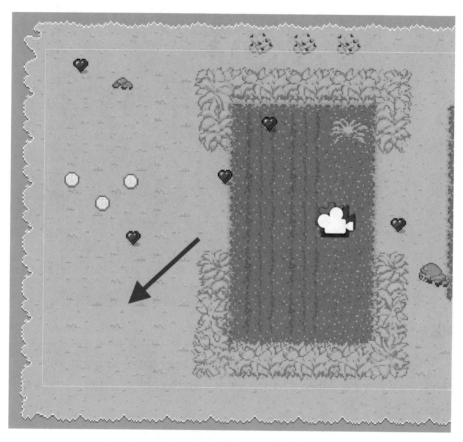

Figure 7-2. *GameObjects without a Sprite are sometimes difficult to see in the Scene view*

Tip   To make Spawn Points easier to locate in the Scene while the game isn't running, select the Spawn Point then press the Icon at the top-left of the inspector as seen in Figure 7-3.

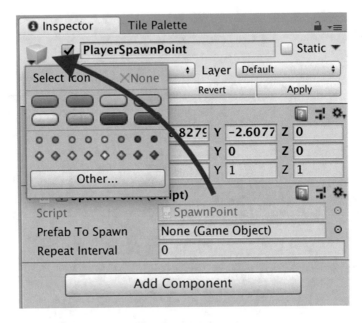

Figure 7-3. *Select the icon in the Inspector*

Choose an icon to visually represent the selected object in the Scene. You should see the selected icon appear over the object in the scene, as seen in Figure 7-4.

Figure 7-4. *Using an icon to make an object easier to find in a Scene*

These icons also can be made visible during runtime by selecting the Gizmos button in the upper-right corner of the Game window, as seen in Figure 7-5.

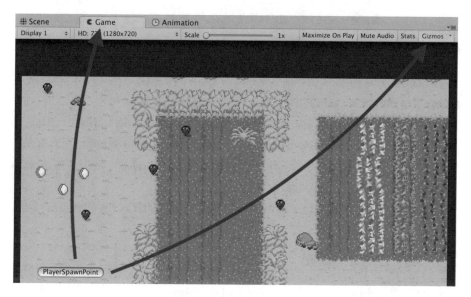

Figure 7-5. *Use the Gizmos button to set the icon visible during runtime*

Configure the Player Spawn Point

We still have to configure the Spawn Point so it knows what prefab to spawn. Set the "Prefab To Spawn" property in the attached Spawn Point script to the PlayerObject prefab by dragging the PlayerObject prefab to the respective property as seen in Figure 7-6. Leave the Repeat Interval set to 0 because we only want to spawn the player once.

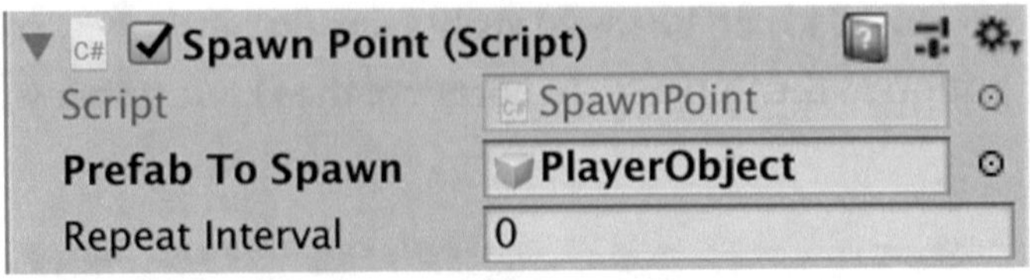

Figure 7-6. *Configure the Spawn Point script*

Because the plan is to use the PlayerSpawnPoint to spawn the player, delete the Player instance from the Hierarchy view.

Press Play and you'll immediately notice that nothing happens. The player is nowhere to be seen. This is because we're not actually calling the SpawnObject() method of the SpawnPoint class anywhere yet. Let's modify the RPGGameManager to call SpawnObject().

Switch back to the Unity Editor and open the RPGGameManager class.

Spawn the Player

Add the following property to the top of the class:

```
public class RPGGameManager : MonoBehaviour
{

// 1
    public SpawnPoint playerSpawnPoint;

        // ...Existing code from the RPGGameManager class...
}

// 1
```

The playerSpawnPoint property will hold a reference to the Spawn Point specifically designated for the player. We're keeping a reference to this specific Spawn Point because we'll want the ability to re-spawn the player when they meet an untimely demise

Add the following method:

```
public void SpawnPlayer()
{
// 1
    if (playerSpawnPoint != null)
    {
// 2
        GameObject player = playerSpawnPoint.SpawnObject();
    }
}
```

// 1

Check if the playerSpawnPoint property is not null before we try to use it.

// 2

Call the SpawnObject() method on the playerSpawnPoint.
SpawnObject to Spawn the player. Store a local reference to the instantiated
player, which we'll be using shortly.

In the SetupScene() method of RPGGameManager, add a single line:

```
public void SetupScene()
{
// 1
    SpawnPlayer();
}
```

// 1

This will invoke the SpawnPlayer() method we just wrote.

Finally we need to configure the RPGGameManager instance in the Hierarchy view with a reference to the Player Spawn Point. Drag and drop the PlayerSpawnPoint from the Hierarchy view, into the Player Spawn Point property in the RPGGameManager instance, as seen in Figure 7-7.

Figure 7-7. *Set the Player Spawn Point property to the PlayerSpawnPoint instance*

Press Play and you should see the Player object appear in the scene at the location of the Player Spawn Point.

In Summary

1. Spawn Points are used to determine what type of object to spawn and the location to spawn in. We've configured the Player Spawn Point instance to reference the PlayerObject prefab.

2. Configure a reference to the Player Spawn Point in the RPGGameManager instance.

3. In the SetupScene() method of RPGGameManager, call the SpawnObject() method of the Player Spawn Point class.

A Spawn Point for Enemies

Let's build a Spawn Point to spawn enemies. Because we've already built a Spawn Point prefab, this will be quick.

1. Drag and Drop a SpawnPoint prefab into the Scene.

2. Rename it EnemySpawnPoint.

   - (Optional) Change the icon to red, so we can view it easily in the Scene view

3. Set the "Prefab to Spawn" property to the Enemy prefab.

4. Set the Repeat Interval to 10 (seconds), to spawn an Enemy every 10 seconds.

After configuring the Enemy Spawn Point, the Scene should resemble Figure 7-8.

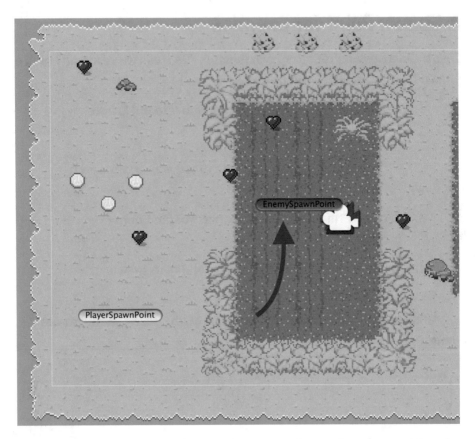

Figure 7-8. *An instance of SpawnPoint configured to spawn Enemies with a custom red icon to make it easily visible*

Press Play and watch as Enemies spawn every 10 seconds. We haven't written any artificial intelligence yet to make the Enemies move around or attack, so the player is safe for the time being.

As you walk the player around the map, you may have noticed that something is off. The camera no longer follows the player around! Catastrophe! This is because we're now spawning the Player dynamically, instead of setting the Player prefab instance in the Cinemachine Virtual Camera—follow property. The Virtual Camera has no follow target and thus remains in the same place.

Camera Manager

To restore the behavior where the camera follows the player as she walks around the map, we're going to create a Camera Manager class and have the Game Manager use it to ensure the Virtual Camera is properly set up. This Camera Manager will be useful in the future as a centralized place for configuring camera behavior instead of embedding that camera code in various places throughout our app.

Create a new GameObject in the Hierarchy and rename it: RPGCameraManager. Create a new script called RPGCameraManager and add it to the RPGCameraManager object. Open the script in Visual Studio.

We'll use the Singleton pattern again, just as we did for the RPGGameManager earlier in this chapter.

Use the following code for the RPGCameraManager class:

```
using UnityEngine;

// 1
using Cinemachine;

public class RPGCameraManager : MonoBehaviour {

    public static RPGCameraManager sharedInstance = null;

// 2
    [HideInInspector]
    public CinemachineVirtualCamera virtualCamera;

// 3
    void Awake()
    {
        if (sharedInstance != null && sharedInstance != this)
        {
            Destroy(gameObject);
        }
```

```
        else
        {
            sharedInstance = this;
        }
```

// 4

```
        GameObject vCamGameObject = GameObject.
        FindWithTag("VirtualCamera");
```

//5

```
        virtualCamera = vCamGameObject.GetComponent<Cinemachine
        VirtualCamera>();
    }
}
```

// 1

Import the Cinemachine namespace so the RPGCameraManager gains access to the Cinemachine classes and data types.

// 2

Store a reference to the Cinemachine Virtual Camera. Make it public so that other classes can access it. Because we'll be setting it programmatically, use the [HideInInspector] attribute so that it doesn't appear in the Unity Editor.

// 3

Implement the Singleton pattern.

// 4

Find the VirtualCamera GameObject in the current Scene. In the following line, we'll get a reference to its Virtual Camera component. We'll also need to create this tag in the Unity Editor and configure the Virtual Camera to use it.

Remember that GameObjects can have multiple components attached to them, with each component providing different functionality. This is known as the "Composition" design pattern.

// 5

All of the Virtual Camera's properties such as the Follow target and Orthographic Size can be configured via script as well as the Unity Editor. Save a reference to the Virtual Camera Component, so we can control these Virtual Camera properties programmatically.

Create a prefab out of the RPGCameraManager but keep an instance in the Hierarchy view.

Using the Camera Manager

In the RPGGameManager class, add the following property to the top of the class:

```
public RPGCameraManager cameraManager;
```

We're making this property public because we're going to set it via the Unity Editor. The RPGGameManager will use this reference to the RPGCameraManager when it spawns the player, as you'll see in the following code.

Still inside the RPGGameManager class, change the SpawnPlayer() method to the following:

```
public void SpawnPlayer()
{
    if (playerSpawnPoint != null)
    {
        GameObject player = playerSpawnPoint.SpawnObject();
```

```
// 1
        cameraManager.virtualCamera.Follow = player.transform;
    }
}
```

```
// 1
```

We've added this line to SpawnPlayer(). Set the Follow property of the virtualCamera to the transform of the player object. This will instruct the Cinemachine Virtual Camera to follow the player once again as she walks around the map.

Switch back to the Unity Editor and select the RPGGameManager instance in the Hierarchy. We're going to configure the Game Manager to use the Camera Manager.

Drag the RPGCameraManager instance into the Camera Manager property of the RPGGameManager in the Hierarchy, as seen in Figure 7-9.

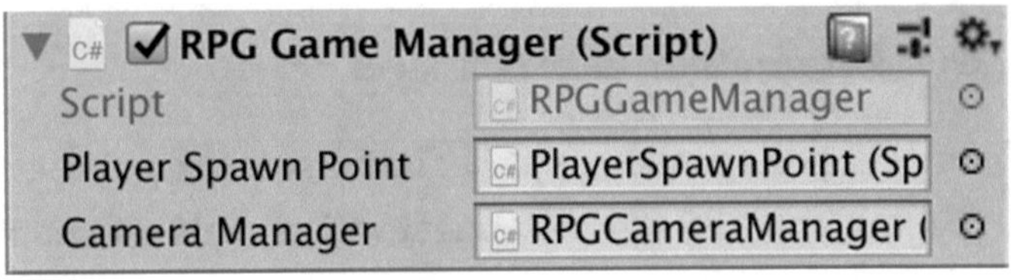

Figure 7-9. *Set the Camera Manager property*

There's one last thing to do before our Virtual Camera will follow the player again: set the Tag on the Virtual Camera so the RPGCameraManager script can find it.

Select the Virtual Camera object in the Hierarchy view. By default, the Virtual Camera will be named: CM vcam1. Click the Tag drop-down menu in the Inspector. If you need a refresher on the location of the Tag drop-down menu, take a look at Figure 7-10.

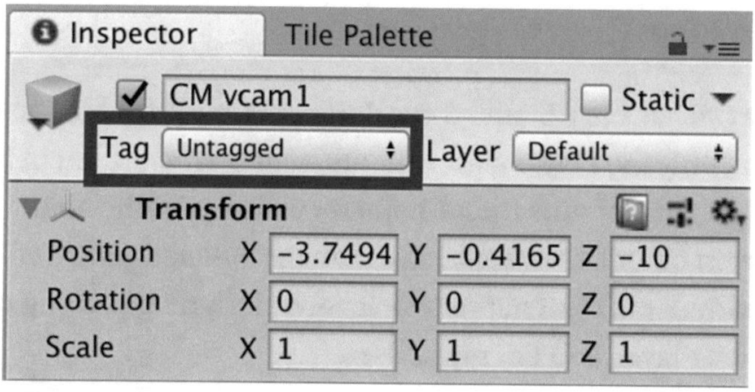

Figure 7-10. *The Tag drop-down menu*

Add a Tag called, "VirtualCamera" to the Tag listing. Then select the Virtual Camera object again in the Hierarchy and set the Tag to the VirtualCamera Tag you just created (Figure 7-11).

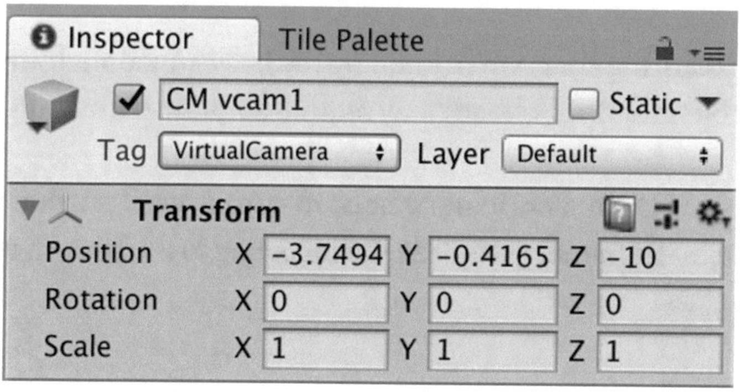

Figure 7-11. *Set the Tag to VirtualCamera so the RPGCameraManager script can find it*

Press Play again and walk the player around the map. The camera should once again follow the player as she walks around the map.

Character Class Design

If you recall back in Chapter 6, we designed a class called: Character. At the moment, only the Player class inherits from Character, but in the future every class that inherits from Character will require the ability to inflict damage on other Characters, have damage inflicted on it, and even die. The remainder of this chapter will involve designing and augmenting the Character, Player, and Enemy classes.

The Virtual Keyword

The "virtual" keyword in C# is used to declare that classes, methods, or variables will be implemented in the current class but **can also** be overridden in an inheriting class if the current implementation is not sufficient.

In the following code, we're building the basic functionality to kill a Character but inheriting classes may require additional functionality on top of this.

Because all Characters in our game are mortal, we'll provide a method to kill them in the parent class. Add the following to the bottom of the Character class:

```
// 1
public virtual void KillCharacter()
{
// 2
    Destroy(gameObject);
}
```

// 1

This method will be called when the characters hit-points reach zero.

// 2

Calling `Destroy(gameObject)` will Destroy the current GameObject and remove it from the Scene when the Character is killed.

The Enemy Class

Part of being a hero is facing adversity and possibly danger. In this section, we're going to build out an Enemy Class and give it the ability to harm our player.

In Chapter 6, we used a neat trick with Scriptable Objects to build a Scriptable Object called `HitPoints` that shares data instantly with the Player's Health Bar. The Character class contains a property of a type of `HitPoints` that is used by the Player class that inherits from Character.

Because the enemies in our game won't have on-screen health bars, they don't require a `HitPoints` ScriptableObject. Only the Player, who has a Health Bar, needs access to a `HitPoints` ScriptableObject. Thus we can simplify the way we keep track of hit-points in the Enemy class by simply using a regular `float variable to track hit-points instead`.

Refactoring

To simplify our class architecture, we're going to refactor some code. *Refactoring* code is simply a term for restructuring existing code without changing its behavior.

Open the Character class and Player class in Visual Studio. Move the `hitPoints` variable from the Character class to the Player class, toward the top where we have the existing properties:

```
public HitPoints hitPoints;
```

Select the EnemyObject prefab and add a script to it called: Enemy. Open the Enemy script in Visual Studio. Remove the default code inside the Enemy class and replace it with the following.

```
using UnityEngine;

// 1
public class Enemy : Character
{
// 2
    float hitPoints;
}
// 1
```

Our Enemy class inherits from Character, which means it gets access to public properties and methods in the Character class.

```
// 2
```

A simplified hitPoints variable of type float.

After these code changes, our Player class will continue to use the HitPoints ScriptableObject we created in Chapter 6. We've also created an Enemy class containing a simplified way of keeping track of hit-points. The Enemy class also gained access to the existing properties in the Character class pertaining to hit-points: startingHitPoints and maxHitPoints.

Tip   When refactoring code, it's best to keep the changes small then test to ensure correct behavior so as to minimize the chance of incorporating new bugs. An iterative cycle of making small changes, then testing, is a good way to maintain your sanity.

The Internal Access Modifier

Notice that we've omitted any access modifier keyword (public, private) in front of the hitPoints variable in the Enemy class. In C# the absence of an access modifier means the internal access modifier will be used by default. The `internal` access modifier restricts access to the variable or method to within the same "assembly." *Assembly* is a term used in C# that can be thought of as encompassing the C# project.

Coroutines

We're going to pause for a moment from building out the Character and Enemy class to talk about an important and useful feature of Unity. When calling a method in Unity, the method runs until completion then returns to the original point of invocation. Everything that happens inside a regular method must happen within a single frame in the Unity Engine. If your game calls a method that would ideally run longer than a single frame, Unity will actually force the entire method to be called within that frame. When that happens, you won't get the result you're looking for. It's even possible that the results of a method that should run over the space of several seconds won't even be visible to the user because it'll run and be completed within a single frame.

To solve this dilemma, Unity offers something called: **Coroutines**. Coroutines can be thought of as functions that can be paused mid-way through execution, and then resume executing in the next frame. Long-running methods that are intended to execute over the course of multiple frames are often implemented as Coroutines.

Declaring Coroutines is as straightforward as using the return type: `IEnumerator` and including a line instructing the Unity engine to pause or "yield" somewhere within the method body. It is this `yield` line that tells the engine to pause execution and return to the same spot in the subsequent frame.

Invoking Coroutines

A hypothetical Coroutine called RunEveryFrame() can be started by enclosing it in the method StartCoroutine() as follows:

```
StartCoroutine(RunEveryFrame());
```

Pausing or "Yielding" Execution

RunEveryFrame() will run up until it reaches a yield statement, at which point it will pause until the next frame, then resume execution. A yield statement could look like:

```
yield return null;
```

A Complete Coroutine

The following RunEveryFrame() method is just an example of a Coroutine. Don't add it to your code anywhere but make sure that you understand how it works:

```
public IEnumerator RunEveryFrame()
{
// 1
    while(true)
    {
        print("I will print every Frame.");
        yield return null;
    }
}
    // 1
```

We're enclosing the print and yield statement in a while() loop to keep the method running indefinitely, that is, to make it long-running and span multiple frames.

Coroutines with Time Intervals

Coroutines also can be used to call code at regular time intervals, such as every 3 seconds, instead of every frame. Instead of using yield return null to pause, we use yield return new WaitForSeconds() and pass a time-interval parameter in this next example:

```
public IEnumerator RunEveryThreeSeconds()
{
    while (true)
    {
        print("I will print every three seconds.");
        yield return new WaitForSeconds(3.0f);
    }
}
```

When this sample Coroutine reaches the yield statement, execution will pause for 3 seconds, then resume. The print statement will be invoked and print every three seconds indefinitely, due to the while() loop.

We're going to write some Coroutines to build out the functionality in the Character, Player, and Enemy classes.

The Abstract Keyword

The "abstract" keyword in C# is used to declare that classes, methods, or variables **cannot** be implemented in the current class and **must** be implemented by an inheriting class.

The Enemy and Player class both inherit from the Character class. By putting the definition of the following methods in the Character class, we require the Enemy and Player class to implement them before the game will compile and run.

Add the following "using" statement to the top of the Character class. We'll need to import System.Collections to work with Coroutines.

```
using System.Collections;
```

Then add the following underneath the KillCharacter() method:

```
// 1
public abstract void ResetCharacter();
```

```
// 2
public abstract IEnumerator DamageCharacter(int damage, float
interval);
```

// 1

Set the character back to its original starting state, so it can be used again.

// 2

Called by other Characters to damage the current character. Takes an amount to damage the character by and a time interval. The time interval can be used in situations when damage is recurring.

As discussed earlier, the return type: IEnumerator is required in a Coroutine. IEnumerator is part of the System.Collections namespace that is why we had to add the import line: using System.Collections earlier.

Remember that all abstract methods must be implemented before the code will compile and run. Because the method is in the parent class of both Player and Enemy, we'll have to implement both methods in both classes.

Implementing the Enemy Class

Now that we're experts in Coroutines and we've built out the Character class, we're going to implement the abstract methods starting with the DamageCharacter() Coroutine.

Imagine a scenario in our game where an enemy runs into the player, and the player doesn't move out of the way. Our game logic says that as long as the enemy keeps in contact with the player, the enemy will continue to damage her. Another scenario where damage would be applied at regular intervals is if the player walked over molten lava. That's just science.

To implement this scenario, we've declared the DamageCharacter() method as a Coroutine to allow the method to apply damage at regular intervals. In the implementation of DamageCharacter() we will leverage: yield return new WaitForSeconds() to pause execution for a specified amount of time.

The DamageCharacter() method

Add the following import to the top of the class:

```
using System.Collections;
```

We need to import System.Collections to work with Coroutines.

Implement the DamageCharacter() method inside the Enemy class:

```
// 1
public override IEnumerator DamageCharacter(int damage, float
interval)
{

// 2
    while (true)
    {
```

```
// 3
        hitPoints = hitPoints - damage;

// 4
        if (hitPoints <= float.Epsilon)
        {
// 5
            KillCharacter();
            break;
        }

// 6
        if (interval > float.Epsilon)
        {
            yield return new WaitForSeconds(interval);
        }
        else
        {
// 7
            break;
        }
    }
}

// 1
```

When implementing an abstract method in a derived (inheriting) class, use the override keyword to indicate the method is overriding the KillCharacter() method from the base (parent) class.

This method takes two parameters: damage and interval. Damage is the amount of damage to inflict on the Character, and interval is the time to wait between inflicting damage. Passing an interval = 0, as we'll see, will inflict damage a single time then return.

// 2

This while() loop will continue inflicting damage until the character dies, or if the interval = 0, it will break and return.

// 3

Subtract the amount of damage inflicted from the current hitPoints and set the result to hitPoints.

// 4

After adjusting the Enemy's hitPoints, we'd like to check if the hitPoints are less than 0. However, hitPoints is of type: float, and floating-point arithmetic is prone to rounding errors due to the way floats are implemented under the hood. For this reason, in some cases it's better to compare a float value to: float.Epsilon, which is defined as the "smallest positive value greater than zero" on the current system. For purposes of enemy life and death, if the hitPoints are less than float. Epsilon, then the character has "zero" health.

// 5

If hitPoints is less than float.Epsilon (effectively 0), then the enemy has been vanquished. Call KillCharacter() then break out of the while() loop.

// 6

If interval is greater than float.Epsilon, then we want to yield execution, wait for interval seconds, then resume executing the while() loop. In this scenario, the loop will only exit when the character dies.

```
// 7
```

If interval is not greater than float.Epsilon (effectively equal to 0), then this break statement will be hit, the while() loop will be broken, and the method will return. The parameter interval will be zero in situations where damage is not continuous, such as a single hit.

Let's implement the rest of the abstract methods declared in the Character class.

In the Enemy class:

ResetCharacter()

Lets build out the method to set the Character variables back to their original state. It's important to do this if we want to use the Character object again after it dies. This method can also be used to set up the variables when the Character is first created.

```
// 1
public override void ResetCharacter()
{
// 2
    hitPoints = startingHitPoints;
}
```

```
// 1
```

Because the Enemy class inherits from the Character class, we override the ResetCharacter() declaration in the parent class.

```
// 2
```

When resetting the character, set the current hit-points to startingHitPoints. We set startingHitPoints on the prefab itself in the Unity Editor.

Calling ResetCharacter() in OnEnable()

The Enemy class inherits from Character, which inherits from MonoBehaviour. The OnEnable() method is part of the MonoBehaviour class. If OnEnable() is implemented in a class, it will be called every time an object becomes both enabled and active. We will use OnEnable() to ensure that certain things occur every time an Enemy object becomes both enabled and active.

```
private void OnEnable()
{
// 1
    ResetCharacter();
}
```

// 1

Call the method we just wrote to reset the enemy. At the moment, "resetting" the enemy just means setting it's hitPoints to startingHitPoints, but we could also include other things in ResetCharacter() as well.

KillCharacter()

Because we've implemented KillCharacter() as a virtual method in the Character class, and Enemy inherits from Character, there's no need to implement it in the Enemy class. Enemy doesn't require any additional functionality beyond what the Character implementation provides.

Updating the Player Class

Next we'll implement the abstract methods in the Player class. Open the Player class in Visual Studio and use the following code to implement the abstract methods from the Character parent class.

Add the following import to the top of the class:

```
using System.Collections;
```

Then add the following method to the Player class:

```
// 1
public override IEnumerator DamageCharacter(int damage, float
interval)
{
    while (true)
    {
        hitPoints.value = hitPoints.value - damage;

        if (hitPoints.value <= float.Epsilon)
        {
            KillCharacter();
            break;
        }

        if (interval > float.Epsilon)
        {
            yield return new WaitForSeconds(interval);
        }
        else
        {
            break;
        }
    }
}
// 1
```

Implement the DamageCharacter() method, as we did in the Enemy class.

```
public override void KillCharacter()
{
// 1
    base.KillCharacter();

// 2
    Destroy(healthBar.gameObject);
    Destroy(inventory.gameObject);
}
```

// 1

Use the base keyword to refer to the parent or "base" class that the current class inherits from. Calling base.KillCharacter() calls the KillCharacter() method inside the parent class. The parent KillCharacter() method destroys the current gameObject associated with the player.

// 2

Destroy the health bar and inventory associated with the Player.

Refactoring Prefab Instantiation

In Chapter 6, we were initializing instances of the health bar and inventory prefabs inside the Start() method. This was before we had the method: ResetCharacter(). Remove the following three lines from Start() and place them inside ResetCharacter() as seen in the following:

Remove these three lines from Start():

```
inventory = Instantiate(inventoryPrefab);
healthBar = Instantiate(healthBarPrefab);
healthBar.character = this;
```

Then create the method ResetCharacter() as in the following, **overriding** the abstract method in the Character parent class:

```
public override void ResetCharacter()
{
// 1
    inventory = Instantiate(inventoryPrefab);
    healthBar = Instantiate(healthBarPrefab);
    healthBar.character = this;

// 2
    hitPoints.value = startingHitPoints;
}
```

// 1

The three lines we removed from the Start() method. These three lines initialize and set up the health bar and inventory.

// 2

Set the hit-points of the Player to the starting hit-points value. Remember—because the starting hit-points is public, we can set it in the Unity Editor.

Review

Let's review what we've just built:

- The Character class provides basic functionality for all the various character types in our game including the Player and her Enemies.

- Character class functionality includes:

  - Basic functionality for killing a character

  - An abstract method definition for resetting a character

  - An abstract method definition for damaging a character

Using What We've Built

We've built out some pretty core functionality but we're not actually using it yet. The enemy has methods that can damage the player, but they're not being invoked at the moment. To see the **DamageCharacter()** and **KillCharacter()** methods in action, we're going to add functionality to the Enemy class that will invoke the DamageCharacter() method when the Player runs into it.

In the Enemy class, add these two variables to the top of the class:

```
// 1
public int damageStrength;
```

```
// 2
Coroutine damageCoroutine;
```

// 1

Set in the Unity Editor, this variable will determine how much damage the enemy will do when it runs into the Player.

// 2

References to running Coroutines can be saved to a variable and stopped at a later time. We'll use **damageCoroutine** to store a reference to the **DamageCharacter()** Coroutine so we can stop it later on.

OnCollisionEnter2D

`OnCollisionEnter2D()` is a method included with all MonoBehaviours and is called by the Unity Engine whenever the current objects `Collider2D` makes contact with another `Collider2D`.

```
// 1
void OnCollisionEnter2D(Collision2D collision)
{

// 2
    if(collision.gameObject.CompareTag("Player"))
    {

// 3
        Player player = collision.gameObject.
        GetComponent<Player>();

// 4
        if (damageCoroutine == null)
        {
            damageCoroutine = StartCoroutine(player.
            DamageCharacter(damageStrength, 1.0f));
        }
    }
}
```

// 1

The collision details are passed as the parameter: `collision`, into `OnCollisionEnter2D()`.

// 2

We want to write game logic such that Enemies can only damage the Player. Compare the Tag on the object that the enemy has collided with to see if it's the Player object.

// 3

At this point we've determined that the other object is the Player, so retrieve a reference to the Player component.

// 4

Check to see if this Enemy is already running the DamageCharacter() Coroutine. If it is not, then start the Coroutine on the player object. Pass into DamageCharacter() the damageStrength and the interval, because the enemy will continue to damage the player for as long as they are in contact.

We're doing something here that we haven't seen before. We're storing a reference to the running Coroutine in the variable damageCoroutine. We can call StopCoroutine() and pass it the parameter: damageCoroutine, to stop the Coroutine at any time.

OnCollisionExit2D

OnCollisionExit2D() is called when another object's Collider2D stops touching the current MonoBehaviour object's Collider2D.

```
// 1
void OnCollisionExit2D(Collision2D collision)
{

// 2
    if (collision.gameObject.CompareTag("Player"))
    {

// 3
        if (damageCoroutine != null)
        {
```

```
// 4
            StopCoroutine(damageCoroutine);
            damageCoroutine = null;
        }
    }
}
```

// 1

The collision details are passed as the parameter: collision, into OnCollisionEnter2D().

// 2

Check the Tag on the object that the enemy has stopped colliding with, to see if it's the Player object.

// 3

If damageCoroutine is not null, that means the coroutine is running and should be stopped, then set to null.

// 4

Stop the damageCoroutine that is actually DamageCharacter() and set it to null. This stops the Coroutine immediately.

Configure the Enemy Script

Flip back to the Unity Editor and configure the Enemy script as seen in Figure 7-12. Remember that the Damage Strength is how much damage the Enemy will cause to the Player when it runs into her.

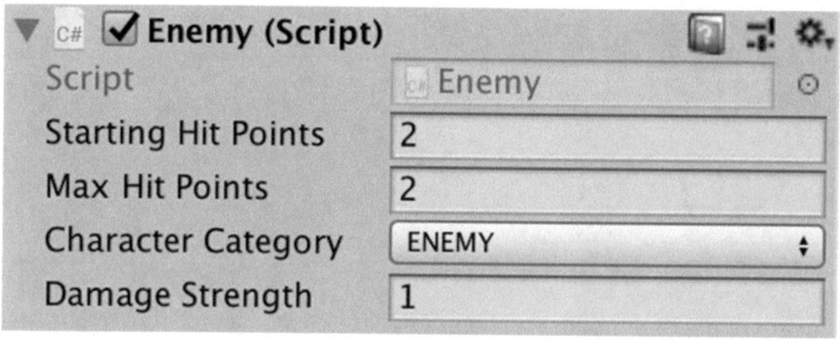

Figure 7-12. *Configure the Enemy Script*

Press Play and walk the Player over to an Enemy Spawn Point. Run the Player into an Enemy and you'll notice that the Player takes some damage, but also pushes the Enemy away. This is because both the Player and the Enemy have RigidBody2D components attached to them and are under the control of Unity's Physics Engine.

Eventually the Enemy will chase after the Player, but for now, push the Enemy into the corner and maintain contact with it. Watch as the health bar decreases down to 0 until the inventory, health bar, and the player disappear off the screen.

Summary

Our sample game is really starting to come together. We've created an architecture for the various types of characters throughout the game and picked up a few pointers on using C# in the process. Our game now has a central game manager responsible for setting up a Scene, spawning the player, and ensuring the camera is set up properly. We've learned how to write code to control the Camera programmatically, where we previously had to set up the Camera via the Unity Editor. We built a Spawn Point to spawn different character types, and learned about Coroutines, an important tool in the Unity developer's toolbox.

CHAPTER 8

Artificial Intelligence and Slingshots

This chapter covers a lot but by the end, you'll have a functioning prototype of a game. We'll build some interesting features such as a reusable artificial intelligence component with chasing behavior. Our courageous Player also will finally receive her weapon of choice: a slingshot, to defend herself with. You'll learn a widely used optimization technique in game programming called Object Pooling, as well as put some of that high-school math to use that you never thought you'd need. This chapter also demonstrates the usage of Blend Trees, which are a more efficient way of doing animations and better for your game architecture in the long-term. We'll wrap things up by showing you how to compile your game to run outside of Unity and talk a little bit about what's next in your game programming adventures.

The Wander Algorithm

In this section we'll leverage what we've learned about Coroutines to write a script that makes an enemy wander randomly around the board. If the enemy detects that the Player is close-by, the enemy will pursue her until she runs away, kills the enemy, or the player dies.

© Jared Halpern 2019
J. Halpern, *Developing 2D Games with Unity*, https://doi.org/10.1007/978-1-4842-3772-4_8

The Wander algorithm may sound complicated but when we break it down step-by-step, you'll see that it's all very achievable.

Figure 8-1 is a diagram of the Wander algorithm. We'll implement each part in stages and explain as we go along, so you won't feel overwhelmed.

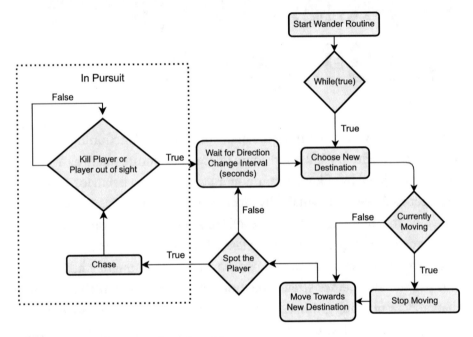

Figure 8-1. *The Wander algorithm*

Getting Started

Select the Enemy prefab and drag it into the scene to make our lives easier. Select the EnemyObject and add a CircleCollider2D component to it. Check the Is Trigger box on the Circle Collider and set the radius of the collider to be: 1. The Circle Collider should look like Figure 8-2.

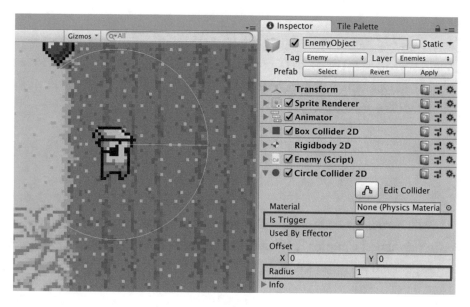

Figure 8-2. *Set Is Trigger and Radius*

This Circle Collider represents how far the Enemy can "see." In other words, when the Player's collider crosses the Circle Collider, the Enemy can see the Player. Remember how trigger colliders work: because we've checked the Is Trigger box on the Circle Collider, it can pass through other objects. The Enemy will "see" the Player cross the collider, then change course and pursue her.

Create the Wander Script

We'll create the Wander script as a MonoBehaviour so it can be re-used and attached to other GameObjects in the future besides the Enemy.

Add a new Script called: "Wander". Open the script in Visual Studio and add the following:

```
// 1
using System.Collections;
using UnityEngine;
```

```
// 2
[RequireComponent(typeof(Rigidbody2D))]
[RequireComponent(typeof(CircleCollider2D))]
[RequireComponent(typeof(Animator))]
public class Wander : MonoBehaviour
{

}
```

```
// 1
```

We'll be using Coroutines and IEnumerator in the Wander algorithm. As mentioned in Chapter 7, IEnumerator is part of the System.Collections namespace, so we import it here.

```
// 2
```

Ensure that whatever GameObject we attach the Wander script to in the future has a Rigidbody2D, a CircleCollider2D, and an Animator. All three of these components are necessary for the Wander script.

By using RequireComponent, any script that this script is attached to will automatically have the required component added if it is not already present.

Wander Variables

Next we're going to sketch out the variables needed for the Wander algorithm. Add the following variables to the Wander class:

```
// 1
    public float pursuitSpeed;
    public float wanderSpeed;
    float currentSpeed;
```

```
// 2
    public float directionChangeInterval;
```

// 3

```
    public bool followPlayer;
```

// 4

```
    Coroutine moveCoroutine;
```

// 5

```
    Rigidbody2D rb2d;
    Animator animator;
```

// 6

```
    Transform targetTransform = null;
```

// 7

```
    Vector3 endPosition;
```

// 8

```
    float currentAngle = 0;
```

// 1

These three variables will be used to set the speed at which the Enemy pursues the Player, the general wandering speed when not in pursuit, and the current speed that will be one of the previous two speeds.

// 2

The directionChangeInterval is set via the Unity Editor and will be used to determine how often the Enemy should change wandering direction.

// 3

This script can be attached to any Character in the game to add wandering behavior. You may want to eventually create a type of Character that doesn't chase the player and only wanders about. The followPlayer flag can be set to turn on and off the player-chasing behavior.

// 4

The variable moveCoroutine is where we'll save a reference to the currently running movement Coroutine. This Coroutine will be responsible for moving the Enemy a little bit each frame, toward the destination. We need to save a reference to the Coroutine because at some point we'll need to stop it, and to do that we need a reference.

// 5

The RigidBody2D and Animator attached to the GameObject.

// 6

We use `targetTransform` when the Enemy is pursuing the Player. The script will retrieve the transform from the PlayerObject and assign it to `targetTransform`.

// 7

The destination where the Enemy is wandering.

// 8

When choosing a new direction to wander, a new angle is added to the existing angle. That angle is used to generate a vector, which becomes the destination.

Build Out Start()

Now that we have all the variables we'll need for the moment, let's build the Start() method.

```
    void Start()
    {
// 1
        animator = GetComponent<Animator>();
```

```
// 2
        currentSpeed = wanderSpeed;
// 3
        rb2d = GetComponent<Rigidbody2D>();
// 4
        StartCoroutine(WanderRoutine());
    }
// 1
```

Grab and cache the Animator component attached to the current GameObject.

```
// 2
```

Set the current speed to wanderSpeed. The Enemy starts off wandering at a leisurely pace.

```
// 3
```

We'll need a reference to the Rigidbody2D to actually move the enemy. Store a reference instead of retrieving it every time we need it.

```
// 4
```

Start the WanderRoutine() Coroutine, the entry point into the Wander algorithm. We'll write WanderRoutine() next.

The Wander Coroutine

The WanderRoutine() Coroutine contains all of the high-level logic from the Wander Algorithm described in Figure 8-1 seen earlier in this chapter, aside from the pursuit logic. We'll still need to write some of the methods called from within WanderRoutine() but this Coroutine is the brains of the Wander Algorithm.

```
// 1
public IEnumerator WanderRoutine()
{
// 2
    while (true)
    {
// 3
        ChooseNewEndpoint();

//4
        if (moveCoroutine != null)
        {
// 5
            StopCoroutine(moveCoroutine);
        }
// 6
        moveCoroutine = StartCoroutine(Move(rb2d,
        currentSpeed));

// 7
        yield return new WaitForSeconds(directionChangeInterval);
    }
}
```

// 1

This method is a Coroutine because it'll doubtlessly run over multiple frames.

// 2

We want the Enemy to wander indefinitely, so we'll use while(true) to loop through the steps indefinitely.

// 3

The ChooseNewEndpoint() method does exactly what it sounds like. It chooses a new endpoint but doesn't start the Enemy moving toward it. We'll write this method next.

// 4

Check if the Enemy is already moving by checking if moveCoroutine is null or has a value. If it has a value then the Enemy may be moving, so we'll need to stop it first before moving in a new direction.

// 5

Stop the currently running movement Coroutine.

// 6

Start the Move() Coroutine and save a reference to it in moveCoroutine. The Move() Coroutine is responsible for actually moving the Enemy. We'll write it shortly.

// 7

Yield execution of the Coroutine for directionChangeInterval seconds, then start the loop over again and choose a new endpoint.

Choosing a New Endpoint

We've written out the starting point and the Wander Coroutine, so it's time to start filling in the methods called by the WanderCoroutine(). The ChooseNewEndpoint() method is responsible for choosing a new endpoint at random for the Enemy to travel to.

```
// 1
void ChooseNewEndpoint()
{
// 2
    currentAngle += Random.Range(0, 360);
// 3
    currentAngle = Mathf.Repeat(currentAngle, 360);
// 4
    endPosition += Vector3FromAngle(currentAngle);
}
```

// 1

Make this method private by omitting the access modifier, because it'll only be needed inside the Wander class.

// 2

Choose a random value between 0 and 360 to represent a new direction to travel toward. This direction is represented as an angle, in degrees. We add it to the current angle.

// 3

The method Mathf.Repeat(currentAngle, 360) will loop the value: currentAngle so that it's never smaller than 0, and never bigger than 360. We're effectively keeping the new angle in the range of degrees: 0 to 360, then replacing the currentAngle with the result.

// 4

Call a method to convert an Angle to a Vector3 and add the result to the endPosition. The variable endPosition will be used by the Move() Coroutine, as we'll soon see.

Angles to Radians to Vectors!

This method takes an angle parameter in degrees, converts it to radians, and returns a directional Vector3 used by the ChooseNewEndpoint().

```
Vector3 Vector3FromAngle(float inputAngleDegrees)
{
// 1
    float inputAngleRadians = inputAngleDegrees * Mathf.Deg2Rad;
// 2
    return new Vector3(Mathf.Cos(inputAngleRadians),
    Mathf.Sin(inputAngleRadians), 0);
}
```

// 1

Convert the input angle from degrees to radians by multiplying by the degrees-to-radians conversion constant. Unity provides this constant so we can do quick conversions.

// 2

Use the input angle in radians to create a normalized directional vector for the enemy direction.

Enemy Walk Animation

Up until this point, the Enemy only had one animation: idle. It's time to utilize the Enemy walking animation clip we created way back in Chapter 3.

Select the Enemy prefab then open the Animation window as seen in Figure 8-3.

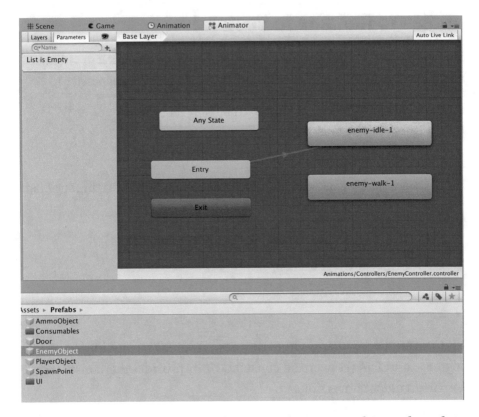

Figure 8-3. *The Animator window with the EnemyObject selected*

If the Idle state is the default state, it will be colored Orange. If it isn't the default state, right-click on the "enemy-idle-1" state and select: Set as Layer Default State.

As you can see, the enemy-walk-1 state exists, with an animation clip, but isn't being used at the moment. The plan is to create an Animation Parameter and use that parameter to switch between the idle and walking state.

Click on the plus-symbol in the Parameters section of the Animator and select Bool, as seen in Figure 8-4.

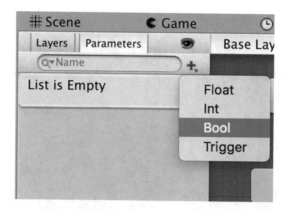

Figure 8-4. *Select Bool to create an Animation Parameter of type: Bool*

Name this parameter: "isWalking", as seen in Figure 8-5.

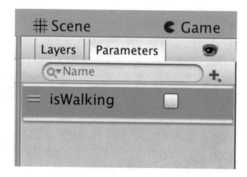

Figure 8-5. *Create the isWalking Bool parameter*

Our Wander script will use this parameter to switch the Enemy's animation state between idle and walking. To keep things simple, the walking animation will serve as a stand-in for running, when in pursuit of the Player, as well as leisurely walking.

Right-click on enemy-idle-1 state and select: Make Transition. Create a transition between the idle state and the walking state. Then create another transition between the walking state and the idle state. When you're done, the Animator State window should look like Figure 8-6.

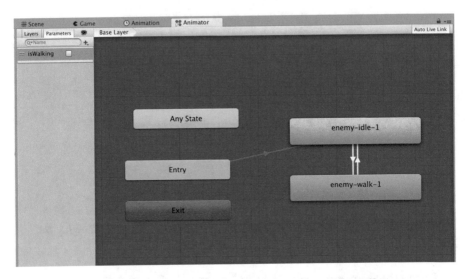

Figure 8-6. *Create transitions between the idle and walk states*

Click on the transition state going from enemy-idle-1 to enemy-walk-1, and use the following settings, as seen in Figure 8-7.

Has Exit Time	☐
▼ Settings	
Exit Time	0.4
Fixed Duration	☐
Transition Duration	0
Transition Offset	0
Interruption Source	Current State Then Next State ⬍
Ordered Interruptio	☑

Figure 8-7. *Transition settings*

Click on the transition from enemy-walk-1 to enemy-idle-1 and configure it using the same settings from Figure 8-7 as well.

Set up each transition to use the Animation Parameter: isWalking, that we just created. Set the condition: isWalking to true, in the transition from enemy-idle-1 to enemy-walk-1 as seen in Figure 8-8.

Figure 8-8. *If isWalking == true, this condition is met*

Set isWalking to false, in the enemy-walk-1 to enemy-idle-1 transition.

That's it! The Enemy walking animation is set up. To use the new animation state, we just need to change isWalking to true, in our Move() Coroutine, as you'll soon see.

Press Apply in the Inspector to apply these changes to all the Enemy prefabs.

The Move() Coroutine

The Move() Coroutine is responsible for moving a RigidBody2D at a given speed from its current location to the endPosition variable.

Add the following method to the Wander script.

```
public IEnumerator Move(Rigidbody2D rigidBodyToMove, float
speed)
{

// 1

    float remainingDistance = (transform.position -
    endPosition).sqrMagnitude;

// 2

    while (remainingDistance > float.Epsilon)
    {
```

```
// 3
        if (targetTransform != null)
        {
            endPosition = targetTransform.position;
        }
// 4
        if (rigidBodyToMove != null)
        {
// 5
            animator.SetBool("isWalking", true);
// 6
            Vector3 newPosition = Vector3.
            MoveTowards(rigidBodyToMove.position, endPosition,
            speed * Time.deltaTime);
// 7
            rb2d.MovePosition(newPosition);
// 8
            remainingDistance = (transform.position -
            endPosition).sqrMagnitude;
        }
// 9
        yield return new WaitForFixedUpdate();
    }
// 10
    animator.SetBool("isWalking", false);
}
```

`// 1`

The equation: (`transform.position - endPosition`) results in a
Vector3. We use a property called: `sqrMagnitude`, which is available on the
Vector3 type, to retrieve the rough distance remaining between the current
position of the Enemy and the destination. Using the `sqrMagnitude`
property is a Unity-provided approach to performing quick Vector
magnitude calculations.

`// 2`

Check that the remaining distance between the current location
and the endPosition is greater than `float.Epsilon,` which is effectively
equivalent to zero.

`// 3`

When the Enemy is in pursuit of the Player, the value `targetTransform`
will be set to the Players transform instead of null. We then overwrite
the original value of the `endPosition` to use `targetTransform` instead.
When the Enemy moves, it will move toward the Player, instead of toward
the original `endPosition`. Because the `targetTransform` is actually the
Player's transform, it will be constantly updated with the Players new
position. This allows the Enemy to dynamically follow the Player.

`// 4`

The `Move()` method requires a `RigidBody2D` and uses it to move
the Enemy. Before we go any further, ensure that we actually have a
`RigidBody2D` to move.

`// 5`

Set the Animation Parameter: `isWalking`, of type `Bool`, to `true`. This
will initiate the state transition to the walking state and play the Enemy
walking animation.

293

// 6

The Vector3.MoveTowards method is used to calculate the movement for a RigidBody2D. It doesn't actually move the RigidBody2D. The method takes three parameters: a current position, an end position, and the distance to move in the frame. Remember that the variable: speed will change, depending on whether the Enemy is in pursuit or leisurely wandering around the Scene. That value will be changed in the pursuit code, which we haven't written yet.

// 7

Use MovePosition() to move the RigidBody2D to the newPosition, calculated in the previous line.

// 8

Use the sqrMagnitude property to update the distance remaining.

// 9

Yield execution until the next Fixed Frame update.

// 10

The Enemy has reached endPosition and waiting for a new direction to be selected, so change the Animation State to idle.

Save this script and switch back to the Unity Editor.

Configure Wander Script

Select the Enemy prefab and configure the Wander script to look like Figure 8-9. Set the Pursuit Speed to a slightly faster speed than the Wander Speed. The Direction Change Interval is how often the Wander Algorithm will call ChooseNewEndpoint() to choose a new direction to wander in.

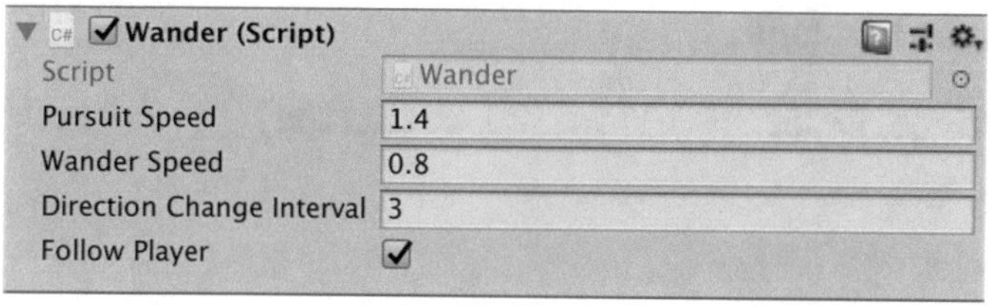

Figure 8-9. *Use these settings in the Wander script*

Press Apply in the Inspector then delete the EnemyObject out of the Hierarchy view.

Now press play. Notice how the enemy wanders around the scene. If the Player walks up close to an enemy they won't pursue her yet. We're going to add the Pursuit logic next.

OnTriggerEnter2D()

So we've implemented nearly all of the Wander algorithm except for the Pursuit logic. In this section we'll write some simple logic to plug into the Wander algorithm to make the Enemy pursue the Player.

The Pursuit logic hinges on the OnTriggerEnter2D() method, which is provided with every MonoBehaviour. As we learned in Chapter 5, Trigger Colliders (colliders with the Is Trigger property set) can be used to detect that another GameObject has entered the collider. When this occurs, the OnTriggerEnter2D() method is called on the MonoBehaviours involved in the collision.

When the Player enters the CircleCollider2D attached to the Enemy, the Enemy can "see" the Player and should pursue her.

Let's write that logic.

```
void OnTriggerEnter2D(Collider2D collision)
{
// 1
    if (collision.gameObject.CompareTag("Player") &&
    followPlayer)
    {
// 2
        currentSpeed = pursuitSpeed;

// 3
        targetTransform = collision.gameObject.transform;

// 4
        if (moveCoroutine != null)
        {
            StopCoroutine(moveCoroutine);
        }

// 5
        moveCoroutine = StartCoroutine(Move(rb2d,
        currentSpeed));
    }
}
```

// 1

Check the tag on the object in the collision to see if it's the PlayerObject. Also check that followPlayer is current true. This variable is set via the Unity Editor and used to turn on and off the pursuit behavior.

// 2

At this point, we've determined that the collision is with the Player, so change the currentSpeed to the pursuitSpeed.

// 3

Set `targetTransform` equal to the Player's transform. The `Move()` coroutine will check if `targetTransform` is not null, and then use it as the new value of endPosition. This is how the Enemy continuously pursues the Player instead of wandering aimlessly.

// 4

If the Enemy is currently moving, the `moveCoroutine` will not be null. It needs to be stopped before started again.

// 5

Because `endPosition` is now set to the PlayerObject's transform, calling `Move()` will move the Enemy toward the player.

OnTriggerExit2D()

Provided the Enemy `pursuitSpeed` is less than the Player `movementSpeed`, the Player can outrun any Enemy. As the Player runs away from the Enemy, she will exit the Enemy Trigger Collider, causing the `OnTriggerExit2D()` to be called. When this occurs, the Enemy effectively loses sight of the Player and resumes wandering aimlessly.

This method is nearly identical to `OnTriggerEnter2D()` with just a few tweaks.

```
void OnTriggerExit2D(Collider2D collision)
{
// 1
    if (collision.gameObject.CompareTag("Player"))
    {
// 2
        animator.SetBool("isWalking", false);
```

```
// 3
    currentSpeed = wanderSpeed;

// 4
    if (moveCoroutine != null)
    {
        StopCoroutine(moveCoroutine);
    }

// 5
    targetTransform = null;
    }
}
```

// 1

Check the tag to see if the Player is leaving the collider.

// 2

The Enemy is confused after losing sight of the Player and pauses for a moment. Set isWalking to false, to change the animation to idle.

// 3

Set the currentSpeed to the wanderSpeed, to be used the next time the Enemy starts moving.

// 4

Because we want the Enemy to stop pursuing the Player, we need to stop the moveCoroutine.

// 5

The Enemy is no longer following the Player, so set the targetTransform to null.

Save this script and flip back to Unity Editor. Press Play.

Move the Player into sight of the Enemy and notice how the Enemy will pursue her until she runs out of sight.

Gizmos

Unity supports the creation of visual debugging and setup tools called Gizmos. These tools are created via a set of methods and only appear in the Unity Editor. They won't appear in your game when it's compiled and running on a user's hardware.

We're going to create two Gizmos to aid in visually debugging the Wander algorithm. The first Gizmo we'll create will show a wire outline of the Circle Collider 2D, used to detect when the Player is within sight of the Enemy. This Gizmo will make it easier to see when the pursuit behavior is supposed to begin.

Add the following variable toward the top of the Wander class, where we have the other variables:

```
CircleCollider2D circleCollider;
```

Then add the following line to Start(). It can be placed anywhere within the method:

```
circleCollider = GetComponent<CircleCollider2D>();
```

This line retrieves the CircleCollider2D component of the current Enemy object. We'll use it to draw a circle on-screen to visually represent the current circle collider.

To implement the Gizmo, implement the method provided by MonoBehaviour called OnDrawGizmos():

```
void OnDrawGizmos()
{
// 1
    if (circleCollider != null)
    {
```

```
// 2
      Gizmos.DrawWireSphere(transform.position,
      circleCollider.radius);
   }
}
// 1
```

Be sure that we have a reference to the Circle Collider before we try to use it.

```
// 2
```

Call `Gizmos.DrawWireSphere()` and provide a position and a radius for it, to draw a sphere.

Save the script and flip back to the Unity Editor. Be sure the Gizmos button is pressed, and then press Play. Notice the Enemy Gizmo surrounding the Enemy as it wanders about, as seen in Figure 8-10. The circumference and position of this Gizmo corresponds to the `CircleCollider2D`.

Figure 8-10. *A Gizmo representing the* `CircleCollider2D` *surrounding the Enemy*

If you don't see the Circle Gizmo appear, make sure you have Gizmos enabled in the upper-right corner of the Game window, as seen in Figure 8-11.

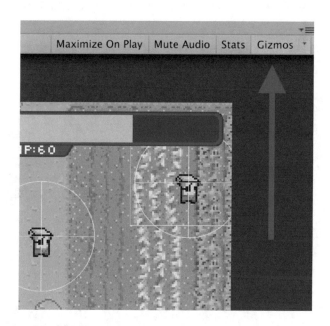

Figure 8-11. *Enable Gizmos*

It would be easier to see how the Wander algorithm moves an Enemy toward a location if we had a line showing an Enemy's destination. Let's draw a line on-screen from the current Enemy position to the end position.

We'll use the Update() method so the line is draw with every frame.

```
void Update()
{
// 1
    Debug.DrawLine(rb2d.position, endPosition, Color.red);
}
```

```
// 1
```

The result of the method Debug.DrawLine() is visible when Gizmos are enabled. The method takes a current position, an end position, and a line color.

As we can see in Figure 8-12, a red line is drawn from the center of the Enemy to the destination (endPosition).

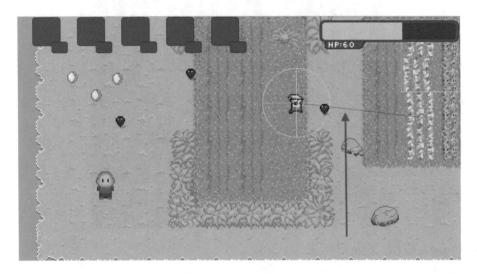

Figure 8-12.   *A red line is drawn from the Enemy position to the end point*

Self-Defense

Our brave player will be armed with nothing more than her wits to guide her and a slingshot for defense. Each press of the mouse button will have our player fire off a single round of slingshot ammo toward the location of the mouse click. We'll script the behavior of the ammo so that as it flies through the air, it travels along an arc toward the target instead of a straight line.

Classes Needed

We'll need a combination of three different classes to give the player the ability to defend herself.

The **Weapon** class will encapsulate the slingshot functionality. This class will be attached to the Player prefab and will be responsible for a few different things:

- Determining when the mouse button is pressed and using the location of the button press as the target

- Switching from the current animation to the firing animation

- Creating ammunition and moving it toward the target

We'll need a class to represent the ammunition fired from the slingshot. This **Ammo** class will be responsible for:

- Determining when the attached Ammo GameObject collides with an Enemy

- Keeping track of how much damage it causes when it collides with an Enemy

We'll also build an **Arc** class responsible for moving the Ammo GameObject in an exaggerated arc from the starting position to the end position. Otherwise the ammo would travel in a straight line.

Ammo Class

At the moment, we want the Ammo in our game to only damage Enemies, but you could just as easily extend the functionality in the future to damage other things as well. Each AmmoObject will expose a property in the Unity Editor describing the amount of damage it causes. We'll turn the AmmoObject into a prefab. If you ever wanted to provide the player with two different types of Ammo, it's a simple task to create a second Ammo prefab, change the Sprite on it and the damage done.

Create a new GameObject in the Project hierarchy and rename it, "AmmoObject". We're going to create the AmmoObject, configure it, write the script, and then turn it into a prefab.

Import the Assets

From the assets you've downloaded to accompany this book, drag the spritesheet titled, "Ammo.png" into the Assets ➤ Sprites ➤ Objects folder.

Select the Ammo spritesheet and use the following import settings in the Inspector:

Texture Type: Sprite (2D and UI)

Sprite Mode: Single

Pixels Per Unit: 32

Filter Mode: Point (no filter)

Be sure the Default button is selected at the bottom and set Compression to: None

Press the Apply button.

The Unity Editor will automatically detect the sprite boundaries, so there's no need to open the Sprite Editor or slice the sprite.

Add Components, Set Layers

Add a Sprite Renderer component to AmmoObject.

On the Sprite Renderer, set the Sorting Layer to: Characters, and set the Sprite property to: Ammo. Ammo is the sprite we just imported.

Add a CircleCollider2D to the AmmoObject. Be sure the "Is Trigger" setting is checked and set the Radius to 0.2. If you need to adjust the

Collider, click the Edit Collider button and move the handles until you're satisfied that the collider surrounds the Ammo sprite.

Create a new Layer called, "Ammo" and use it to set the Layer on AmmoObject as seen in Figure 8-13.

Figure 8-13. *Set the Layer to: Ammo*

Update the Layer Collision Matrix

If you recall back in Chapter 5, we learned about Layer-Based Collision Detection. To summarize, two colliders in different Layers will only interact if the Layer Collision Matrix is configured so that they're aware of each other.

Go to the Edit Menu ➤ Project Settings ➤ Physics 2D and configure the Layer Collision Matrix to look like Figure 8-14.

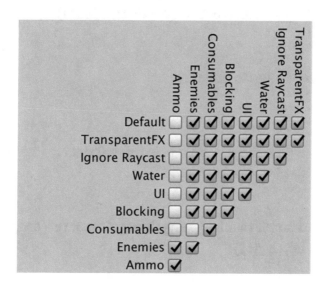

Figure 8-14. *Configure the Ammo Layer*

We want to allow an Ammo collider to interact with an Enemy collider, but not interact with any other colliders. Back in Chapter 5, we configured Enemies to use the Enemies Layer, and we've configured AmmoObject to use the Ammo Layer.

Build the Ammo Script

Add a new Script to AmmoObject called, "Ammo". Open the Ammo script in Visual Studio.

Use the following code to build out the Ammo class.

```
using UnityEngine;

public class Ammo : MonoBehaviour
{

// 1
    public int damageInflicted;

// 2
    void OnTriggerEnter2D(Collider2D collision)
    {
// 3
if (collision is BoxCollider2D)
        {

// 4
            Enemy enemy = collision.gameObject.
            GetComponent<Enemy>();

// 5
            StartCoroutine(enemy.DamageCharacter(damageInflict
            ed, 0.0f));
```

```
// 6
        gameObject.SetActive(false);
    }

  }
}
```

// 1

The amount of damage the ammunition will inflict on an Enemy.

// 2

Called when another object enters the Trigger Collider attached to the Ammo GameObject. A Trigger Collider is simply a Collider with the: Is Trigger property set. In this case, it's a `CircleCollider2D`.

// 3

It's important to check if we hit the `BoxCollider2D` inside the enemy. Remember that the Enemy also has a `CircleCollider2D` that is used in the Wander script to detect if the Player is nearby. The `BoxCollider2D` is the collider we use to detect objects that actually collide with the Enemy.

// 4

Retrieve the Enemy script component of the `gameObject` from the collision.

// 5

Start the Coroutine to damage the Enemy. If you recall from Chapter 7, the method signature for `DamageCharacter()` looks like this:

```
DamageCharacter(int damage, float interval)
```

The first parameter: damage, is the amount of damage to inflict on the Enemy. The second parameter: `interval`, is the time to wait between inflicting damage. Passing `interval = 0` will inflict damage a single time.

We pass the variable damageInflicted, an instance variable on the Ammo class that will be set via the Unity Editor, as the first parameter.

// 6

Because the ammo has struck the Enemy, set the gameObject of the AmmoObject to be inactive.

Why are we are setting the gameObject to be inactive instead of calling Destroy(gameObject) and getting rid of it altogether?

Good question—glad you asked. We're setting AmmoObject to be inactive so we can use a technique called **Object Pooling** to maintain good performance in our game.

Before We Forget ... Make the AmmoObject Prefab

One last thing before we get into Object Pooling—let's turn the AmmoObject into a prefab. Follow the same process we've always used to create prefabs out of GameObjects:

1. Drag AmmoObject from the Hierarchy view into the prefabs folder to create a prefab.

2. Delete the original AmmoObject from the Hierarchy View.

Object Pooling

If your game has a large number of objects being instantiated then destroyed in a short amount of time, you might see pauses in gameplay, slowdowns, and overall poor performance. This is because Instantiating and Destroying objects in Unity is more performance intensive than simply activating and deactivating objects. Destroying an object will invoke

Unity's internal memory cleanup process. Invoking this process repeatedly in short succession, especially in memory constrained environments such as mobile devices or the web, can affect performance. These effects on performance won't show up with a small number of objects, but if your game involves spawning a large number of enemies or bullets, you'll want to consider a more optimized approach.

To avoid the performance issues associated with object creation and destruction, we'll use an optimization technique called Object Pooling. To use Object Pooling, pre-instantiate multiple copies of an object for the Scene ahead of time, de-activate them, and add them to an object pool. When the Scene requires an object, loop through the object pool and return the first inactive object found. When the Scene is finished using the object, place it inactive, and return it to the object pool to be re-used by the Scene in the future.

Simply put, Object Pooling reuses objects, minimizing performance degradation due to runtime memory allocation and cleanup. Objects will initially be set to inactive, and only activated when used. When the scene is done using an object, the object is set inactive once again, signaling that it can be re-used when needed.

By clicking the mouse button repeatedly, the slingshot weapon will fire multiple rounds in quick succession. This is a textbook scenario where object pooling would improve runtime performance.

The following are the three key steps in using Object Pooling in Unity:

- Pre-instantiate a collection (a "pool") of objects ahead of time before they're needed and set them inactive

- When gameplay needs an object, instead of instantiating a new object, grab an inactive object from the pool and activate it

- When finished using the object, simply place it inactive to return it to the pool

Building the Weapon Class

We're going to create and store the Ammo object pool inside the Weapon class. As described earlier, this class will encompass the slingshot functionality as well as eventually control the animations showing the Player firing the slingshot.

We'll start off building the basic slingshot functionality by creating the Object Pool to hold Ammo.

Select the PlayerObject prefab and add a new script called, "Weapon". Open this script in Visual Studio. Use the following code to begin building the Weapon class.

```
// 1
using System.Collections.Generic;
using UnityEngine;

// 2
public class Weapon : MonoBehaviour
{

// 3
    public GameObject ammoPrefab;

// 4
    static List<GameObject> ammoPool;

// 5
    public int poolSize;

// 6
    void Awake()
    {
```

// 7

```
        if (ammoPool == null)
        {
            ammoPool = new List<GameObject>();
        }
```

// 8

```
        for (int i = 0; i < poolSize; i++)
        {
            GameObject ammoObject = Instantiate(ammoPrefab);
            ammoObject.SetActive(false);
            ammoPool.Add(ammoObject);
        }
    }
}
```

// 1

We'll need to import System.Collections.Generic so we can use the List data structure. A variable of type: List, will be used to represent the object pool—the collection of pre-instantiated objects.

// 2

Weapon inherits from MonoBehaviour and thus can be attached to a GameObject.

// 3

The property ammoPrefab will be set via the Unity Editor and used to instantiate copies of the AmmoObject. These copies will be added to a pool of objects in the Awake() method.

// 4

The property ammoPool of type: List is used to represent the object pool.

A List in C# is an ordered collection of strongly typed objects. Because they're strongly typed, you must declare ahead of time what type of object the List will hold. Attempting to insert any other type of object will result in an error when compiling, and your game will not run. This List is declared to hold only GameObjects.

The variable ammoPool is a static variable. If you recall from Chapter 7, static variables belong to the class itself, and only one copy exists in memory.

// 5

The poolSize property allows us to set the number of objects to be pre-instantiated in the object pool. Because this property is public, it can be set and easily tweaked via the Unity Editor.

// 6

The code to create the Object Pool and pre-initialize the AmmoObjects will be contained in the Awake() method. Awake() is called one time in the lifetime of a script: when the script is being loaded.

// 7

Check to see if the ammoPool object pool has been initialized already. If it has not been initialized, create a new ammoPool of type: List to hold GameObjects.

// 8

Create a loop using poolSize as the upper limit. On each iteration of the loop, instantiate a new copy of ammoPrefab, set it to be inactive, and add it to the ammoPool.

The Object Pool (ammoPool) has been created and is ready for use in a Scene. As you'll soon see, whenever the Player uses her slingshot to fire ammo, we'll grab an inactive AmmoObject from ammoPool and activate it. When the Scene is done using the AmmoObject, it's deactivated and returned to ammoPool.

Stubbing-Out Methods

Method stubs are substitutes for code that hasn't been developed yet.
They also can be helpful for figuring out the required methods for specific
functionality. Let's stub-out the various methods we'll need for the rest of
the basic weapon functionality.

Add the following code to the Weapon class.

```
// 1
    void Update()
    {

// 2
        if (Input.GetMouseButtonDown(0))
        {

// 3
            FireAmmo();
        }
    }

// 4
    GameObject SpawnAmmo(Vector3 location)
    {
        // Blank, for now...
    }

// 5
    void FireAmmo()
    {
        // Blank, for now...
    }
```

```
// 6
    void OnDestroy()
    {
        ammoPool = null;
    }
```

// 1

Inside the Update() method, check every frame to see if the user has clicked the mouse to fire the slingshot.

// 2

The GetMouseButtonDown() method is part of the Input class and takes a single parameter. This method will check if the left mouse button has been clicked and released. The method parameter, 0, indicates that we are interested in the first (left) mouse button. If we were interested in the right mouse button, we would pass the value: 1 instead.

// 3

Because the left mouse button has been clicked, call the FireAmmo() method, which we're about to write.

// 4

The SpawnAmmo() method will be responsible for retrieving and returning an AmmoObject from the object pool. The method takes a single parameter: location, indicating where to actually place the retrieved AmmoObject. SpawnAmmo() returns a GameObject—the activated AmmoObject retrieved from the ammoPool Object Pool.

// 5

FireAmmo() will be responsible for moving the AmmoObject from the starting location where it was spawned in SpawnAmmo(), to the end-position where the mouse button was clicked.

// 6

Set the `ammoPool` = `null` to destroy the Object Pool and free up memory. The `OnDestroy()` method comes with `MonoBehaviour` and will be called when the attached `GameObject` is destroyed.

The SpawnAmmo Method

The SpawnAmmo method will loop through the collection or "pool" of pre-instantiated AmmoObjects and find the first inactive object. It will then activate the AmmoObject, set the `transform.position`, then return the AmmoObject. If no inactive AmmoObjects exist, it returns `null`. Because the ammo pool was initialized with a set number of AmmoObjects, there is an inherent limit on the number of AmmoObjects that can be on-screen at once. This limitation can be tweaked via changing the `poolSize` in the Unity Editor.

Tip   The best way to figure out the ideal number of Objects to pre-instantiate in the Object Pool is by playing your game a lot, then tweaking the number accordingly.

Let's implement the SpawnAmmo() method in the Weapon class.

```
public GameObject SpawnAmmo(Vector3 location)
{
```
// 1
```
    foreach (GameObject ammo in ammoPool)
    {
```
// 2
```
        if (ammo.activeSelf == false)
        {
```

315

// 3

```
                ammo.SetActive(true);
```

// 4

```
                ammo.transform.position = location;
```

// 5

```
                return ammo;
            }
        }
```

// 6

```
        return null;
    }
```

// 1

Loop through the pool of pre-instantiated objects.

// 2

Check if the current object is inactive.

// 3

We've found an inactive object, so set it to be active.

// 4

Set the transform.position on the object to the parameter: location. When we call SpawnAmmo(), we'll pass a location to make it appear as though the AmmoObject was fired from the slingshot.

// 5

Return the active object.

// 6

No inactive object was found, so all objects from the pool are currently being used. Return null.

The Arc Class and Linear Interpolation

The Arc script will be responsible for actually moving the AmmoObject.
We want the ammunition to travel in an arc toward the target. We'll create
a new MonoBehaviour called, "Arc" to contain this functionality. Because
we're creating Arc as a separate MonoBehaviour, we can attach this script
to other GameObjects in the future to make them travel in an arc as well.

To keep things simple, we'll implement the Arc script to travel in a
straight line at first. After we have things working, we'll add a small tweak
to make the Ammo travel in a nice-looking arc.

Select the AmmoObject prefab in the Project view and add a new
script called: "Arc" to it. Open the Arc script in Visual Studio and write the
following code:

```
using System.Collections;
using UnityEngine;

// 1
public class Arc : MonoBehaviour
{
// 2
    public IEnumerator TravelArc(Vector3 destination, float
    duration)
    {
// 3
        var startPosition = transform.position;
// 4
        var percentComplete = 0.0f;
// 5
        while (percentComplete < 1.0f)
        {
```

```
// 6
            percentComplete += Time.deltaTime / duration;

// 7
            transform.position = Vector3.Lerp(startPosition,
            destination, percentComplete);

// 8
            yield return null;
        }
// 9
        gameObject.SetActive(false);
    }
}
```

// 1

Because Arc is a MonoBehaviour, it can be attached to GameObjects.

// 2

TravelArc() is the method that will move the gameObject along an arc. It makes sense to design TravelArc() as a Coroutine because it will execute over the course of several frames. TravelArc() takes two parameters: destination and duration. The definitions are as follows: destination is the end position and duration is the desired amount of time to move the attached gameObject from the starting position to destination.

// 3

Grab the current gameObject's transform.position and assign it to startPosition. We will use startPosition in the position calculation.

// 4

The percentComplete is used in the Lerp, or Linear Interpolation, calculation used later in this method. We'll explain its usage then.

`// 5`

Check that the `percentComplete` is less than 1.0. Think of 1.0 as the decimal form of 100%. We only want this loop to run until `percentComplete` is 100%. This will make sense when we explain Linear Interpolation in the next line.

`// 6`

We want to move the AmmoObject smoothly toward its destination. The distance the Ammo will travel each frame is dependent on the duration we want the movement to take place over, and the time already elapsed.

The amount of time elapsed since the last frame, divided by the total desired duration of the movement, equals a percentage of the total duration.

Take a look at this line again: `percentComplete += Time.deltaTime / duration;`

`Time.deltaTime` is the amount of time elapsed since the last frame was drawn. The result in that line: `percentageComplete`, is what we get when we add the percentage of total duration, to the previous percentage complete, to get the total percentage of the duration that has been completed thus far.

We'll use this total percentage complete in the next line to move the AmmoObject smoothly.

`// 7`

To achieve the effect where the AmmoObject appears to move smoothly between two points at a constant speed, we use a widely used technique in game programming called **Linear Interpolation**. Linear Interpolation requires a starting position, an end position, and a percentage. When we use Linear Interpolation to determine the distance to travel per frame, the percentage parameter of the Linear

Interpolation method: `Lerp()`, is the percentage of duration completed (`percentComplete`).

Using the duration `percentComplete` in the `Lerp()` method means that no matter where we fire the AmmoObject, it will take the same amount of time to get there. This is obviously unrealistic for a real-world simulation but for a video game we can suspend the real-world rules.

The `Lerp()` method will return a point between the start and end, based on this percentage. We assign the result to the `transform.position` of the AmmoObject.

`// 8`

Pause execution of the Coroutine until the next frame.

`// 9`

If the arc has reached its destination, deactivate the attached `gameObject`.

Don't forget to save this script!

Screen Points and World Points

Before we write the next method, we should talk about Screen Points and World Points.

Screen Space is the space that is actually visible on-screen and is defined in pixels. For example, our Screen Space is currently 1280 × 720 or 1280 pixels horizontally by 720 pixels vertically.

World Space is the actual game world and has no limitations in terms of size. Its size is theoretically infinite and defined in units. We configured the camera to map world units to screen units when we set the PPU in Chapter 4.

When we move objects around our game, because they can move anywhere and aren't limited to only moving on screen, we move them with respect to World Space. Unity provides some handy methods to convert from Screen to World Space.

The FireAmmo Method

Now that we've built out the Arc component to move the AmmoObject, switch back to the Weapon class and let's implement the FireAmmo() method using the following code.

First, add the following variable to the top of the Weapon class, after the poolSize variable. This variable will be used to set the velocity of the ammo fired from the slingshot:

```
public float weaponVelocity;
```

Then use the following code to implement the FireAmmo() method:

```
void FireAmmo()
{
```

// 1

```
    Vector3 mousePosition = Camera.main.
    ScreenToWorldPoint(Input.mousePosition);
```

// 2

```
    GameObject ammo = SpawnAmmo(transform.position);
```

// 3

```
    if (ammo != null)
    {
```

// 4

```
        Arc arcScript = ammo.GetComponent<Arc>();
```

// 5

```
        float travelDuration = 1.0f / weaponVelocity;
```

```
// 6
            StartCoroutine(arcScript.TravelArc(mousePosition,
            travelDuration));
        }
    }
```

// 1

Because the mouse uses Screen Space, we convert the mouse position from Screen Space to World Space.

// 2

Retrieve an activated AmmoObject from the Ammo Object Pool via the SpawnAmmo() method. Pass the current weapon's transform.position as the starting position for the retrieved AmmoObject.

// 3

Check to make sure SpawnAmmo() returned an AmmoObject. Remember, it's possible that SpawnAmmo() returns null if all the pre-instantiated objects are already in use.

// 4

Retrieve a reference to the Arc component of the AmmoObject and save it to the variable arcScript.

// 5

The value weaponVelocity will be set in the Unity Editor. Dividing 1.0 by weaponVelocity results in a fraction that we'll use as the travel duration for an AmmoObject. For example, 1.0 / 2.0 = 0.5, so the Ammo will take half a second to travel across the screen to its destination.

This formula results in speeding up the velocity of ammunition when the destination is further away. Imagine a scenario where the Player was firing at something close-by. If we didn't ensure that the travel time always took 0.5 seconds regardless of distance to travel, it's possible that the ammo would fire from the slingshot to the enemy so quickly that you really wouldn't see it. If we were making a first-person shooter, that might be ok. But in our RPG, we'd like to visibly see the ammo fired from the slingshot at all times. It simply seems more "fun" this way.

// 6

Call the TravelArc method we wrote earlier on arcScript. Recall the method signature: TravelArc(Vector3 destination, float duration). For the destination parameter, pass the location of the mouse-click. For the duration parameter, pass travelDuration that we calculated in the previous line:

```
float travelDuration = 1.0f / weaponVelocity;
```

Recall that duration parameter in TravelArc() is used to determine how long it will take for the AmmoObject to travel from the starting location to the destination. We're going to set the value of weaponVelocity when we configure the Weapon Script in the next step.

Configure the Weapon Script

We're nearly done! Just a few more things to tidy up before the player can use the slingshot. Save the Weapon script, switch to the Unity Editor, and select the PlayerObject. Because we've already added the Weapon script to the PlayerObject, drag the AmmoObject prefab into the Ammo Prefab property on the Weapon script. Set the Pool Size to 7, and the Weapon Velocity to 2 as seen in Figure 8-15.

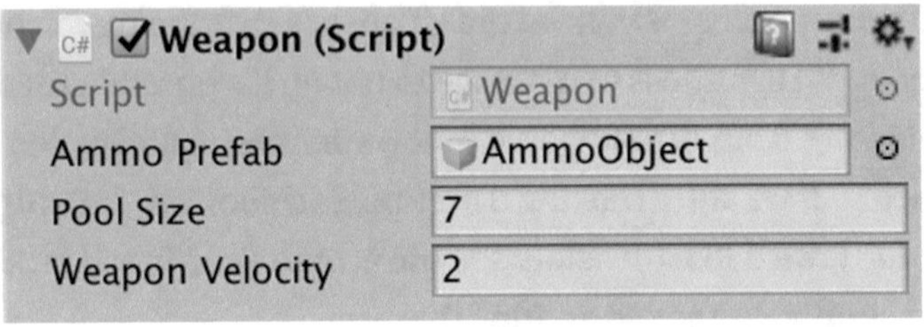

Figure 8-15. *Configure the Weapon script*

We've chosen to use 0.5 for the Weapon Velocity because it feels like a natural amount of time for a slingshot bullet to travel. Feel free to tweak this value to something that seems natural and fun to you.

We're ready to go. Press Play and click on an Enemy to fire the slingshot and rain down pixelated death.

Fantastic! The slingshot fires ammo, but it doesn't travel in an arc. Let's fix that.

Arcing

Switch back to the Arc script in Visual Studio. We're going to tweak the script a bit to make the Arc script live up to its name and actually travel in an arc trajectory.

Revise the while() loop in the Arc script to resemble the following:

```
while (percentComplete < 1.0f)
{
        // Leave this existing line alone.
        percentComplete += Time.deltaTime / duration;

// 1
        var currentHeight = Mathf.Sin(Mathf.PI *
        percentComplete);
```

// 2

```
    transform.position = Vector3.Lerp(startPosition,
    destination, percentComplete) + Vector3.up *
    currentHeight;

            // Leave these existing lines alone.
    percentComplete += Time.deltaTime / duration;
    yield return null;
}
```

// 1

To understand what's happening here, we'll need a tiny bit of high-school trigonometry. The "period" of a wave is the time it takes to complete one complete cycle. The period of a sine wave is (2 * π), and half the period of a sine wave is just (π) as per Figure 8-16.

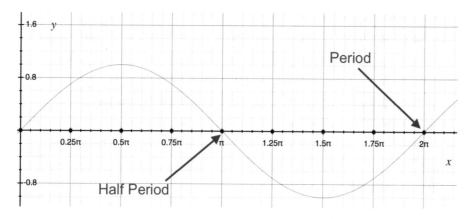

Figure 8-16. *The sine curve*

By passing the result of (percentComplete × Mathf.PI) to the sine function, we are effectively traveling PI distance down the sine curve every duration second. The result is assigned to currentHeight.

`// 2`

Vector3.up is a Unity-provided variable representing Vector3(0, 1, 0). Adding `Vector3.up * currentHeight` to the result of `Vector3.Lerp()` adjusts the position so that instead of traveling in a straight line, the AmmoObject moves up then down along the Y axis toward the `endPosition`.

Save the script, return to the Unity Editor, and press Play. Fire the slingshot and notice how it travels in an arc.

You'll notice that we're not actually playing any type of firing animation as the Player shoots her slingshot. We'll fix that in the next section.

Animating the Slingshot

We've created a weapon and written the code to fire it, but the Player looks a bit odd because she just stands there as the ammo mysteriously materializes and goes flying at the target. In this section, we're going to build functionality to play the animations of the player firing the slingshot. You'll also learn a new approach to simplifying the animation state management.

To keep things simple, we'll start by applying this new state management approach to the walking animations because we're already familiar with how that state machine works, and how the animations should look. Once we're comfortable with the new approach, we'll apply it to firing the slingshot.

Animation and Blend Trees

Back in Chapter 3 we set up an Animation State Machine for the Player consisting of animation states containing animation clips. These states were connected by transitions, which we controlled by setting animation parameters on the Animator component.

The state machine for the player currently resembles Figure 8-17.

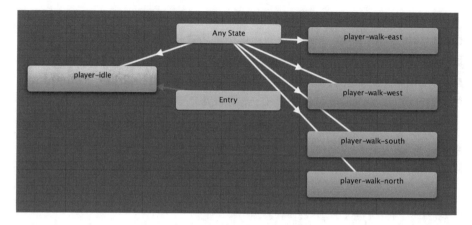

Figure 8-17. *The Player Animation State Machine*

Because the player can walk in four different directions, it stands to reason that she can fire the slingshot in four different directions as well. If we added another four animations states for the four firing directions, this state machine would start to look rather crowded. If we eventually wanted to add even more states to the state machine, things would quickly become difficult to manage, visually confusing, and slow down development overall.

Fortunately, Unity provides us with a solution—enter: Blend Trees.

Blend Trees

Game programming frequently requires blending between two animations, such as when a character is walking, then gradually begins to run. Blend Trees can be used to smoothly blend multiple animations into one smooth animation. Although we won't be blending multiple animations in our game, Blend Trees also have a secondary use that we'll be using.

When used as part of an Animation State Machine, Blend Trees can be used to **transition** smoothly from one animation state to another. The Blend Tree can bundle together various animations into a single node, making your game architecture cleaner and more manageable. A Blend Tree is controlled by variables that are configured in the Unity Editor and set in code.

We're going to create two Blend Trees. As we're already familiar with the walking animation state machine, the first Blend Tree we create will be used to re-create the walking states. We'll also update the Player's MovementController code to use this Blend Tree. Rebuilding something familiar will be a good way to get comfortable with Blend Trees.

Once we have the walking Blend Tree working, we'll add the four firing states as their own Firing Blend Tree and update the Weapon class to use the Firing Blend Tree.

Clean Up the Animator

It's time to say goodbye to the old way of managing animation state. With the PlayerObject selected, open the Animator view. Delete the four original player walking states from the Animation State Machine. Remove the transition between Any State and Idle State, as we won't need that anymore either.

When you're done, the Animator view should look like Figure 8-18.

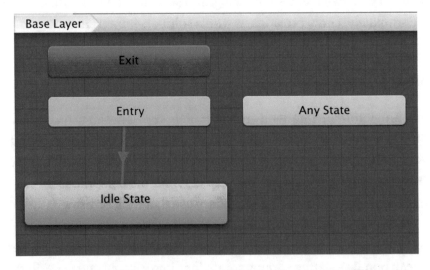

Figure 8-18.   *The Animator view with the old player walking states removed*

We're going to create a Blend Tree node that will act as a sort of container for the various walking animation states within it. The Blend Tree node containing all four walking animations will appear as a single node in the Animator view. As you can imagine, this approach makes it much easier for the developer to visualize and manage the states as their number grows.

Build the Walking Blend Tree

1. Right-click in the Animator window and select: Create State ➤ from New Blend Tree.

2. Select the created **Blend Node** and change its name in the Inspector to: "Walk Tree".

3. Double-click the Walk Tree node to view the Blend Tree Graph.

The Blend Tree should look like Figure 8-19.

Figure 8-19. *An empty Blend Tree Graph*

4. Select the Blend Tree node and change the **Blend Type** in the Inspector to: 2D Simple Diectional. We'll talk more about Blend Types after we finish configuring the Blend Tree.

5. Select the Blend Tree node, right-click, and select:
Add Motion. A **Motion** holds a reference to an
animation clip and corresponding input parameters.
When we use a Blend Tree for Transitions, the input
parameters are used to determine what motion
should be played.

6. In the Inspector, click the dot (Figure 8-20) next to
the Motion we just added to open the Select Motion
selector.

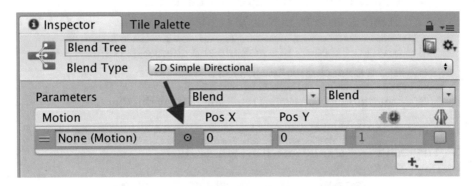

Figure 8-20.   *Click the dot to open the Select Motion selector*

7. With the Select Motion selector open, select the
player-walk-east animation clip. The Motion should
now look like Figure 8-21.

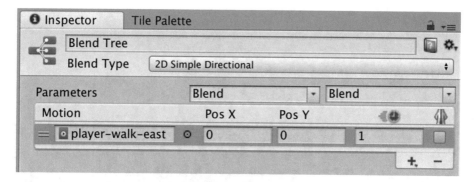

Figure 8-21. Use the player-walk-east animation clip in the Motion

8. Add three more motions and add the following
    animation clips: player-walk-south, player-walk-
    west, and player-walk-north, as seen in Figure 8-22.

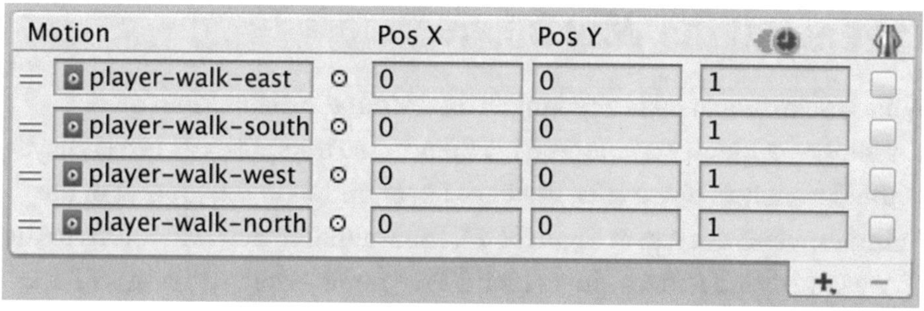

Motion		Pos X	Pos Y		
= ▣ player-walk-east	⊙	0	0	1	☐
= ▣ player-walk-south	⊙	0	0	1	☐
= ▣ player-walk-west	⊙	0	0	1	☐
= ▣ player-walk-north	⊙	0	0	1	☐

Figure 8-22. Four Motions with four animation clips in the Blend
Tree

The Animator window should look like Figure 8-23 when all four
motions have been added. Each motion appears as a child node of the
Blend Tree node.

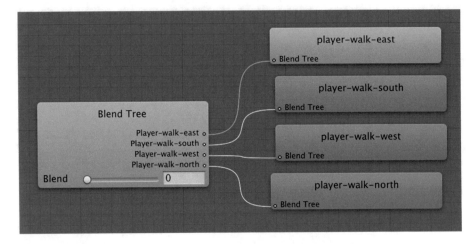

Figure 8-23. *Blend Tree with four Motion nodes, containing animation clips*

Layers, All the Way Down

What we've done here is wrap up all four animation states into a container—a Blend Tree node. This Blend Tree node sits inside a sublayer of the Base Layer. If you click the Base Layer button in the top-left of the Animator view, as seen in Figure 8-24, the Animator view will return to the "Base Layer" and show a single Blend Tree node. When working with the Animator, you can nest layers inside layers inside layers, if it serves your architecture.

Figure 8-24. *Click the Base Layer button to go back to the base Animator view*

As we can see in Figure 8-25, this simplified approach to managing state will keep your game architecture clean and manageable in the future. The Walk Blend Tree is a single node in the Animator.

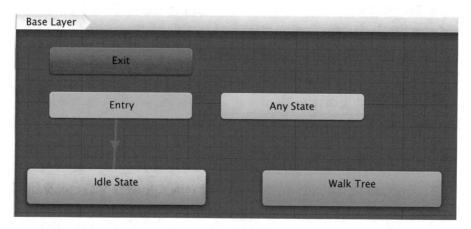

Figure 8-25. *The Base Layer in the Animator with a single Blend Tree (Walk Tree) node*

A Note About Blend Types

Blend Types are used to describe how the Blend Tree should blend motions. As you know, we're not actually blending motions so the term *Blend Type* is a bit misleading. We're transitioning between them, so we've configured the Blend Tree to use the 2D Simple Directional Blend. This blend type takes two parameters, and works best with animations that represent *different* directions, such as walk north, walk south, and so forth. Because we're using the Blend Tree to transition between walking north, south, east, and west, the 2D Simple Directional Blend is perfect for our use case.

Animation Parameters

We've worked with Animation Parameters in the past, when we first configured the Animation State Machine for the Player and created the "AnimationState" parameter.

Delete the AnimationState parameter on the left of the Animator window. We've already deleted the animation transitions that depend on it. We're going to replace this parameter and the associated states with a Blend Tree and its own parameters. These parameters will be used in the code we'll write in the Weapon class.

Create these three Animation Parameters. Capitalization matters, because we'll be referring to these in code:

- isWalking of type: Bool

- xDir of type: Float

- yDir of type: Float

The parameter: Blend was created when the Animator was created. Feel free to delete that parameter, as we won't be needing it.

The Animation Parameters section of the Animator should look like Figure 8-26.

Figure 8-26. *New animation parameters for the walking blend tree*

Tip   When creating Animation Parameters, a common source of error is to create them with the wrong data type.

Use the Parameters

With the Blend Tree selected, select the xDir and yDir parameters from the dropdown in the Inspector as seen in Figure 8-27. We're about to use these two parameters in the next step.

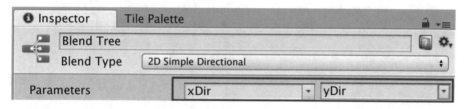

Figure 8-27. *Choose the parameters: xDir and yDir from the drop-down menu*

With the Blend Tree node selected, look at the Visualization Window in the Inspector, underneath the Parameters. The Visualization Window will automatically appear once you've added more than one motion to the Blend Tree.

Imagine a Cartesian coordinates plane with (0, 0) running through the center of the window (Figure 8-28). The four coordinates (1,0), (0, -1), (-1, 0), and (0, 1) can be mapped accordingly to the ends of the dotted lines in the following. The purpose of the Visualization Window is to help the developer visualize the configuration.

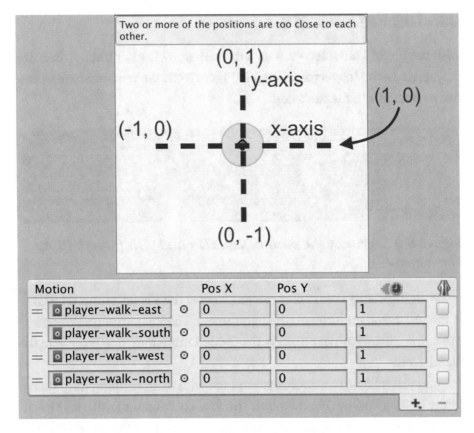

Figure 8-28. *Imagine a Cartesian coordinate plane*

In Figure 8-28, there are four blue dots clustered together at 0, 0 that you can't see because they're covered by the red center dot. Each one of those dots represents one of the four motions that we added earlier.

Set the Pos X and Pos Y for the first motion so that the blue dot representing the player-walk-east motion is located at Position: (1, 0), as seen in Figure 8-29.

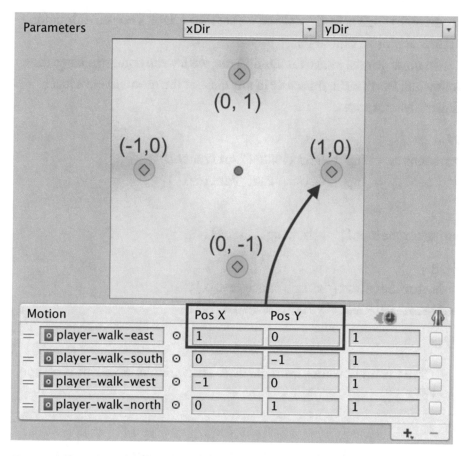

Figure 8-29. *Set the positions X and Y for all four motions*

We also want to set the X and Y positions for the other three motions accordingly. For example, the player-walk-south motion positions should be set to (0, -1). Set the positions for all four motions as seen in Figure 8-29.

Ok, but *Why*?

So we've set up the Blend Tree to use our animation parameters, and taken care to set the Pos X and Pos Y for each motion, but *what's it all for*?

As we mentioned at the beginning of this section, we can manage 2D state transitions in a Blend Tree by setting the variables on the animator component. This is just like when we set the variables on the Animation State Machine in Chapter 3.

In other words, to use the Blend Tree, we'll write code similar to the following. Don't write this code in any class at the moment—it's just for illustrative purposes.

```
// 1
movement.x = Input.GetAxisRaw("Horizontal");
movement.y = Input.GetAxisRaw("Vertical");
```

```
// 2
animator.SetBool("isWalking", true);
```

```
// 3
animator.SetFloat("xDir", movement.x);
animator.SetFloat("yDir", movement.y);
```

```
// 1
```

Grab the input values from the user. The variable: movement is of type: Vector2.

```
// 2
```

Set the Animation Parameter: isWalking, to signify the Player is walking. This will transition to the Walking Blend Tree.

```
// 3
```

Set the Animation Parameters used by the Blend Tree to transition into a specific Motion. These are of type: Float because the movement Vector2 contains Floats.

When the user presses to the right, the input values will be (0, 1). We set this on the Animator, and the Blend Tree plays the player-walk-right animation clip.

Loop Time

Select each one of the four child nodes of the blend tree and if it is not checked by default, check the Loop Time property as seen in Figure 8-30. This property tells the Animator to continuously loop the animation clip when in this state.

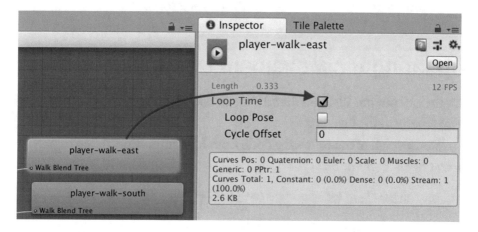

Figure 8-30. *Check the Loop Time property*

If we didn't check this box, the animation would play through once and then stop.

Create the Transitions

Last but not least, we need to create the transitions between the Idle state and the new Walking Blend Tree.

Right-click on the Idle State node in the Animator and select: Make Transition. Connect the transition to the Walking Blend Tree. Select the transition and use the following settings:

> Has Exit Time: unchecked
>
> Fixed Duration: unchecked
>
> Transition Duration: 0

Transition Offset: 0

Interruption Source: None

Create a Condition using the isWalking variable we created. Set it to: true.
Create another transition between the Walking Blend Tree and the
Idle state. Select the transition and use the same settings as earlier, except
when you create the isWalking condition, set it to: false.

Updating the Movement Controller

It's time to put the Walking Blend Tree to use. Open the
MovementController class.

Remove all of the following code from MovementController, as we
won't need it anymore:

```
string animationState = "AnimationState";
```

And also remove the entire CharStates enum:

```
enum CharStates
{
    walkEast = 1,
    walkSouth = 2,
 // etc
}
```

Replace the existing UpdateState() method with:

```
void UpdateState()
{
// 1
    if (Mathf.Approximately(movement.x, 0) && Mathf.
    Approximately(movement.y, 0))
    {
```

```
// 2
        animator.SetBool("isWalking", false);
    }
    else
    {
// 3
        animator.SetBool("isWalking", true);
    }
// 4
    animator.SetFloat("xDir", movement.x);
    animator.SetFloat("yDir", movement.y);
}
```

// 1

Check if the movement vector is approximately equal to 0, indicating the player is standing still.

// 2

Because the player is standing still, set isWalking to false.

// 3

Otherwise movement.x, movement.y, or both, are non-zero numbers, which means the player is moving.

// 4

Update the animator with the new movement values.

Save this script and switch back to the Unity Editor. Press play and walk the Player around the scene. You've gotten rid of the old animation states and rebuilt the walking animations using a Blend Tree.

Import the Fight Sprites

The first step is to import the sprites used for the Player fight animations. Drag the spritesheet called, "PlayerFight32x32.png" into the Sprites ➤ Player folder.

Select the Player Fight spritesheet and use the following import settings in the Inspector:

> Texture Type: Sprite (2D and UI)
>
> Sprite Mode: Multiple
>
> Pixels Per Unit: 32
>
> Filter Mode: Point (no filter)
>
> Be sure the Default button is selected at the bottom and set Compression to: None

Press the Apply button, then open the Sprite Editor.

From the Slice menu, select Grid By Cell Size and set the Pixel Size to 32. Press Apply and close the Sprite Editor.

Create Animation Clips

The next step is to create the animation clips. In previous chapters, we created animation clips by selecting the sprites for each frame of the animation, then dragging them onto the GameObject. Unity would automatically create an animation clip and add an animation controller if one didn't already exist.

We're going to create animation clips a little differently this time because we'll be creating a Blend Tree to manage the animations.

Go to the Sprites ➤ Player folder and expand the spritesheet that we just sliced. Select the first four frames, as seen in Figure 8-31. These sprites correspond with the Player pulling back the slingshot and firing it.

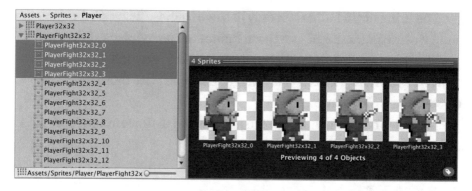

Figure 8-31. *Select the first four player fight sprites in the Project view*

Right-click and select Create ➤ Animation as seen in Figure 8-32.

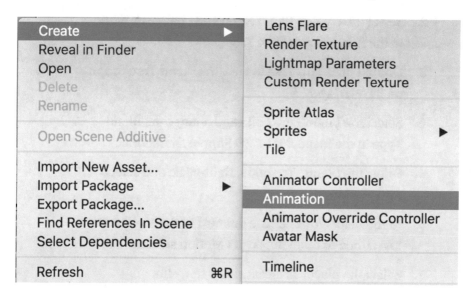

Figure 8-32. *Creating an animation manually*

Rename the created animation: "player-fire-east". Select the next four sprites and follow the same steps. Name the resulting animation: "player-fire-west".

The firing north animation only has two frames: "PlayerFight32x32_8" and "PlayerFight32x32_9". Use those frames to create "player-fire-north".

The firing south animation has three frames: "PlayerFight32x32_10", "PlayerFight32x32_11", and "PlayerFight32x32_12". Use those frames to create "player-fire-south".

Move all the animation clips we just created to the Animations ➤ Animations folder.

Build the Fighting Blend Tree

1. Right-click in the Animator window and select: Create State ➤ From New Blend Tree.

2. Select the created Blend Node and change its name in the Inspector to: "Fire Tree".

3. Double-click Fire Tree to view the Blend Tree Graph on its own layer.

4. Select the Blend Tree node and change the Blend Type in the Inspector to: 2D Simple Directional.

5. Select the Blend Tree node, right-click, and select: Add Motion.

6. In the Inspector, click the dot next to the Motion we just added to open the Select Motion selector.

7. Select the player-fire-east animation clip.

8. Add 3 more motions and add the animation clips for player-fire-south, player-fire-west, and player-fire-north.

9. Create the following Animation Parameters:
   isFiring (type: Bool), fireXDir (type: Float),
   fireYDir (type: Float), and delete the Blend
   parameter.

10. Configure the Blend Tree to use the Animation
    Parameters in the drop-down box, as seen in
    Figure 8-33.

Figure 8-33. *Configure the Animation Parameters*

11. Set Pos X and Pos Y for each Motion as seen in
    Figure 8-34.

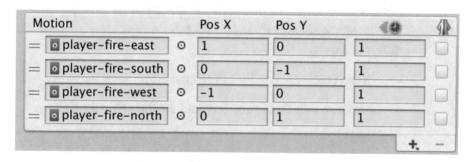

Figure 8-34. *Set Pos X and Pos Y for each Motion*

12. Do not check the loop time box in the Blend Tree
    child nodes. We want to play a firing animation only
    once.

13.   Create the transition between the Idle state and the new Fire Blend Tree. Select the transition and use the following settings:

— Has Exit Time: unchecked

— Fixed Duration: unchecked

— Transition Duration: 0

— Transition Offset: 0

— Interruption Source: None

Create a Condition in the transition using the isFiring variable we created. Set it to: true.

14.   Create another transition between the Fire Blend Tree and the Idle state. Select the transition and use the same settings as earlier, except for two differences:

— When you create the isFiring condition, set it to: false.

— Check the Exit Time property and set the value for Exit Time to: 1.

Exit Time

The Exit Time property on a transition is used to tell the animator after what percentage of the animation has played should the transition take effect. By setting the Exit Time property on the fire ➤ idle transition to: 1, we are saying we want 100% of the firing animation to play before transitioning.

Update the Weapon Class

The next step is to update the Weapon class to take advantage of the Fire Blend Tree we just built.

Add the `RequireComponent` attribute to the top of the Weapon class:

```
[RequireComponent(typeof(Animator))]
public class Weapon : MonoBehaviour
```

The code we're about to add requires an Animator component, so make sure there's always one available.

Add the Variables

We'll need a few additional variables to animate the player. Add the following variables to the top of the Weapon class.

```
// 1
bool isFiring;
```

```
// 2
[HideInInspector]
public Animator animator;
```

```
// 3
Camera localCamera;
```

```
// 4
float positiveSlope;
float negativeSlope;
```

```
// 5
enum Quadrant
{
    East,
    South,
    West,
    North
}
```

// 1

A bool to describe if the Player currently firing the slingshot.

// 2

Use the [HideInInspector] attribute along with the public accessor so the animator can be accessed from outside this class but won't show up in the Inspector. There's no reason to show animator in the Inspector because we plan to programmatically retrieve a reference to the Animator component.

// 3

Use localCamera to store a reference to the Camera so we don't have to retrieve it each time we need it.

// 4

Store the slope of the two lines used in the quadrant calculation we'll do later in this chapter.

// 5

An enum used to describe the direction the Player is firing in.

Start()

Add the Start() method, which we'll use to initialize and set variables that we'll need throughout the Weapon class.

```
void Start()
{
// 1
    animator = GetComponent<Animator>();
// 2
    isFiring = false;
// 3
    localCamera = Camera.main;
}
```

// 1

Optimize by grabbing a reference to the Animator component so we don't have to retrieve it every time we need it.

// 2

Set the isFiring variable to false to start with.

// 3

Grab and save a reference to the local Camera so we don't have to retrieve it each time it's needed.

Update Update()

Make two small changes to the Update() method as seen in the following:

```
void Update()
{
    if (Input.GetMouseButtonDown(0))
    {
// 1
        isFiring = true;
        FireAmmo();
    }
// 2
    UpdateState();
}
```

// 1

When the left mouse button has been pressed and lifted, set the isFiring variable to true. This variable will be checked inside the UpdateState() method.

// 2

The UpdateState() method will update the animation state every frame, regardless of whether the user has pressed the mouse button or not. We'll write this method shortly.

Determining Direction

To determine which animation clip to play, we need to determine the direction that the user clicked relative to the Player. It wouldn't look very good if the user clicked west of the player, only to play the animation firing the slingshot east.

To determine the direction the user clicked in, we will divide the screen into four quadrants: North, South, East, and West. We should think of all user clicks as being relative to the player, so these four quadrants are centered on the player as seen in Figure 8-35.

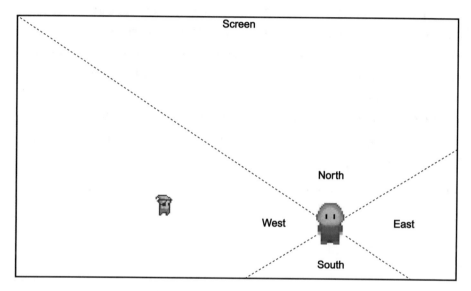

Figure 8-35. *Four quadrants based on the current player location*

We can check which quadrant the user clicked in to determine the direction the player fires the slingshot, and the proper animation clip to play.

Dividing the screen into quadrants based on the player location makes sense, but how do we actually programmatically determine which quadrant the user clicked in?

Think back to the slope-intercept form for a line from your high-school math days:

$$y = mx + b,$$

where:

m = slope (can be a positive slope or a negative slope)

x and y are the coordinates of a point

b = is the y-intercept, or the point where the line crosses the y-axis.

This form allows us to find any point along a line. As we saw in Figure 8-35, we've created two lines by dividing the screen into quadrants. If we think about the user clicking the mouse on any point in the screen, we can imagine another set of two lines emerging from that clicked point.

Here's the trick: we can determine what quadrant the user clicked in based on whether or not the positive sloped line from the mouse-click is above or below the player's positive sloped line. Likewise, we check if the negative sloped line from the mouse-click is above or below the player's negative sloped line.

Take a look at Figure 8-36 for help in visualizing this. Remember that lines slanting upward have a positive slope, and lines slanting downward have a negative slope.

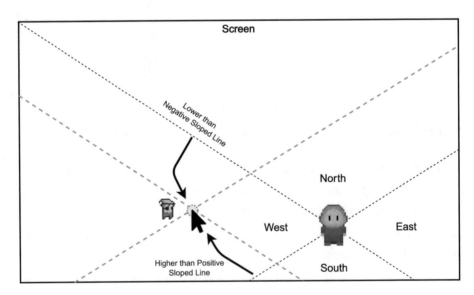

Figure 8-36. *Clicking in the west quadrant*

Two lines with equivalent slopes mean that the lines run parallel to each other.

To check if one line is above another line with an equivalent slope, we simply compare their y-intercepts. As seen in Figure 8-36, if the y-intercept of the mouse-click line is below the negative player line but above the positive player line, then the user clicked in the west quadrant.

There's a few things you should internalize about this approach. If the player were standing in the exact center of the screen, each line would go from corner to corner. As the player moves around the scene, the lines move with her. The visible size of the quadrants change, but the slopes of the two lines dividing the screen remain the same. The slope of each line remains constant because the screen size never changes—only her location changes.

When we write the code, we'll rearrange the slope-intercept form $y = mx + b$ to make it easier to compare the y-intercepts. Because we're comparing y-intercepts, we need to solve for b. So the rearranged form is: $b = y - mx$.

Let's continue writing the code.

The Slope Method

Given two points in a line, the standard equation for calculating the slope of a line is: $(y2 - y1) / (x2 - x1) = m$, where $m = $ slope.

Written out, that's: the second y-coordinate minus the first y-coordinate, divided by the second x-coordinate minus the first x-coordinate.

Add the following method to the Weapon class to calculate the slope of a line:

```
float GetSlope(Vector2 pointOne, Vector2 pointTwo)
{
    return (pointTwo.y - pointOne.y) / (pointTwo.x - pointOne.x);
}
```

Calculate the Slopes

Let's put the GetSlope() method to use. Add the following to the Start() method.

```
// 1
Vector2 lowerLeft = localCamera.ScreenToWorldPoint(new
Vector2(0, 0));
Vector2 upperRight = localCamera.ScreenToWorldPoint(new
Vector2(Screen.width, Screen.height));
Vector2 upperLeft = localCamera.ScreenToWorldPoint(new
Vector2(0, Screen.height));
Vector2 lowerRight = localCamera.ScreenToWorldPoint(new
Vector2(Screen.width, 0));

// 2
positiveSlope = GetSlope(lowerLeft, upperRight);
negativeSlope = GetSlope(upperLeft, lowerRight);
```

// 1

Create four Vectors to represent the four corners of the Screen. Unity Screen Coordinates (which are different from the GUI coordinates we used to create the Inventory and Health Bars) start with (0,0) in the lower-left.

We also convert each point from Screen to World Coordinates before assigning it. We do this because the slopes we're about to calculate will be used in relation to the Player. The Player moves around in World Space, which uses World Coordinates. As we described earlier in this chapter, the World Space is the actual game world, and has no limitations in terms of size.

// 2

Use the GetSlope() method to get the slope of each line. One line goes from the lower-left to the upper-right, and the other line goes from the upper-left to the lower-right. Because the screen size will remain the same, so too will the slope. We calculate the slope and save the result to a variable so we don't have to recalculate it each time we need it.

Comparing *y*-Intercepts

The HigherThanPositiveSlopeLine() method is where we calculate if the mouse-click is higher than the positive-sloped line running through the Player. Add the following to the Weapon class.

```
bool HigherThanPositiveSlopeLine(Vector2 inputPosition)
{
// 1
    Vector2 playerPosition = gameObject.transform.position;
// 2
    Vector2 mousePosition = localCamera.ScreenToWorldPoint(input
    Position);
// 3
    float yIntercept = playerPosition.y - (positiveSlope *
    playerPosition.x);
// 4
    float inputIntercept = mousePosition.y - (positiveSlope *
    mousePosition.x);
// 5
    return inputIntercept > yIntercept;
}
// 1
```

Save a reference to the current transform.position for clarity. This script is attached to the Player object, so this will be the Players position.

// 2

Convert the `inputPosition`, which is the mouse position, to World Space and save a reference.

// 3

Rearrange $y = mx + b$ a bit to solve for b. This will make it easy to compare the y-intercept of each line. The form on this line is: $b = y - mx$.

// 4

Using the rearranged form: $b = y - mx$, find the y-intercept for the positive sloped line created by the `inputPosition` (the mouse).

// 5

Compare the y-intercept of the mouse-click to the y-intercept of the line running through the player and return if the mouse-click was higher.

HigherThanNegativeSlopeLine()

The `HigherThanNegativeSlopeLine()` method is identical to `HigherThanPositiveSlopeLine()` except we compare the y-intercept of the mouse-click to the negative-sloped line running through the Player. Add the following to the Weapon class.

```
bool HigherThanNegativeSlopeLine(Vector2 inputPosition)
{
    Vector2 playerPosition = gameObject.transform.position;
    Vector2 mousePosition = localCamera.ScreenToWorldPoint(inpu
    tPosition);

    float yIntercept = playerPosition.y - (negativeSlope *
    playerPosition.x);
```

```
float inputIntercept = mousePosition.y - (negativeSlope *
mousePosition.x);

return inputIntercept > yIntercept;
}
```

We'll forgo the explanation of the HigherThanNegativeSlopeLine()
method because it's nearly identical to the previous method.

The GetQuadrant() method

The GetQuadrant() method is responsible for determining which
of the four quadrants the user has tapped in and returning a
Quadrant. It utilizes the HigherThanPositiveSlopeLine() and
HigherThanNegativeSlopeLine() methods that we wrote earlier.

```
// 1
Quadrant GetQuadrant()
{
// 2
    Vector2 mousePosition = Input.mousePosition;
    Vector2 playerPosition = transform.position;
// 3
    bool higherThanPositiveSlopeLine = HigherThanPositiveSlopeL
    ine(Input.mousePosition);

    bool higherThanNegativeSlopeLine = HigherThanNegativeSlopeL
    ine(Input.mousePosition);
// 4
    if (!higherThanPositiveSlopeLine &&
    higherThanNegativeSlopeLine)
    {
```

```
// 5
        return Quadrant.East;
    }
    else if (!higherThanPositiveSlopeLine &&
    !higherThanNegativeSlopeLine)
    {
        return Quadrant.South;
    }
    else if (higherThanPositiveSlopeLine &&
    !higherThanNegativeSlopeLine)
    {
        return Quadrant.West;
    }
    else
    {
        return Quadrant.North;
    }
}
```

`// 1`

Return a Quadrant describing where the user clicked.

`// 2`

Grab references to where the user clicked and the current player position.

`// 3`

Check if the user clicked above (higher than) the positive sloped and negative sloped lines.

// 4

If the user's click is not higher than the positive sloped line, but is higher than the negative sloped line, the user clicked in the east quadrant. If this doesn't quite make sense yet, refer back to Figure 8-36.

// 5

Return the Quadrant.East enum.

The rest of the if-statements check the remaining three quadrants and return their respective Quadrant values.

The UpdateState() Method

The UpdateState() method checks if the Player is firing, checks which quadrant the user clicked in, and updates the Animator so the Blend Tree can show the correct animation clip.

```
void UpdateState()
{
// 1
    if (isFiring)
    {
// 2
        Vector2 quadrantVector;
// 3
        Quadrant quadEnum = GetQuadrant();
// 4
        switch (quadEnum)
        {
```

// 5

```
            case Quadrant.East:
                quadrantVector = new Vector2(1.0f, 0.0f);
                break;
            case Quadrant.South:
                quadrantVector = new Vector2(0.0f, -1.0f);
                break;
            case Quadrant.West:
                quadrantVector = new Vector2(-1.0f, 1.0f);
                break;
            case Quadrant.North:
                quadrantVector = new Vector2(0.0f, 1.0f);
                break;
            default:
                quadrantVector = new Vector2(0.0f, 0.0f);
                break;
        }
```

// 6

```
        animator.SetBool("isFiring", true);
```

// 7

```
        animator.SetFloat("fireXDir", quadrantVector.x);
        animator.SetFloat("fireYDir", quadrantVector.y);
```

// 8

```
        isFiring = false;
    }
    else
    {
```

// 9

```
        animator.SetBool("isFiring", false);
    }
}
```

// 1

Inside the Update() method, we check if the user clicked the mouse button. If so, the isFiring variable is set equal to true.

// 2

Create a Vector2 to save the values that we'll pass to the Blend Tree.

// 3

Call GetQuadrant() to determine which quadrant the user clicked in and assign the result to quadEnum.

// 4

Switch on the quadrant (quadEnum).

// 5

If the quadEnum is East, assign the quadrantVector the values (1, 0) in a new Vector2.

// 6

Set the isFiring parameter inside the animator to true, so it transitions to the Fire Blend Tree.

// 7

Set the fireXDir and fireYDir variables in the animator, to the corresponding value for the quadrant the user clicked in. These variables will be picked up by the Fire Blend Tree.

// 8

Set isFiring back to false. The animation will play all the way through before stopping, because we set Exit Time in the transition to 1.

// 9

If isFiring is false, set the isFiring parameter inside the animator to false as well.

Save the Weapon script and return to the Unity Editor.

Press the Play button and click the mouse in various places around the scene to fire the slingshot. Notice how the Player animation shows her firing the slingshot in a specific direction, then returning to the idle state.

Flicker When Damaged

When a character is damaged in a video game, it's helpful to have a visual effect signifying that they've been damaged. To add a bit of polish to our game, let's create an effect to tint any character red for just a moment, perhaps one-tenth of a second, to show that they've been injured. This flickering effect will take place over several frames so it makes sense to implement as a Coroutine.

Open the Character class and add the following code to the bottom:

```
public virtual IEnumerator FlickerCharacter()
{
// 1
    GetComponent<SpriteRenderer>().color = Color.red;

// 2
    yield return new WaitForSeconds(0.1f);
```

```
// 3
    GetComponent<SpriteRenderer>().color = Color.white;
}
```

// 1

Assigning Color.red to the SpriteRenderer component will tint the sprite red.

// 2

Yield execution for 0.1 seconds.

// 3

By default, the SpriteRenderer uses a tint color of white. Change the SpriteRenderer tint back to the default color.

Update the Player and Enemy Classes

Open the Player and Enemy class and update the DamageCharacter() method in each class to look like the following. When updating DamageCharacter(), be sure to add the StartCoroutine call to the top of the while() loop.

```
public override IEnumerator DamageCharacter(int damage, float
interval)
{
    while (true)
    {
```

```
// 1
        StartCoroutine(FlickerCharacter());

        //... Pre-existing code
// 1
```

Start the `FlickerCharacter()` Coroutine to tint momentarily tint the Character red.

That's it! Press Play and fire the slingshot at an Enemy. It should flash red momentarily when hit. If an Enemy manages to catch up to the Player and damage her, she'll flicker red as well.

Building for Platforms

In this section, we're going to learn how to compile your game to run on several platforms outside of the Unity Editor.

Go to File ➤ Build Settings in the Menu Bar. You should be presented with a screen that looks like Figure 8-37.

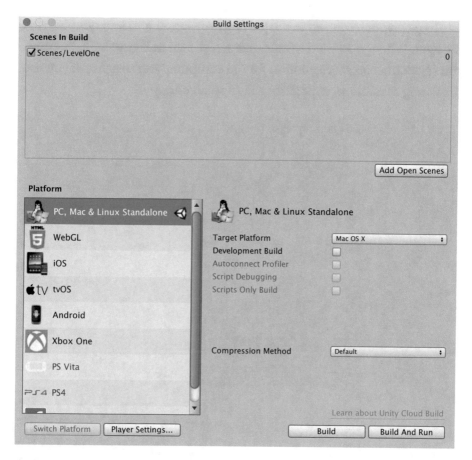

Figure 8-37. *The Build Settings screen*

The Build Settings screen allows you to choose a target Platform, adjust a few settings, choose which Scenes to include in the build, and then create the build. If your game consists of multiple scenes, click the Add Open Scenes button to add them.

We'll select Mac OS X but if you're working on a PC, that should already be selected.

Press the Build button. Choose a name for the binary and a location to save it, then press the Save button. Unity will create the build and let you know when it's successful.

To play your game, go to the location you saved it in and double-click the icon. When presented with the screen shown in Figure 8-38, be sure you select the correct resolution for the computer you're using. If you use the wrong resolution, your game may appear choppy.

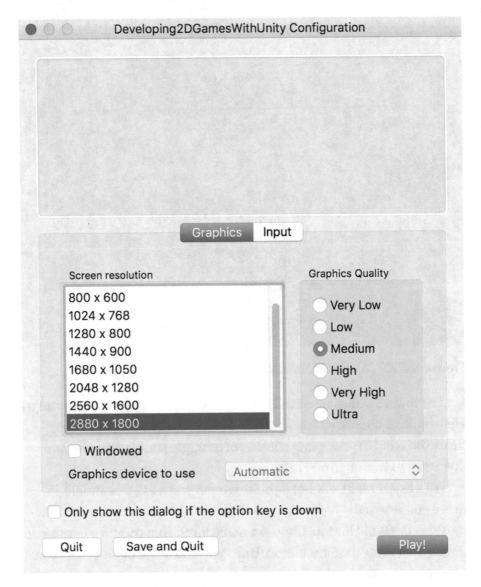

Figure 8-38. *Select the resolution for your computer*

This screen also allows the user to select the graphics quality, which is important if they have an older machine.

Press the Play! button to play your game!

Exiting the Game

All good things must come to an end, and at some point, the user will want to quit your game. In this section, we'll learn how to build functionality that allows the user to press the Escape key to exit your game.

This game-ending functionality will not work when playing the game inside the Unity Editor—it's only meant for when you've built your game to run outside the editor.

Open the RPGGameManager class and add the following:

```
void Update()
{
    if (Input.GetKey("escape"))
    {
        Application.Quit();
    }
}
```

The Update() method will check with every frame to see if the user has pressed the escape key. If so, quit the application.

Summary

Whew—we've covered a lot in this chapter. You've used Coroutines to build intelligent chasing behavior and in doing so, constructed the first real challenge for the gamer. The player can die now and needs to be able to defend herself, so we built a slingshot that fires ammunition at the Enemies. The slingshot utilizes a widely used optimization technique called Object Pooling. We took advantage of some high-school level trigonometry for the trajectory arc. We learned about Blend Trees and how they can help us to better organize our game architecture and streamline the state machine if we want to add additional animations in the future. We also learned how simple it is to build our game for the PC or Mac and run it outside of Unity.

You probably have some ideas about how to change around and improve your game. The great thing is: you now have the skills to do so! Experiment, break things, tinker with the scripts, read the documentation, and examine other people's code to learn from it. The only limitations to what you can build is how much effort you're willing to put into it.

What's Next

You may be wondering what's next—how do you advance your game development knowledge and build better games. A great place to start is by engaging with the game developer community.

Communities

No one is born an expert at anything. The key to becoming a better developer is learning from more experienced developers. You never want to be the best developer in the room. And if you are, make sure the other developers are great as well so you can learn from them.

Meetup.com is a great place to find monthly game developer gatherings. Meetup also has listings for the Official Unity User Group Meetups. It's possible that your city has a Unity Meetup and you didn't know about it. There are Official Unity Users Groups all over the world. If there isn't a local Unity Meetup in your city or town, consider starting one!

Discord is a voice and text chat application designed specifically for gamers. It's also a great place to virtually meet developers as well. Discord communities can answer questions as well as provide helpful interactions with the community. Sometimes game developers will create their own Discord server dedicated to their game, where they gather feedback, gather bug reports, and distribute early builds.

Any discussion of community would be remiss without mentioning Twitter. Twitter can be helpful for getting the word out and marketing your game as well as connecting with other Unity developers.

Reddit maintains two active sub-reddits of use to game developers: */r/ unity2d* and */r/gamedev*. These sub-reddits can be a great place to post demos of your work and gather feedback, as well as engage in discussion with other passionate game developers. The */r/gamedev* sub-reddit also has its own Discord server.

Learn More

Unity hosts a wide range of frequently updated educational content on their site at: `https://unity3d.com/learn/`. The content ranges from absolute beginner to advanced, so you should definitely check it out.

This website: `https://80.lv`, has great articles on a wide variety of subjects that are of interest to game developers. Some articles are Unity-specific while others are more generic techniques.

YouTube also can be helpful for learning new techniques, though the quality of content can vary widely. Many talks from past Unity conferences can be easily found on YouTube.

Where to Find Help

Everyone at some point will run into a problem that no matter what, they just can't seem to solve. For that situation, there are several important resources to know about.

Unity Answers (`https://answers.unity.com`) is a helpful resource, structured for questions and answers (Q&A) instead of extended discussions. For example, a question might be titled: "Trouble debugging this movement script."

The Unity Forums (`https://forum.unity.com`) are active message-boards frequented by Unity employees and other game developers. The Forums are designed for discussions around topics rather than straight-up Q&A interactions. You'll find plenty of helpful "What are some techniques for optimizing this" discussions, with more back and forth than you'd find in Unity Answers.

Last but not least, `https://gamedev.stackexchange.com` is part of the Stack Exchange network of Q&A websites. It's not as busy as the Unity sites, but absolutely worth your time if you run into an issue.

Game Jams

Game Jams are hackathons for building video games. They usually have a time constraint such as 48 hours, which is meant to put pressure on participants to focus on only what is necessary in a game as well as encourage creativity. Game jams need all types of participants: artists, programmers, game designers, sound designers, and writers. Sometimes game jams have a specific theme, which is usually kept secret ahead of time.

Game jams can be a fantastic way to meet local (or remote) game developers, push yourself, expand your knowledge, and walk away with (hopefully) a finished game. The Global Game Jam (`https://globalgamejam.org`) is a yearly global game jam with various sites around the world and hundreds of participants. Ludum Dare (`https://ldjam.com`) is a weekend-long game jam that runs every four months. Both of these game jams are great to participate in if you want to see and make some amazing games. Another good place to find online game jams is itch.io/jams.

News and Articles

Gamasutra.com is the standard bearer as far as game news, jobs, and industry happenings. Another good site is indiegamesplus.com with news, reviews, and interviews with indie game developers.

Games and Assets

As we mentioned way back in Chapter 1, the Unity Asset Store contains thousands of free and paid game assets, as well as scripts, textures, and shaders. The common criticism that you should be aware of with regards to the Asset Store is that games made strictly with assets from the store tend to look "same-y."

Itch.io is a widely known community for publishing indie games as well as assets. You can upload games you've made, play other indie games for free, or support other developers by purchasing their games. Itch.io is also a great place to buy art or sound assets for your game. Gamejolt.com is similar to itch.io, but focuses entirely on indie games, and doesn't have assets.

OpenGameArt.org has a tremendous amount of user-posted game art that is available under a variety of licenses.

Beyond!

If you've stuck with me this long, then you have the tenacity to read through a several hundred page programming book. This tenacity will serve you well in game programming, because although there are plenty of examples and books out there teaching the fundamentals of game programming, the really unique and fun games often involve elements for which there is no tutorial. Building interesting and fun games can be very difficult, but there are few other creative ventures as rewarding. The most important thing to remember about getting better at game programming is to **keep making games!** Game development is just like any other discipline—if you keep practicing, one day you'll look back to where you started and amaze yourself.

Index

A

AAA game development studios, 8

Ammo class
- Ammo layer, configuration, 305
- AmmoObject, 308
- import assets, 304
- layer collision matrix (*see*
  Layer-based collision
  detection)
- script, build, 306–307
- Sprite Renderer
  component, 304–305

Animation
- Can Transition to Self, 82
- clips, creation, 342–344
- components, 46, 47
- conditions, 82
- creation, 46
- dragging sprites,
  PlayerObjects, 45
- Exit Time, 82, 346
- Fixed Duration, 82
- Has Exit Time, 82
- parameter, 78, 288
  - AnimationState, 80
  - animator window, 79
  - CharStates, 86
  - condition, settings, 82

- hard-coding, 86
- inspector window, 88
- MovementController.cs
  script, 82–85
- names and types,
  displaying, 89
- SetInteger() method, 87
- transition, configuration, 81
- trigger state changes, 82
- SetInteger() method, 87
- state objects, 75
  - player-idle, default, 76
  - transition, creation, 77–78
  - window organization, 76
- transition duration, 82

Animation Controller, 46, 48–49

Animator State Machine
- Any state, 50, 77
- controller, 49
- Entry state, 50
- Layer Default State, 76
- Make Transition, 77
- speed, changing, 53
- window, 49

Anisotropic filtering, 106

Anti-aliasing, 106

Arcing, 324–326

Awake() method, 312

B

Bethesda Game Studios, 8
Blend trees
    animation
        parameters, 333–334, 338
    animator view, 328
    base layer, 332–333
    build, walking blend tree, 329
    coding, 338
    creation, 328
    2D state transitions, 337
    loop time property, 339
    MovementController class
        (*see* Movement Controller)
    parameters, 335–337
    player-walk-right
        animation clip, 338
    transitions, creation, 327, 339–340
    types, 333
    walking animation states, 329
Blend types, 333
Blizzard Entertainment, 8
Boolean stackable property, 160

C

C#, 10, 17, 66
    abstract keyword, 145, 261, 270
    base keyword, 269
    casting, 88
    comments, 67
    const keyword, 219
    enumerated constants, 86
    internal access modifier, 258
    List, data structure, 312
    namespaces, 68
    override keyword, 264, 270
    using keyword, 68
Camera manager
    character class design, 256
    property, 254
    RPGCameraManager
        class, 251–253, 255
    virtual keyword, 256
Canvas, 175
    Canvas Scaler, 177
    Pixel Perfect, 207
    Reference Pixels Per Unit, 177
    Render Mode, 176
    UI Scale Mode, 177, 207
Character class, 144–145, 271
ChooseNewEndpoint() method, 285
    angles to radians, 287
    directional vector, 287
    enemy walk animation, 287
    Gizmos, 299–302
    Move() Coroutine, 291, 293–294
    OnTriggerEnter2D(), 295–297
    OnTriggerExit2D(), 297–298
    Wander script, 294–295
Cinemachine
    Adam Myhill, 110
    installation
        component, 113
        unity 2017, 111–112
        unity 2018, 112–113
    virtual camera (*see* Virtual
        camera)

Circle collider 2D, 148–149
Colliders, 54–55, 106, 130–132,
    151, 153–155
Communities, 368–369
Composite collider, 134–136
Console view, 21
Consumable script, 161
Consumables layer, 154
Coroutines
    abstract methods, 262
    DamageCharacter()
        method, 263, 265–266
    Enemy class, 263
    explanation, 259
    IEnumerator, 262, 280
    KillCharacter(), 267
    OnEnable() method, 267
    ResetCharacter() declaration, 266
    return type, 259
    RunEveryFrame(), 260
    StopCoroutine(), 273
    storing references, 271
    time intervals, 261
    while() loop, 261
    yield statement, 260
Cross-platform compilation, 2
Custom Editor, 22
Custom Fonts, 188

D

DamageCharacter()
    method, 263, 265–266,
        271, 363

Data-oriented design, 35
Dynamic rigidbody, 56

E

Edit Mode, 26–27
Enemy class
    access modifier
        keyword, 258
    DamageCharacter(), 263
    HitPoints, 257
    player's health bar, 257
    refactoring code, 257–258
Entity-Component design, 33–35
EventSystem, 176
Exiting game, 367
Exit Time property, 346

F

FireAmmo()
    method, 314, 321–323
First-person shooter (FPS), 8
FixedUpdate() method, 70, 73
Flickering effect, 362
float.Epsilon, 265
Framerate, 73

G

Game engines
    Adrian Carmack, 8
    advantages, 1
    blast furnace, 5

Game engines (*cont.*)
   Chip Morningstar, 6
   component-based
      architecture, 2
   cross-platform compilation, 2
   description, 1
   functionality, 3
   historically, 6–7
   impact, 8
   John Carmack, 8
   John Romero, 8
   Maniac Mansion, 7
   proprietary in-house game
      engine, 9
   Ron Gilbert, 6
   SCUMM game engine, 7
   Tom Hall, 8
   types, 3
   Wolfenstein 3D engine, 8
Game jams, 370
Game manager, 233
GameObject, 19–20, 24, 31
   add script, 74
   Animation Controller, 46, 48–49
   entity-component
      design, 33–35
   hierarchy view, 32
   icons for visibility, 244
   "parent–child"
      relationship, 19–20
   Prefabs
      folder, 63–64
      instances, 65
   transform component, 35

Game play code, 2
Game View, 19
GetAxisRaw() method, 73, 87
GetComponent()
   method, 73, 165
GetMouseButtonDown()
   method, 314
GetQuadrant() method, 357–359
GetSlope() method, 354
Git, 16
Gizmos, 245, 299–302
   OnDrawGizmos(), 299

H

Handle position controls, 24–26
Health bar
   anchor points, 179–184
   building, 176
      background image,
         adjusting, 178
      resizing, 179
      UI Scale Mode,
         setting, 177
   canvas object, 175–176
   character script, 193
   component, 202–206
   custom fonts, 188
   Fill Amount, 201
   hit-points, 189
      HPText anchor object, 191
      HPText object, 190
      text component,
         configuration, 190

image masks, 184
  BarMask, 185
  components, 186
  meter object, 187
  source image, 185
player script
  AdjustHitPoints()
    method, 197
  Start() method, 194
scriptable objects, 192–193
script, creation, 198–202
UI elements, 176
HealthBarObject, 176–178, 191, 202, 203
Health points, 143
HideInInspector
  attribute, 200, 348
Hierarchy Window, 19–20
HigherThanNegativeSlopeLine()
  method, 356
HigherThanPositiveSlopeLine()
  method, 355
hitObject property, 171
Hit-points, 144–145
HitPoints script, 192

I

IEnumerator, *see* Coroutines
Image component, 210
Inspector window, 21
  locking, 206
  preview multiple
    sprites, 167

Inventory script
  AddItem() method, 223–226, 230–231
  Player Script, updation, 228–229
  properties, 218–219
  slot Prefabs, 220–222
  Start() method, 222
Inventory slot
  configuration
    background, 211
    ItemImage, 210
    QtyText, 213–214
    tray object, 212–213
  Prefabs, creation, 214–215
  script, building, 215, 217
Is Trigger property, 123, 154, 278, 304

J

Jittering effect, 125

K

Kinematic rigidbody, 56

L

Layer-based collision
  detection, 305
  collider components, 151
  configuration, 153
  enemies layer, addition, 152
  layer, creation, 151
  usage, 151

Layer collision matrix, 305

Layers

blocking, 59

collision detection, 58

drop-down menu, 58

sorting, 59, 148

addition, 61

characters, 62

orthographic

perspective, 60

window, 58

Lerp() method, 320

Linear Interpolation, 319

Lucasfilm Games, 7

M, N

Materials, Sprite2D, 129–130

Method stubs, 313

MonoBehaviour, 69, 144

MonoDevelop, 17

Move() Coroutine, 291, 293–294

Movement Controller, 82

animation clips,

creation, 342–344

CharStates enum, 340

direction determination,

350, 352–353

Exit Time property, 346

fighting blend tree,

build, 344–346

GetQuadrant()

method, 357–359, 361

GetSlope() method, 354

HigherThanNegative

SlopeLine() method, 356

HigherThanPositive

SlopeLine() method, 355

movement vector, 341

player fight spritesheet, 342

quadrants, player location, 351

slope method, 353

Start() method, 349

Update() method, 350

UpdateState()

method, 340, 359–362

variables to animate player, 347

y-intercept, 355–356

Weapon class, update, 347

Move() method, 293

MovePosition(), 294

O

Object pooling, 308–309

ammoPool, 312

description, 308

poolSize (see Weapon class)

OnCollisionEnter2D() method, 272

OnCollisionExit2D() method, 273

OnDestroy() method, 315

OnTriggerEnter2D()

method, 154, 295–297

OnTriggerExit2D()

method, 297–298

Orthographic cameras

custom resolution, 110

3D projects, 107

screen resolution, 107, 109
size, 107
Orthographic size, 253

P, Q

Pixels Per Unit (PPU), 40, 127
Platforms, building, 364–366
Player animation state
    machine, 327
Player class, 145–146
    DamageCharacter()
        methods, 271
    enemy script,
        configuration, 274–275
    OnCollisionEnter2D()
        method, 272–273
    OnCollisionExit2D()
        method, 273–274
    ResetCharacter(), 269–270
    updation, 267, 269
Play Mode, 26–27
Play, Pause, and Step
    controls, 26
Prefabs, 64, 147, 227, 228
    advantages, 63
    circle collider 2D, set up,
        148–149
    coin, creation, 147–148
    custom tag, set up, 149–150
    import settings, 147
    SpawnPoint GameObject, 242
Primitive collider, 54
Project Window, 20

R

Raycasting, 8
Refactoring, 257
Renderer component, 102
RequireComponent attribute, 347
ResetCharacter(), 269
Rigidbody 2D component, 140
    dynamic, 56
    Freeze Rotation, 134
    kinematic, 56
    static, 56
RPGCameraManager, *see* Camera
    manager
RPGGameManager, *see* Singletons

S

Scene, 31, 38
    Saving, 38
Scene view, 19
Screen Coordinates, 354
Screen Space, 320
Script
    GetAxisRaw() method, 74
    MonoBehaviour class, 70
    MovementController, 66–67
    movementSpeed, 72
    UnityEngine namespace, 69
Scriptable objects
    consumable item, 162–163
    consumable script, build, 161
    CreateAssetMenu, 158–159
    creation, 157, 159, 160

Scriptable objects (*cont.*)
heart power-up,
creation, 165–166
heart prefab, 168
multiple sprites, 168
OnTriggerEnter2D()
method, 170–171
player's hit-points, 172
prefab settings, 169
player collisions, 164–165
ScriptableObject class, 157
string property, 156
use cases, 156
Script Editor, 17
SCUMM game engine, 7
Separation of concerns, 33
Singletons
benefits, 234
creation, 235–236
SetupScene() method, 237
Start() method, 237
downsides, 234
GameManager prefab,
build, 238
rationale, 234
RPGGameManager class, 235
software design pattern, 234
unified access point, 234
Slingshots
animations, 326
defense, 302–303
Weapon class (*see* Weapon
class)
Sorting layers, 101, 102

SpawnAmmo() method,
314–316, 322
Spawn points
configuration, 245
InvokeRepeating() method, 240
MonoBehaviours, 238–240
playerSpawnPoint
property, 246
prefab, build, 241
Gizmos button, 245
icon, selection, 244
renaming, 242
scene view, 243
quaternion, 241
repeatInterval, 240
spawn enemies, 249–250
SpawnObject() method, 247
SpawnPlayer() method, 247
Sprite Editor tool
grid by cell size, 42
pixel size, 42
slice button, 42
Sprite Renderer, 37, 46, 102
Sprites, 35
add component, 37
import settings, 39
compression, 40
filter mode, 40
texture type, 40
physics shape, 138–140
Player GameObject, 38–40
pixel size, 42
properties, 41
resulting sliced sprites, 43

scene view, 44
Sprite Selector screen, 43
Stardew Valley, 36
Stabilization, 125–126
Start() method, 70, 349

T

Tags, 57
Text object
alignment, 213
Font Style, 213
Tilemap Collider 2D, 130–132
Tilemap Renderer, 93, 102, 103,
116, 119, 129, 130
Tilemaps, 106
Active Tilemap, 101
characters sorting layer, 105
component, 93
ground layer, 102
material properties, 129
multiple, 101
organization, 92
outdoor objects tile palette, 103
pixel-perfect location, 129
Sprite2D material, 130
Sprite Import Settings, 92
Tile palettes
creation, 93–95
Erase tool, 103
navigating, 96
organization, 93
painting, 96–101
rotate tiles, 103

Transform component, 35, 80
Transform tools, 23–24
TravelArc() method, 318, 323
Triggers and scripting, 154–155

U

UI Elements
Anchor Points, 179–184
BarMask, 184–187
Fill Amount, 187
Fill Method, 187, 188
Rect Transform, 176
render order, 188
Unity
configuration, 14–15, 17
cross-platform support, 10
documentation, 29
drag-and-drop, 10
Editor Extension
functionality, 11
game engine, 10–11
graphics APIs, 10
installation, 13–14
interface, 18
licenses, 10
preferences menu, 28
project structure, 28–29
script editor, 17
Unity Asset Store, 11, 19
Unity Meetup, *see* Communities
Unity Package Manager, 111, 112
Unity Physics Engine, 54, 56
Unity Screen Coordinates, 354

UnityScript, 67

Unity Teams, 15

Unity Users Groups, 368

Update() method, 70, 73, 314, 350, 367

UpdateState() method, 359–362

V

Vector2, 73

Vector3

  sqrMagnitude, 293

  up keyword, 326

Virtual camera, 252

  background color, 117

  Body section, 118

  Cinemachine Brain, 114

  Cinemachine Confiner, 120–122

    Bounding Shape 2D, 123

    Composite Collider 2D, 122

    dead zone, 117–118, 124

    polygon collider 2D, 121–123

  damping properties, 119

  Game Window Guides, 117

  post-processing pipeline, 128

  target, 115

  tracking point, 117

Visual Studio, 17

  auto-completion, pop-up, 89

  MovementController script, 66–67

W, X, Y, Z

Wander algorithm

  ChooseNewEndpoint() method, 285

  Circle Collider, 278

  Move() Coroutine, 285

  pursuit logic, 295

  script, creation, 279–280

  Start() method, 282–283

  trigger and radius, 279

  variables, 280–282

  WanderRoutine() Coroutine, 283, 285

Weapon class

  ammoPool and ammoPrefab, 311

  Arc class, 317

  Arc script, 324–325

  Awake() method, 312

  code, build, 310–311

  FireAmmo() method, 321–323

  Lerp() method, 320

  linear interpolation, 319

  screen points and world points, 320

  SpawnAmmo method, 315–316

  stubbing-out methods, 314–315

Weapon script, configuration, 323–324

Window views
    asset store, 19
    console, 21
    game view, 19
    hierarchy view, 19
    inspector window, 21
    project, 20
    scene view, 19
Wolfenstein 3D
    engine, 8
World Space, 320, 354
World units, 107, 108

<barcode>||| || || ||||||||||| ||||| ||| || || || ||||||||||| || || || |||</barcode>

Printed in the United States
By Bookmasters